CHRYSLER, DODGE & PLYMOUTH
MUSCLE

Anthony Young

MBI Publishing Company

First published in 1999 by MBI Publishing Company,
729 Prospect Avenue, PO Box 1, Osceola, WI 54020-0001USA

MBI Publishing Company books are also available at discounts in bulk quantity for industrial or sales-promotional use. For details write to Special Sales Manager at Motorbooks International Wholesalers & Distributors, 729 Prospect Avenue, PO Box 1, Osceola WI, 54020 USA.

Library of Congress Cataloging-in-Publication Data

Young, Anthony.
     Chrysler, Dodge and Plymouth muscle / Anthony Young.
          p. cm.
     Includes index.
     ISBN 0-7603-0533-1 (hardbound : alk. paper)
     1. Chrysler automobile—History. 2. Dodge automobile—History. 3. Plymouth automobile—History. 4. Automobiles—Performance—History. 5. Muscle cars—History. I. Title.
  TL215.C55Y6696   1999
  629.222--dc21   99-27349

On the front cover: Not too many cars in the late 1960s dared to challenge these two beasts at a traffic light. Leading this duo is a 1968 Plymouth Road Runner, which is followed by a 1968 Dodge Coronet Super Bee. *Tom Shaw*

On the frontispiece: After years of big-block muscle, an era passed. The 1971 440-6 'Cuda was the last of the big-block Mopars. *Tom Shaw*

On the title page: Nothing shows the brute strength of a muscle car more than a smoking tire. This 1971 440-6 'Cuda makes it easy; all you have to do is floor it! *Tom Shaw*

On the back cover: In 1970, Dodge introduced the Challenger, and the Challenger R/T was added to the 1970 Scat Pack. Fewer than 1,000 R/T ragtops were built that year. Blackout hood paint was optional, making this model even more rare. *Tom Shaw*

On the back cover, inset: A 1967 magazine advertisement for Dodge's new Coronet R/T.

Edited by Christopher Batio

Designed by Tom Heffron

Printed in Hong Kong

CONTENTS

ACKNOWLEDGMENTS

The idea for this book was suggested to me by my editor, now publishing director at MBI, Zack Miller. Zack and I talked about doing a full color, expanded sequel to *Mighty Mopars*, my first book for Motorbooks International, which was published in 1984. Despite being entirely black and white, it was a very popular book

The Dodge 1970 Coronet R/T was counted among the Dodge Scat Pack. Resplendent in Green Go paint, optional 426 Hemi with functional Ramcharger dual hoodscoops, this was Mopar musclecar heaven. While expensive to insure, it was a very entertaining, and winning, street machine.

This Plymouth ad appeared in the March 31, 1941, issue of LIFE magazine. Life in America, as reflected in this ad, was carefree. All that would end on December 7th with the bombing of Pearl Harbor. Chrysler Corporation converted to wartime vehicle production and development. Out of this came the first generation hemispherical combustion chamber V-8, which later influenced design and development of the 426 Hemi.

with Mopar enthusiasts and remained in print for more than 10 years. Zack felt a color book on the subject with more in-depth history of the famous cars themselves would prove even more popular. This book is the result.

All of the superb color photography in this book (except for Chapter Six) was shot by Tom Shaw, the editor of *Muscle Car Review*. Tom has the enviable task of driving and photographing the most desirable cars ever built, and many of them are Mopars. He generously opened his personal files to me, and the quality of his work is evident throughout the book.

Dodge and Plymouth produced some of the most eye-catching and clever musclecar ads to ever grace the pages of the enthusiast magazines. All the ads reproduced in the book were loaned to me by Bob Ashton. Bob, along with his wife, Vicki, operate Auto Know in Utica, Michigan, just north of Detroit. This store truly is an automotive enthusiast's candy store and is worth a trip whenever you are in Motor City.

When I traveled to Detroit to view the Viper and Prowler assembly lines and interview those involved with producing the cars, I received tremendous cooperation.

Sharon Hayden, craft manager of the Conner Avenue Assembly Plant where these cars are built, arranged for my personal tour of the plant. Dwight Kennedy walked me through all the phases of Prowler and Viper assembly. A few blocks away at the Mound Road Engine Plant, Rod Romain showed me the steps that went into the assembly of the Viper's V-10 engine.

Many men and women have worked on the Dodge Viper and Plymouth Prowler programs and I was able to interview some of the key people involved. At the DaimlerChrysler Corporation headquarters, Charlie Brown III, Viper powertrain supervisor, gave me a wealth of information regarding the V-10 development. Richard Winkles, who was development and test cell engineer on the engine, successfully supervised the engine's evolution from the brazed-block prototype to the final production unit; he discussed the engine in detail with me. Winkles was assisted in the test cell by test engineer Bob Zeimis who recalled the more memorable moments in the Viper V-10's development. Peter M. Gladysz, today senior

1951

The Chrysler Hemi-head V-8 was released for production in 1951. It was offered in various displacements and outputs as the Chrysler FirePower, Dodge Red Ram, and the DeSoto FireDome. Eventually the wedge-head V-8 replaced it, but high-performance development of this engine led to the new racing Hemi released in 1964.

Over the years, Dick Maxwell, Tom Hoover, and Larry Shepard have continued to support my work documenting Chrysler, Dodge, and Plymouth performance history. They have always been eager to answer my questions and volunteer information regarding Chrysler Corporation's rich performance legacy.

I would like to thank several people who were supportive of this book project. Peter Schwartz of Schwartz Engineering Company in San Antonio, Texas, generously loaned me one of his laptop computers in order to complete the book. When my home computer died as I was working on Chapter Six, my good friend Frank Molinari loaned me one of his machines, and I was able to meet the deadline. I am most grateful to Jimmy Dollar, the Red Adair of the aircraft refurbishment business, for his endless optimism and encouragement. Thanks "Pops."

There were others who must be mentioned. Mike McNamara, David Combs, Eric Vandergrift, Will Benoist, Todd Bailey, and the others at Jet Aviation became friends and made memories.

Finally, I want to thank my wife, Annie, daughters Erin and Katie, and my father for their support, encouragement, and love.

—Anthony Young

manager of PL Vehicle Development & Synthesis and one of the charter Team Viper members, recalled many exciting events regarding the Viper's development, and his input was invaluable. Bob Champine, senior manager of Dodge Car Marketing Plans, rolled out the Viper red carpet for me and arranged for me to obtain the photography I needed for that car. Peter Hollinshead in Chrysler Plymouth Jeep Division gave me the Plymouth Prowler product information and transparencies I needed. Dennis Peters, manager of Prowler Body Engineering, answered my many questions regarding Plymouth's production street rod.

Bill Weertman, who had spearheaded the 426 Hemi program and many others over the years, shared with me his contributions to the V-10 engine program. Larry Rathgeb revealed to me the very precise work involved in perfecting the Viper's suspension design and settings.

When I visited Ross Roy Communications in Bloomfield Hills, Michigan, by arrangement of Bob Champine at Dodge Marketing, I was given generous help. Amy Selwa called everyone involved with the Viper account to meet me and sit down to discuss my requirements. Gary LaGuire, Dennis Staszak, Katye Abramson, and Amy herself cleared their schedules on short notice to show me available Viper art. Nancy Peski put me in contact with photographer representative Kent Lund for permission to use Ron Strong's superb shots of the Viper for this book.

Chrysler Corporation saw racing as a means of promoting its production cars. To meet homologation rules, Dodge and Plymouth had to build street equivalents of its racing cars. For Trans Am racing, this resulted in the 1970 Plymouth AAR 'Cuda (shown) and the Dodge Challenger T/A.

INTRODUCTION

The musclecar era holds a unique place in the hearts of American performance enthusiasts, especially for those who grew up during the 1960s and early 1970s. Musclecars ruled the pages of enthusiast magazines like *Car Life, Cars, Hot Rod,* and *Car Craft,* as well as general interest automotive magazines like *Motor Trend, Road & Track,* and *Car & Driver.* It was a great time to be not only a musclecar enthusiast, but also an automotive engineer. The musclecar era provided a rich source for corporate engineering, manufacturing, marketing, and advertising to harness the creative talent of the day. It was an exciting time to be in the automotive

The Dodge Viper, introduced in 1992, restored the performance heritage of Chrysler that had been established in the mid-1950s. The Viper was so well engineered, the car won its class in the 24 Hours of LeMans. *Ron Strong*

business. It was even more exciting to be in the market to buy a high performance American car.

The musclecar virus infected practically all the domestic car manufacturers, but none more powerfully than Chrysler Corporation. Despite being only the third-largest automaker in America, Chrysler built some of the most desirable musclecars of the period. They were able to do so in large part because the extraordinary demands of World War II instigated engineering programs at Chrysler that later formed the performance basis for the high-performance Dodges and Plymouths of the 1960s and early 1970s.

The storm clouds of another World War had been forming since the late 1930s. Americans were torn from their isolationist policies on December 7, 1941, with the bombing of the U. S. Pacific Fleet at Pearl Harbor by Japan, and America's manufacturing base changed, almost overnight. Congress issued legislation halting automobile and truck production to permit conversion to war materiel production; manufacturers were permitted to run limited production lines for car and truck spare parts. Chrysler engineers went to work designing and engineering the machinery needed to win the war.

Chrysler came out of the postwar period with a pent-up desire to market exciting automobiles. A great many engineering projects that commenced as a result of World War II kick-started the dormant but talented engineers and designers at Chrysler. After having experienced demanding, challenging, and rewarding work during the early 1940s and seeing the effort of their labors reach the manufacturing level with unprecedented speed, the people at Chrysler Corporation were straining to implement so much of what had been learned and achieved in the automotive marketplace with the end of World War II.

In actuality, advanced engine projects for Chrysler cars developed during the war. The company realized one day the war would end and Chrysler would get back to the business of building civilian cars and trucks. Two key programs were the research and development of a hemispherical combustion chamber application for passenger cars, and the development of Chrysler's first V-8; these two programs were engineered concurrently and merged, producing the first generation Hemi-head V-8.

The engine, in the form of the Chrysler FirePower, Dodge Red Ram, and DeSoto FireDome, put Chrysler on the performance circuit in the 1950s. By the middle of the decade, the Chrysler 300 was packing them in at National Association for Stock Car Auto Racing (NASCAR) events around the country, setting records, and stocking the trophy case.

Then Chrysler launched a new engine program to build a wedge combustion chamber V-8 to rival the output of its famed Hemi. Gradually the Hemi was superseded by the Wedge in passenger cars on circle tracks and on the quarter-mile strip. However, the limitations of the Wedge on the long-circle tracks of NASCAR became apparent and a new, better-breathing engine was needed. Chrysler turned to its pioneering Hemi V-8, engineered a new Hemi V-8 for racing, and turned the racing world on its ear—all in record time.

The second generation Hemi V-8 became a legend in its own time on the long, high-banked ovals in NASCAR and the quarter-mile strips in National Hot Rod Association (NHRA) and American Hot Rod Association (AHRA) events all across America. It is an engine that remains revered to this day. But the Hemi was not the only engine that made Mopars mighty. The Max Wedge V-8s proved the awesome power available from the Wedge itself. The 340, 383, and 440 Wedge V-8s made Mopars street machines to be respected and even feared on streets and boulevards from New York to California, and from Michigan to Florida.

The musclecar era at Chrysler during the 1960s produced the Dart GTS, Charger, Coronet R/T, and Super Bee, the GTX and Road Runner, the Superbird and Daytona, the Barracuda (or the 'Cuda) and Challenger. Just how did Dodge and Plymouth, with seemingly fewer resources than Ford or General Motors, achieve such a staggering array of desirable musclecars? These two divisions of Chrysler were every bit as clever and aggressive as GM and Ford in garnering their share of the performance market during the 1960s and early 1970s. The engineers, product planners, and designers produced cars that fired the impressionable imaginations of a youthful generation—cars with the looks and muscular performance to pull in buyers to Dodge and Plymouth dealers all across America. With supreme and justifiable belief in their cars, Dodge and Plymouth beat the performance drum loudly, and the sales figures gladdened the Sales Division's heart.

Chrysler succeeded in winning many over to the Mopar camp with a combination of superb engineering, great styling, clever advertising, and even a sense of humor. Behind that tongue-in-cheek humor, however, was a fierce determination to win on the track and on the street. It literally gave Ford and General Motors a run for the money. This lasted until 1971, when insurance premiums and looming emission controls spelled doom for the musclecar. Nevertheless, Chrysler kept the spirit of performance alive through its performance parts program and race promotion through the 1970s and the 1980s.

To prove the corporation's ability to bring a brand new car to market in only three years and offer the highest performance Dodge ever built, that division brought out the outrageous Viper. What magnificent excess—488 cubic inches of V-10 power with acceleration and top speed to rival the most expensive exotic cars in the world. New models of the Viper were introduced to an eager niche market. And then, Plymouth turned the automotive world on its ear with the Prowler.

The legacy of Chrysler performance is one of the richest and most exciting in the automotive world. No doubt Chrysler intends for it to continue.

The Plymouth Prowler was introduced in 1997. The car went from concept to production in record time. It proves that the joy of high performance street cars is still very much a part of Chrysler.
DaimlerChrylser Corporation

CHAPTER ONE

The Dawn of Chrysler Performance

The 1950s ushered in the era of the American V-8 engine. For decades, car manufacturers had installed trustworthy straight sixes or straight eights in their cars. The involvement of auto manufacturers in new designs, materials, manufacturing methods, and production schedules during World War II unleashed a torrent of engineering creativity that might have otherwise laid dormant. With the end of that war, car manufacturers were faced with the daunting task of converting, once again, back to automotive and truck manufacturing.

During World War II, Chrysler had been engaged in the design and development of V-16 aircraft engines and a V-12 tank engine. Both configurations used hemispherical combustion chambers as a means of increasing volumetric efficiency and power. The hemi-head design was not new—in 1904, the Welsh passenger car used a four-cylinder engine having hemispherical combustion chambers. The hemi head was also used by such racing marques as Stutz, Miller, Offenhauser, and Duesenberg. The development of the hemi-head design in the V-12 and V-16 engines by Chrysler showed real promise, but never reached production due to the war's end. Nevertheless, research and development began on a passenger-car Hemi-head engine at Chrysler's Highland Park facilities even before the end of the war.

The First Generation Hemi V-8

Chrysler was blessed with a wealth of engineering talent before, during, and after World War II, and it was all brought to bear in the development of a new engine to put into Chrysler Corporation passenger cars. To offer postwar consumers something different in its cars, Chrysler embarked on an engine program that would increase power and smoothness. What Chrysler did not and could not realize was the impact this engine program would have on Chrysler's image and product line decades later.

Two areas were felt to hold the most promise in achieving the smooth power they were looking for: volumetric efficiency and a higher compression ratio. Upping the compression ratio was easy enough to accomplish but was limited by the octane rating of automotive gasolines. Volumetric efficiency, on the other hand, was inherent in the engine design itself and was a product of combustion chamber design in particular and engine breathing in general. In the postwar era, there was the temptation for Chrysler engineering management to stick with the tried and true, conventional approach to engine design. However, encouraging results were achieved in the development of the V-12 and V-16 hemispherical combustion chamber engines, and Chrysler chose to explore this approach for a new automotive engine.

Dodge benefitted from Hemi power, and the highest performance option in the 1956 Royal Lancer was the D-500. Sporting a 315 ci Hemi, the D-500 pumped out 260 horsepower. Dodge promoted the car's styling as "The Forward Look."

Even in the mid-1950s, Dodge believed in identifying its performance cars. The D-500 option in the Royal Lancer earned this medallion on the trunk lid and the leading edge of the hood.

The hemispherical combustion chamber was a proven power-maker. So why hadn't it achieved more widespread use in cars? There were two basic reasons. Due to the juxtaposition of the intake and exhaust vales and subsequent valvetrain, the cylinder head was complex mechanically and didn't lend itself to mass production at an affordable price. Also, the hemi-head had earned the dubious reputation of running rough and needing high-octane fuel. On the roughness issue Chrysler couldn't turn up much in the way of quantifiable evidence. With regard to the cost of manufacturing a hemi-head engine, Chrysler felt manufacturing efficiencies could be incorporated with the goal of installing such an engine in various displacements in most if not all of Chrysler's automotive lineup.

The engineering talent that would oversee the design and development of this soon to be legendary engine was formidable. James C. Zeder was director of Engineering and Research, who along with his older brother Fred Zeder, O.R. Skelton, and Carl Breer, were lured away from Studebaker in 1920 by Walter P. Chrysler himself to establish the Chrysler Corporation. Reporting to James Zeder was Ray White, in charge of experimental design, William Drinkard, head of laboratory research and development, and Mel Carpentier, in charge of production engine design.

To establish a baseline on engine performance and find out how well other manufacturers' engines were performing, Chrysler engine labs began to test as many domestic and foreign engines it could, including British, French, and German powerplants, among others. One of the most surprising engines was the British Healey. It was a V-type engine with single overhead cam using hemispherical combustion chambers. Dyno results revealed it was the highest-powered and most efficient engine Chrysler had ever tested.

After evaluating various passenger car engines and taking into account the surprising performance of the Healey, Chrysler built a single-cylinder engine with 47.2 ci displacement that could accept interchangeable cylinder heads. This engine was tested with Chrysler's familiar L-head and F-head designs, along with an overhead valve (OHV) design with inline valves, and a cylinder head with spherical combustion chamber with opposed valves.

Chrysler had found with its conventional cylinder head designs in passenger car engines, combustion chamber deposits could significantly reduce power over a given period. A combustion chamber with low surface-to-volume ratio like the hemi minimized these losses. Single cylinder testing also revealed the other cylinder head designs had to run a much higher compression ratio to match the efficiency and power of the hemi-head running at only 7.0:1 compression.

Zeder wrote of this finding in a Society of Automotive Engineers (SAE) paper he presented in March 1952: "It would seem, therefore, that it would have been wise to review this matter of compact combustion chambers periodically during the last twenty years. During this time, while fuel quality was advancing steadily, no one seems to have recognized that the performance of a good hemispherical chamber at borderline knock was getting to be very good indeed; and its over-all performance on any fuel made other chambers look like somewhat backward country cousins. Perhaps some of the failure of the industry to recognize this changing condition may be ascribed to the lack, during this period, of competitive hemispherical chamber engines on which to experiment."

John Platner supervised the lab testing of the single-cylinder engine with the four different cylinder head designs. Platner, who joined Chrysler in 1931, was a member of the first graduating class of the Chrysler Institute of Engineering Graduate School that same year. He worked in Engine Development his entire career with Chrysler, and he was a believer and vocal supporter of the first generation Hemi V-8 that eventually emerged from this research and development phase.

What Platner found regarding the hemi-head was contrary to the prevailing doctrine; the hemi-head actually displayed knock-limiting characteristics. In terms of thermal efficiency, the hemi was the best performer; the L-head, F-head, and the overhead valve head all had to run at higher compression ratios to match the Hemi's performance parameters. With the hemi's intake valve closest to the intake manifold and the exhaust valve directly across from it on the other side of the hemispherical chamber with an included valve angle of 58-1/2 degrees, the fuel-air mixture entered, burned, and exited efficiently. The hemi head also extended valve life and promoted sealing by aiding effective uniform sealing of the valve seats.

The results from testing the single-cylinder hemi were so encouraging that Zeder's team decided to build a straight six-cylinder engine using the hemispherical combustion chamber. A standard Chrysler straight six

The Chrysler 300 was the first high-performance car from Chrysler Corporation in the Postwar era, as described in this ad that appeared in August 1955. First-generation Hemi development reached its apex in the Chrysler 300 with the dual four-barrel 331 ci Hemi developing 300 horsepower.

The Chrysler Windsor line was the basis for the Chrysler 300. The St. Regis model came with a lower output Hemi V-8, but it also came with a lower pricetag as well. The Hemi V-8 was a revelation to Chrysler owners who were used to leisurely straight-six power.

was chosen and a special double overhead camshaft valvetrain designed for it. When tested, this engine showed a significant performance gain over the standard straight six. This new engine, with the designation A161, was installed in a Chrysler for evaluation under real-world conditions. Wallace E. Zierer was in charge of automobile testing. He found the car ran effortlessly on then-current 80 octane regular gasoline. The anticipated roughness was absent, and the engine performed smoothly during all phases of testing. It was a true milestone that would have a profound effect on the Chrysler Corporation for decades.

However, from a production standpoint, the chain-driven dual overhead cam design was complex and expensive, so Chrysler engineers set about to design a pushrod-actuated, overhead-valve, hemi-head straight six. This greatly simplified valvetrain dynamics and lowered anticipated production cost. At this phase, a V-8 was not yet in the picture.

Convincing the Powers that Be

Every new automotive engine design has its supporters and its detractors, and the nascent hemi was no different. While Zeder's team was enthusiastic and supportive, the old guard at Chrysler needed to be convinced. It took some doing. The automotive industry had built V-type engines during the 1920s and 1930s, primarily in pricier Lincolns, Cadillacs, and Packards. By the early 1940s, virtually all domestic carmakers were building straight sixes and eights. The pendulum began to swing the other way and car manufacturers began to seriously consider V-8 development programs after World War II.

Just prior to and after the war, Chrysler had experimented with both 60-degree and 90-degree V-6s and 90-degree V-8s. The V-6s did not have the smoothness that was needed in a passenger car. The straight eights were felt by some engineers at Chrysler to be too long and heavy. The V-8 was the most promising configuration to incorporate the Hemi-head, but the Hemi and the V-8 met with stiff opposition by Chrysler upper management. William Drinkard, as head of the engine research and development lab, knew what a Hemi V-8 was capable of, and was one of the engine's few true believers.

"There were just two guys, as far as I'm concerned, that believed in the idea of the Hemi V-8 engine and tried to sell it," Drinkard remembers most vividly. "Those two guys were John Platner and myself. There

wasn't anybody else. Anytime you work in a big corporation, if you've got some idea and try to sell it, look out for all those guys who are going to sell something else and belittle you. That is exactly what happened. Fred Zeder said, 'Look fellas, I'm not going to have any part of a V-8 engine. We've made our money on a straight eight and that's all we're going to have.' We had all these research guys in there trying to muddy the waters. Finally, K.T. Keller, the chief operating officer, said, 'Bill, I think maybe you've got the right plan.' That was the thing that turned the whole thing around."

The decision by K.T. Keller to move ahead with a Hemi-head V-8 was yet another Chrysler Corporation milestone. Had that decision not been made, the eventual production of a Chrysler V-8 would have been delayed by years, and a Hemi V-8 would probably never have seen the light of day. It was a less than closely guarded secret that General Motors was working on a OHV V-8, and this engine did, in fact, appear first in the Cadillac and Oldsmobile in 1949. Ford had been building its flathead (valve-in-block) V-8 since 1932.

With Keller's sanction, design engineering on the Hemi V-8 commenced in earnest. By 1948, Chrysler had a 330 ci Hemi-head V-8 undergoing testing by Ray White's experimental engine group. This engine project was the A182. After thorough testing and evaluation on Chrysler's dynamometers, one of the engines was installed in a Chrysler and evaluated in the vehicle. Although initially reluctant to back the V-8, the majority of Chrysler's management were suitably impressed with the Hemi V-8 design. Keller felt vindicated. Approval was given for an engine of this type and size to be designed for production.

Mel Carpentier's department refined the engine even further, taking into account the requirements for mass production. The production engine design that finally emerged was the A239, which was shorter and lighter than the A182. It had a slightly larger displacement of 331 ci. Drinkard laid out the specification whereby the engine had to pass a 1,000-hour test on a given test schedule, equivalent to 100,000 miles without having to replace major parts. Specifically, Carpentier wanted the bearings, valves, pistons, and rings to last the equivalent of 100,000 miles.

This engine was Chrysler's first overhead valve engine, and initially the development V-8 suffered accelerated camshaft wear; it did not survive the 100,000-mile durability test. Some engines actually failed after several thousand miles. It took a change in the material of the camshaft lifter to chilled cast iron, coupled with a change in the spherical radius of the lifter. In addition, a graphite-based anti-scuff coating had to be applied to the lifter along with a special additive in the engine oil to finally solve the problem.

In the world of engineering, grand schemes and theories do not see the light of day without drawings. One of the design drafters present at the creation of the first generation Hemi was Fred Shrimpton. He first reported for work at Chrysler in 1929, just months before the great stock market crash. He started work first as a tracer and had risen to chief layout man when interest in the Hemi V-8 as a production engine actually emerged.

"Mel Carpentier came up to me one day," Shrimpton remembers, "and said, 'I want you to lay out a Hemi head.' I laid out all three engines—the Chrysler, the Dodge, and the DeSoto. Then we had a strike, so I rolled all the stuff up. We were gone for 104 days; it was a long strike. When I came back, those drawings were gone, but we had already started on detailing drawings. In fact, we knew so little about them, we made details right off the layout drawings. The big problem was getting spark plugs down through the center of the head and how to seal them."

With the spark plugs located between the intake and exhaust valves and slightly offset from the cylinder's centerline, some means had to be developed to permit changing the plugs without having to remove the large valve covers. A steel tube was designed with a flange at the lower end that acted as a gasket as the spark plug was screwed into the cylinder head. Snapping the spark plug wire onto the spark plug was facilitated by a long ceramic boot. To prevent oil from leaking between the tube and the valve cover, an ignition wire cover compressed a neoprene ring with a steel washer, creating a seal around each tube as the ignition wire cover was screwed into place. The ignition wires were hidden by the wire cover until they exited the back of the valve cover near the distributor, giving the engine a very clean look.

The Hemi had a number of other features that aided its durability and quiet operation. The crankshaft was shot-peened, and the journal fillets were undercut to eliminate tool marks and surface roughness, greatly improving fatigue strength. Hydraulic tappets achieved quiet valve operation. Chrysler worked with Carter to design a water-jacketed carburetor to prevent engine

stalling due to carburetor icing. A dual-breaker distributor provided a reserve of ignition voltage at high speeds.

Just how durable was this new engine? More than 8,000 hours of dyno testing and over 500,000 miles on test cars were involved to ensure the new V-8's long-term durability. Chrysler chose the name FirePower for the new Chrysler Hemi V-8. Scheduled for introduction in the 1951 line of Chrysler cars, DeSoto and Dodge would also get the Hemi, but in smaller and distinct displacements.

Launching the Horsepower Race

The Chrysler FirePower V-8 was introduced in the long-running Chrysler Saratoga and New Yorker, as well as the Chrysler Imperial and Crown Imperial. The FirePower V-8 had a displacement of 331.1 ci and produced 180 horsepower at 4,000 rpm with 312 foot-pounds of torque at 2,000 rpm. This represented more than a 40 percent boost in horsepower and a 16 percent increase in torque over the straight-eight engine of 1950. On top of this, it was nine and a half inches shorter than the straight eight.

While not a high-performance engine per se, it was Chrysler's first V-8 passenger car engine, and it bristled with features that made great advertising copy. It developed more horsepower than either the Cadillac or Oldsmobile V-8s, and didn't require premium grade fuel like its competitors. It gave General Motors fits.

"It was jokingly said," Harold Welch recalls, "that it made the lights on the top floor of the General Motors building burn extra hours at night. It's sometimes blamed for kicking off what was generally referred to as the horsepower race." Welch had joined Chrysler in 1935, went through the Chrysler Institute, and was assigned to the mechanical laboratory in 1937. He moved to engine development in 1940 and became assistant manager under William Drinkard.

As planned, Chrysler expanded availability of the Hemi-head V-8 to other makes. In 1952, the DeSoto FireDome V-8 made its debut with a displacement of 276 ci with 160 horsepower at 4,400 rpm. Dodge received its Red Ram Hemi V-8 in 1953. It was the smallest of all the Chrysler Hemis, with a displacement of 241.3 ci; it generated 140 horsepower at 4,400 rpm. The engine was offered in the 114- and 119-inch wheelbase versions of the V-8-equipped Coronet that year. Chrysler's decision to expand availability of the

Hemi V-8 across its product line was a very smart move—even the average car buyer could experience the pride and pleasure of owning and driving a Hemi V-8.

Chrysler was anticipating road test reports from automotive magazines. The corporation executives were confident the new 1951 line of cars equipped with the Hemi V-8 would get favorable reviews. Their confidence was well placed. *Road & Track,* always partial to foreign cars, nevertheless felt the new V-8 Chrysler significant enough to warrant a road test. The editors tested a Saratoga Club Coupe. It was a very low mileage car with just over 600 miles on the odometer. The leisurely acceleration of most cars of the late 1940s and early 1950s was their only reference, so the editors were stunned by the performance of the Hemi-powered Saratoga. Wrote the editors: "The acceleration was startling—the Chrysler bowing to no other cars." What really threw the editors on their heels was the car's performance against a Jaguar XK120. The Saratoga was faster to 60 miles per hour—only ten seconds. Top speed for the big, 4,200 pound car was also impressive, topping out at 108 miles per hour.

Motor Trend editors tested a 1951 New Yorker for the May issue and were equally surprised by the car's acceleration. In fact, no car they had tested that year could beat it. "Without a doubt," the editors wrote, "the ability of the heavy Chrysler New Yorker to accelerate either from a standing start or at high speeds is the car's most amazing feature."

While these numbers appear rather mundane today, in 1951 they were a revelation. And the Hemi was precisely what Chrysler Corporation needed to draw attention to its product line and garner more market share from GM and Ford.

More Power

Almost immediately, Chrysler engineers started research and development to extract greater levels of power from its new V-8. The engine had untapped reserves of power, and the engineers knew it. Two areas were explored: compression ratio and volumetric efficiency. Running a 12.5:1 compression ratio increased power 15 percent over the baseline, but the engine needed the equivalent of 130 octane. The most dramatic gains were achieved improving volumetric efficiency. Substituting streamlined exhaust manifolds for the stock units netted 13 additional horsepower and 18 additional pounds-feet of torque. Three other areas

looked at were the valve sizes and ports, the intake manifold and carburetor, and the camshaft. Intake valve diameter was increased .125 inch and the exhaust-valve diameter a whopping .250. The cylinder head intake and exhaust ports were increased accordingly.

Two different intake manifolds were designed, both using four large single-barrel carburetors; one manifold was designed for high torque and the other designed for high speed/high horsepower output. With the high-flow cylinder heads and high-torque intake manifold, the engine gained 42 horsepower and 30 foot-pounds of torque. Three camshafts were tested on this engine, with the 270/260/50 degree camshaft giving the best all-around performance increase. This cam helped to bump output from the baseline an amazing 95 horsepower and 60 foot-pounds of torque.

Replacing the high-torque intake manifold with the high-horsepower manifold achieved stunning results. Using the 280/270/60 degree camshaft resulted in 308 horsepower with 341 pounds-feet of torque—with stock pistons! With 12.5:1 pistons and running a special extra high octane fuel, the engine generated 353 horsepower and 385 foot-pounds of torque—all from 331 ci. One of these engines was the K-310 which Chrysler dressed

The 301 ci Chrysler FirePower Hemi V-8 installed in the Windsor St. Regis developed 188 horsepower at 4,400 rpm. More importantly, it produced low-end torque that gave the big Chrysler impressive performance on the street.

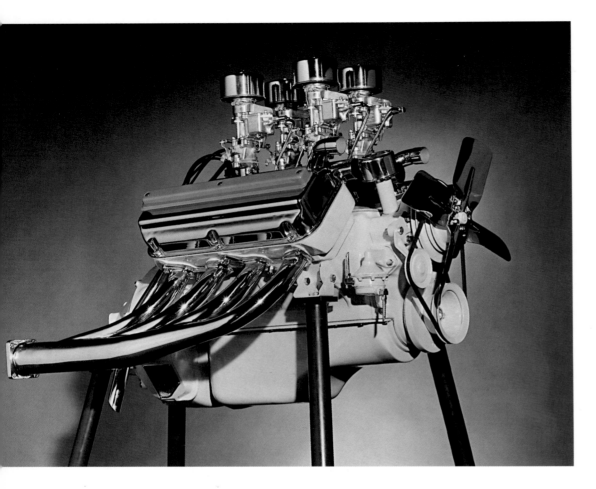

Chrysler did extensive performance development of the first-generation Hemi V-8. The most impressive results were achieved with the K-310 engine program. With four single-barrel carburetors feeding into log-type manifolds, hot cam timing, and over 12:1 compression, the engine developed 353 horsepower from the 331 cubic-inch Hemi.

up with chrome-plated induction and exhaust components and displayed around the country. Zeder included the results of this high-performance development in his SAE paper. Clearly, the Chrysler believers in the Hemi were totally vindicated. The research and development program boded well for future production line offerings. In fact, this research and development program served as a reservoir of technical information used by the Ramchargers a decade later when they used the first generation Hemi in its drag racing program.

The Hemi came along just in time for Briggs Cunningham, a man who was making a name for himself on both sides of the Atlantic. In 1950, Cunningham's racing team placed 10th and 11th at LeMans running mildly modified Cadillacs with that division's new V-8. However, Cadillac was not forthcoming with V-8s the following year and Cunningham was forced to look elsewhere. The Hemi was the answer. He designed and built a special roadster, the C2, using the Hemi V-8. However, he chose to use higher compression Cadillac pistons, and

the car did not fare well on the lower octane French gasoline at LeMans, and he finished 18th in the 1951 race. In the 1952 race, a Cunningham C4-R finished an amazing fourth, routinely surpassing 150 miles per hour down the Mulsanne straight.

Stateside, Carl Kiekhaefer, whose corporation manufactured the Mercury outboard engines, also discovered the Hemi V-8. In 1951 he entered two Chrysler Saratogas in the Carrera PanAmericana, or Mexican Road Race. John Fitch in car No. 32 was actually leading the Ferraris in the first leg of the race until he was forced to retire because of a faulty oil pressure relief valve. Tony Bettenhausen drove No. 7 to 16th place. While disappointing, Bettenhausen did set two-way average speed records of 112.50 miles per hour and 114.33 miles per hour.

The horsepower race was on, as Detroit manufacturers discovered horsepower was a powerful sales tool. But more than that, the automotive press now started making its presence felt by comparing one manufacturer's offerings against another. The point of comparison was not style, appointments, or even price. It was horsepower, so GM and Ford began responding. In 1952, Cadillac countered with a 190 horsepower V-8. Lincoln introduced its 160 horsepower V-8 and the press made its displeasure known. Nevertheless, Lincoln walked away with the first four place finishes in the 1952 Mexican Road Race; for 1953 Lincoln bumped its V-8 output to 205 horsepower.

Chrysler was not overly concerned about this, because the corporation could dial in however much horsepower it wanted. For 1953 Chrysler offered a heavy-duty performance package optional on the New Yorker. The Hemi V-8 featured two four-barrel carburetors, and more aggressive profile camshaft using roller tappets, and a higher compression ratio. The engine was rated very conservatively at 235 horsepower. Underneath, the New Yorker received front and rear anti-roll bars, stiffer suspension, front disc brakes, and other upgrades. So good was this car that it seized impressive wins during the 1953 and 1954 Grand National seasons. Output for the standard 331 cubic inch Chrysler FirePower was bumped up in 1954 to 195 horsepower; a higher compression version of the Dodge Red Ram with 150 horsepower was available and the DeSoto FireDome now developed 170 horsepower. While all these cars were good performers, their styling left something to be desired, mired in the postwar mold.

Chrysler was aware of this and was preparing to turn the automotive world on its ear once again, determined to shake off its conservative image. The high-performance development work that showed the Hemi's potential was about to bear fruit.

The Chrysler 300

Bob Rodger joined Chrysler in 1939 and was enrolled in the Chrysler Institute. Upon graduating in 1941 with a Master's degree in automotive engineering, he worked in the engine development lab. He was closely involved in the development of the Hemi and remained in engine development until 1951. That year he was made assistant chief engineer of the Chrysler division and in 1952 was promoted to chief engineer. One of the engine programs he watched carefully was the A311, or Indianapolis 500 racing engine. This engine began life in the form, ostensibly, as a tire test car first for Firestone, then Goodyear. At least, that was the company line. What it was, actually, was a rolling test-bed that pushed the performance envelope of the Hemi.

"The A311 was made with large ports and roller tappets," says Harold Welch. "John Platner and Don Morre were deeply involved with the project. They used a Hilborn-injection system, which was common at Indianapolis at that time. That car was used for many miles of high-speed testing and it was able to easily run at regular Indianapolis speeds. As part of the dedication of the new Chrysler Proving Grounds [in Chelsea, Michigan] in June of 1954, the first four finishing drivers of that year's Indianapolis 500-mile race were invited to bring their winning cars to try them on the new highly banked 4.7-mile oval track. All of the drivers held their cars wide open through the turns, which was the first time any of them had had an opportunity to do so. Jack McGrath was the fastest, with 179 miles per hour. Even more amazing was that the Chrysler-powered Kurtis Kraft tire-test car then ran 182 miles per hour!"

Bob Rodger was at the dedication ceremonies that day, and the Chrysler test car's performance relative to the exotic Indy race cars made an indelible impression. Before Chrysler could enter the Indy 500 with its stock displacement Hemi, the ruling body changed the displacement rules down to 272 cubic inches. Chrysler engineers complied, but the change was too great a handicap for the pushrod, overhead valve V-8 to overcome. Nevertheless, Rodger wondered what a truly high-performance Chrysler sedan could do for

The Plymouth line of cars did not receive the Hemi V-8, staying with a more or less conventional combustion chamber design. In 1958, Plymouth introduced the Golden Commando V-8 and in 1959, the division announced the Golden Commando 395, the hottest engine in the Plymouth line. The Sport Furys in this ad were photographed at Chrysler's Chelsea, Michigan, proving grounds.

By the early 1960s, the Hemi V-8 had all but vanished from Chryslers and Dodges, replaced by Wedge-head V-8s of ever-increasing displacement. The Max Wedge 413s and later 426s were setting records coast to coast. Dodge used those victories to promote its 426 street Wedge for 1963 in ads like this one.

the corporation. This was helped along by the letters that would cross his desk asking if or when Chrysler would introduce such a car. No doubt he also had his imagination tweaked by the independent racers who were racing Hemi Chryslers with remarks such as, "You know, Bob, if you built a high-performance Hemi and put it in a good-looking Chrysler, you'd really have something. . . ."

Rodger discussed the concept with Ed Braden, Chrysler's sales manager. Braden was enthusiastic to the concept of such a car. Together, they went to Chrysler Division manager Ed Quinn and sold him on the idea. Chrysler's director of styling, Virgil Exner, was called in. Due to the long-lead nature of a uniquely bodied car, however, it was agreed to use sheet metal from the new, forthcoming 1955 Chrysler line with styling elements unique to this car. The engineers worked on extracting 300 stock horsepower from the 331 cubic-inch Hemi, so the car was given the name C-300. This kind of stock horsepower from an American car had not been seen since the mighty Duesenbergs of the early 1930s.

The Chrysler 300 achieved its unique appearance, in simple terms, by starting with the unadorned two-door Windsor model, per Exner's behest, and using the split egg-crate grille from the Imperial. Other chrome trim pieces were deleted or added to further distinguish the car. The medallion between the split grille, on the rear flanks, and the trunk lid of the car identified it as a Chrysler 300.

Under the hood was the highest level of Hemi V-8 development to date. Displacement was still 331 cubic inches, but horsepower output was way up. With dual four-barrel Carter WCFB carburetors and running a 8.5:1 compression ratio, the Chrysler 300 Hemi for 1955 developed 300 horsepower at 5,200 rpm with 345 foot-pounds of torque at 3,200 rpm. Were there any contenders? Well, the Cadillac Eldorado, weighing nearly a half ton more, developed 270 horsepower. In terms of horsepower per cubic inch, the Chrysler 300 was at the top of the heap, with .92 horsepower per cubic inch.

Going Public

The first public display of the Chrysler 300's prowess supervised by a sanctioning body took place in February 1955 at Daytona Beach for the famous Daytona Speed Week. The car could not have had a more conspicuous or successful debut. In the flying mile for American stock cars, the Chrysler 300 took first, second, and third places. Warren Koechling drove his personal C-300 to first place with a two-way average of 127.580 miles per hour. Only one mile per hour, roughly, separated the three Chryslers, proving all three were uniformly stock. In distant fourth was a 1955 Cadillac with a two-way average speed of 120.478 miles per hour.

Carl Kiekhaefer wasted no time preparing a team of C-300s and drivers to campaign during the 1955 NASCAR and AAA racing season. The Kiekhaefer C-300s won 37 races and won both titles for that year. It was a record that Chrysler built upon when it introduced the 300B for 1956. The top-of-the-line Hemi in the top-of-the-line Chrysler was bumped to 354 cubic inches and now pumped out 340 horsepower with 385 foot-pounds of torque at 3,400 rpm. However, there was an optional high compression version with 10.0:1 compression, 355 horsepower, and 405 foot-pounds of torque. There was an almost bewildering array of Hemi power in various displacements among the Chrysler, Dodge, and DeSoto lines of cars for 1956, and Hemi was on the lips of enthusiasts, magazine editors, and, most important, car buyers across America.

The Chrysler 300 really did have mystique about it. With its now-legendary racing victories and awesome horsepower, the 300B turned heads wherever it was seen. The legend grew in 1956, with Chrysler again taking the NASCAR title. The Kiekhaefer-sponsored team won 16 races in a row. Chrysler capitalized on the success of its 300 in its advertising. In an ad picturing a 300B getting the checkered flag under the bright lights of a nighttime race, the copy read, "Let's get one thing straight . . . Chrysler had won every major competition in 1956! And don't confuse Chrysler's Grand Slam wins in all the big events with those 'in their class' wins that you may have read about. When Chrysler competes it competes against all comers!"

All of Chrysler Corporation's car divisions received all-new sheet metal for 1957, and the Fin era was now in full swing. Chrysler reduced its offerings from seven distinct models to four: Windsor, Saratoga (absent since 1953), New Yorker, and the 300C. Horsepower kept climbing, as did compression ratios. The venerable 331 Hemi was dropped. The Windsor was now powered by a 285-horsepower 354 cubic-inch Hemi. The Saratoga had 10 more horsepower this year. And now, there was a new Hemi: the 392 cubic-inch V-8. This was a raised-block design with a 4.00-inch bore and 3.90-inch stoke. It had bigger valves and ports. In single four-barrel trim it developed 325 horsepower and churned out 430 foot-pounds of torque; this engine was standard in the New Yorker.

The most powerful Chrysler 392 that year was reserved for the 300C. The dual four-barrel, radically cammed 392 Hemi with 9.25:1 compression developed 375 horsepower at 5,200 rpm with 420 foot-pounds of torque at 4,000 rpm. The optional 10.0:1 compression version developed 390 horsepower with 430 foot-pounds of torque.

The Hemi Sputters

Some automotive pundits felt the late 1950s were an era of excess in terms of horsepower and styling, and that is true. This is evident in model names as well. DeSoto was a prime example. For 1957, you could choose from the Firesweep, FireDome, Fireflight, and Adventurer. For less fanciful types, there was also the Explorer and Shopper station wagons. This was to be the last year for the Hemi engine in DeSotos; it would be replaced by the Turboflash V-8—no joke—in 1958. The Turboflash V-8 was a Wedge combustion-chamber design and was a portent of things to come at Chrysler. All this fire and flash was to no avail, however, as DeSoto ceased car production with its 1961 line.

The days for the Chrysler Corporation Hemi were indeed numbered, although the venerable 300 model would continue well into the next decade. The company had been working on a less-expensive Wedge-head design, and engines with the new cylinder head made their debut in 1958. For that year at Dodge, the lone Hemi offering was the 325, which was at a distinct disadvantage when stacked up against the new 350 and 361 cubic-inch Wedge engines that developed more horsepower. The Hemi still dominated the engine lineup at Chrysler for 1958 and all the 354 and 392 Hemis sported 10.0:1 compressions. This was the last year for the first-generation Hemi in the Chrysler line of cars.

Why was such a thoroughly proven and successful engine design scrapped? Mel Drinkard frankly states that the Hemi was replaced for purely economic reasons. Harold Welch agrees, but says there were other reasons involved.

"To our chagrin," Welch recalls, "our management thought we were spending more producing our engine than Ford and General Motors were with their wedge-shaped combustion chambers, and manufacturing was interested in building a new, central engine plant to build engines [for all divisions]. So, for primarily economic reasons, the B and raised-B engines built at Trenton eventually replaced the Hemi. They were somewhat lighter than the Hemi and more economical as far as material is concerned, and then, of course, the cars began to get heavier, so that the V-8 for Dodge and DeSoto ended up being too small. That combination of things replaced the first generation family of Hemis with the B and raised-B engines."

The Rise of the Wedge

The unadorned truth was Chrysler had made dramatic gains in the power output of combustion chambers other than the Hemi in V-8 engines in its engine labs. All during the mid-1950s, the dyno rooms in Highland Park were resounding with the sound of more conventional V-8s in development test-running at full tilt. The improvement in performance relative to Chrysler's previous conventional combustion chamber designs clearly put the Hemi in peril.

The first of these new V-8s with poly-sphere-shaped combustion chambers was introduced in 1956. It was a small-displacement, 277 cubic-inch V-8 with a 3.75-inch bore and 3.12-inch stroke, the first V-8 in a series Chrysler called the "A" engine family. These were to be small-block V-8s built in various displacements. Concurrently, Chrysler was engineering big-block V-8s with wedge-shaped combustion chambers; these would be the "B" engine family. In standard trim the 277 cubic-inch V-8 developed 187 horsepower. It was offered in the Plymouth line of cars.

In 1957, the 301 replaced the 277 cubic-inch V-8 and the 318 cubic-inch V-8 was introduced. The 301 was also short-lived, being offered in 1957 only. The two-barrel version of the 318 developed 230 horsepower while the four-barrel version introduced in 1958 was rated at 260 horsepower. The 318 was also available with a dual four-barrel carburetor setup in 1957 that developed 290 horsepower. The 318 remained in production until 1966 and was referred to as the "old style" 318. Lightweight casting techniques were finally adopted in 1967 and the first of "L.A." engines was the 273 cubic-inch V-8 introduced that year. A high-performance four-barrel version of this engine followed. Still, performance enthusiasts in the late 1950s and early 1960s knew even then there was no substitute for cubic inches.

The "B" series big-block Wedge V-8 was introduced in 1958 in both 350 and 361 cubic-inch displacements. These were bread and butter V-8s but with the introduction of the 383 in 1959, the real performance using a wedge-type combustion chamber was launched. Chrysler made sure it had a hot runner available among the 383s offered in 1959, with a dual four-barrel version

that produced 345 horsepower at 5,000 rpm with 420 foot-pounds of torque at 3,600 rpm. This engine was offered only in Dodges; the largest V-8 offered in Plymouths was the 305-horsepower, 361 cubic-inch V-8. During the first few years of the 383's production life, Chrysler worked to get the engine sorted out. The low-block version of the 383 had a 4.25-inch bore by 3.38-inch stroke. The high-block version of the 383 had a 4.03-inch bore by 3.75-inch stroke. The short stroke, low-block version of the 383 replaced the high-block version in 1960 and was manufactured through 1971.

The Longhorn Cross-ram 383

Chrysler ushered in the 1960s with one of the wildest-looking engines anyone had ever seen. Known to enthusiasts as the longhorn cross-ram 383, the engine bespoke performance with a capital P. Chrysler had been doing some remarkable things in its engine labs with regard to induction systems, and this engine reflected the success of that work. A four-barrel carburetor was suspended over each side of the engine via a cast-aluminum manifold; the carburetor fed into a plenum beneath each carburetor with two Siamese runners crossing over the valve covers to the cylinder head on the opposite side of the engine.

Two versions of this manifold were manufactured, a short-ram and a long-ram design. Only the long-ram version was offered in the standard passenger cars. The short-ram versions were only offered over the Mopar parts counter to be used in racing. What was the difference between the two? Actually, the long- and short-ram manifolds were identical dimensionally, but they differed internally. In the long-ram manifold, the wall between the pair of passages reached all the way from the plenum chamber beneath the carburetor to the cylinder head surface; this was done to achieve maximum torque. In the short-ram manifold, this wall extended only 10-1/2 inches from the cylinder head surface. The long-ram version, known as the D-500 Ram Induction, tuned at a lower rpm than the short-ram unit. In other words, the long ram was designed for the street and the short ram was designed for the strip and circle-track racing.

The D-500 383 with long-ram manifolds produced 330 horsepower at 4,800 rpm with 460 foot-pounds of torque at 2,800 rpm. With short-ram manifolds, it produced 340 horsepower at 5,000 rpm with 440 foot-pounds of torque at 2,800 rpm. Dodge had just the right

car to put it in—the restyled Dart. This option made the automotive magazine editors sit up and take notice. *Motor Trend* and *Hot Rod* both tested the Dart with the D-500 optional V-8 and it bowled them over. Despite the four-door Dart Phoenix's weight of 4,005 pounds, the editors at *Motor Trend* achieved a 0-60 miles per hour time of 6.8 seconds and a quarter-mile time of 16.0 seconds at 94 miles per hour in their D-500 equipped Dart with TorqueFlight transmission. "For all-out performance," the editors wrote, "the 1961 car buyer has to look no further than Dodge's newest Dart with its optional powerplant, the brutal D-500 ram-induction engine."

Hot Rod magazine decided to hop up the engine and check its top speed capability using over-the-counter Chrysler parts. With the short-ram manifolds, 284-degree mechanical camshaft, and other modifications, the D-500 Dart streaked across the dry El Mirage lakebed at 134.12 miles per hour.

Chryslers continued to be offered with Hemis but the 383 and 413 cubic-inch Wedge V-8s were offered for the first time. The 413 was a Raised Block (RB) design having a 4.18-inch bore and a 3.75-inch stroke. Very soon, the 413 would put Dodge and Plymouth on the drag racing map. Also available in Dodges were the 383s and 413s that composed the Maximum Special Police Packages. These included a single four-barrel 325-horsepower 383 and 350-horsepower 413; a dual four-barrel short-ram 340-horsepower 383 and 375-horsepower 413; and a dual four-barrel "Runner"-type manifold 330-horsepower 383 and 375-horsepower 413. The AMA specifications did not define the difference between the "Runner"-type manifold and the Ram-type manifolds. It was an almost bewildering selection to go through.

Plymouth's equivalent to the Dodge Dart was the Sport Fury. It was available with many of the same powertrain options as the Dart. The Sport Fury didn't have the same performance image as the Dart, however, and Plymouth sales in general were at their lowest levels in years. Fortunately for both Dodge and Plymouth, the musclecar era was just a few years away and both makes would become famous for building some of the most powerful and imaginative cars in North America.

The 383 continued to be a good all-around V-8 in Dodges and Plymouths, and in high-performance versions, a very respectable performer on the street. The 383 gained renewed prominence with the advent of the Plymouth

In 1966, Dodge released the Charger. From its vacuum-operated concealed headlights (with headlights turned on for this publicity shot) to the trailing edge of its sleek fastback roofline, it was the closest thing yet to a showcar hitting the streets.

This is Dodge Charger

Watch out for the fastback that's full-sized and fully loaded. Dodge Charger is one dream car that sprang to life with all the excitement and fresh ideas intact. With styling that swivels heads in your neighborhood as fast and often as it did in auto shows a year ago. With comfort that won't quit and standard features that usually cost extra—tach, a racing-style steering wheel, bucket seats all around. Plus power choices all the way up to the hot, optional 426 Street Hemi. Leave it to Dodge to do things right, right? So do right by yourself. Check out Charger, the Dodge Rebellion's hot new leader that's stirring up excitement on streets and highways everywhere. Do it now. The Dodge Rebellion wants you.

Dodge Charger

DODGE DIVISION   CHRYSLER MOTORS CORPORATION

Put down undersized, underequipped personal cars ...go Charger.

YOU HAVE A CHANCE OF WINNING A DODGE CHARGER—REGISTER AT YOUR DODGE DEALER'S.

The advertising budget for the 1966 Charger was considerable, and Dodge placed numerous color ads throughout the enthusiast magazines. This ad announces the fact the 426 Hemi was now available to drive on the street. Ford and General Motors were not happy.

Road Runner and Dodge Super Bee in 1968, but in the early 1960s, Chrysler began a big push in the 400-plus cubic inch Wedge V-8s. It was with these largest Wedge V-8s that Chrysler would spend the most advertising dollars promoting its fledgling performance image.

Large Wedge V-8s

The 413 was introduced first in Chryslers in 1959, then in Dodges in 1961. The Ramchargers were putting Chrysler on the performance map and the Dodge name

before drag strip enthusiasts. With the introduction in 1962 of the Dodge 413 Ramcharger and Plymouth Super Stock 413 for drag racing, Chrysler became the hottest name at drag strips from coast to coast. That winning performance image rubbed off on the street 413, and that was the whole idea.

In an effort to build its showroom traffic and sales, Plymouth loudly touted its restyled, top-of-the-line 1962 Sport Fury. A brochure issued to dealers read: "Sport Fury—for the man who wants to go first class—fast! The luxury leader of the low-priced field—with sizzling performance to make your prospects' eyes pop!" How could a car be the "luxury leader of the low-priced field"? It sounded like an oxymoron, but it was classic automotive promotion. In fact, the Sport Fury was simply a dressier Belvedere. The Sport Fury interior featured bucket seats with center console and distinctive interior trim. The car was laden with chrome trim inside and out. The paint colors were inviting: Silhouette Black, Ermine White, Cherry Red, Pale Gray, Pale Blue, Luminous Blue, and Luminous Brown. The 305-horsepower 361 V-8 was the standard powerplant. Available was the four-barrel 383 that had the same horsepower but met the needs of the street with more torque at a lower rpm. The more powerful 340-horsepower 413 was on tap to boost the car's performance even further.

Rocket-fueled Development

America in the early 1960s was going through an engineering renaissance on numerous fronts. After the shock of the Russians launching Sputnik into orbit around the earth on October 4, 1957, the United States embarked on its own space program. But when Russia put the first man into space on April 12, 1961, America started a crash program to beat the Soviets, and the Space Race was launched. After Alan Shepard's suborbital flight and John Glen's orbital flights as part of the Mercury space program, pride and confidence returned to America. Nevertheless, the largest rockets the world was to ever see were on the drawing boards with the eventual goal of landing American astronauts on the moon first.

The same engineering mood was coursing through the automotive firms in Detroit. While it was important to make and market cars for "everyman," performance fever had gripped General Motors, Ford, and Chrysler. The engine displacement war was raging by 1963, driven by the stock car and drag racing sanctioning bodies issuing displacement limits that encouraged manufacturers to raise the bar.

For Chrysler, that meant bringing out a new 426 cubic-inch V-8 in various states of tune for 1963. The 426 had the same 3.75-inch stroke of the 413 but had a larger 4.25-inch bore to get the increased displacement. Depending on the model of Dodge or Plymouth you chose, the 426 was available in four different states of tune. For example, in the full-size Dodge 330, 440, Polara, and Polara 500, you could order the 426 with single four-barrel carb and 11.0:1 compression having 370 horsepower or with a 12.5:1 compression version for drag racing having 385 horsepower. As the Ramcharger 426 with dual four-barrel carbs on the cross-ram intake manifold, the engine was offered in 11.0:1 compression having 415 horsepower, while the same engine with optional 13.5:1 pistons produced 425 horsepower.

Conceivably, you could drive the 11.0:1 compression 426 Ramcharger on the street with the right super-premium gasoline, but the cross-ram manifold was really for high rpm applications encountered at the strip—above 4,000 rpm—which made driving it on the street difficult. Still, it made for a tremendous street racer in 1963. There was no question, however, that the Dodge Ramcharger 426 and Plymouth Super Stock 426 were engineered solely for the quarter-mile strip.

Annual model changes were a fixture with Detroit manufacturers because it gave buyers a reason to go look at the new models. The car manufacturers considered this a necessary expense of doing business, and few challenged the conventional wisdom. Actually, it permitted them the opportunity to correct past mistakes when the car buyers voted with their dollars.

For 1963, the styling of both Dodges and Plymouths was improved from the forced lines on the 1962 models. The biggest news at Dodge, for example, was the downsizing of the Dart to a compact. To performance enthusiasts, however, what was under the hood was of more interest than the car's appearance.

Besides the aforementioned 426, there were four 383s to choose from. The two-barrel 383 was rated at 305 horsepower, there were 330- and 360-horsepower, four-barrel 383s, and the top-rated 383 was the dual four-barrel longhorn cross-ram version with 390 horsepower. The 413 was caught in the middle of the displacement lineup, but its existence was not immediately threatened. The four-barrel 413 available developed 340 horsepower. More 413s were on the drawing boards and due for release in 1964.

Not all developments were in the realm of engine engineering, however. Chrysler had a brand new model in the wings, to be released by Plymouth division. It was a decision that would have long-term ramifications when the golden era of musclecar mania reached its apex in the late 1960s and early 1970s.

Turning Up the Heat

Plymouth product planners were not caught entirely off-guard by the release of the Ford Mustang, but watched with concern as it sold to many eager young buyers, and those young at heart. That was because they were working on a sporty compact of their own, to be called the Barracuda. Joe Sturm, Chrysler product planner at the time, says, "The Valiant was a fine car for Mr. and Mrs. America, but there was a feeling around the studio that a sportier derivative was needed."

Introduced in May 1964, the Barracuda employed the "something borrowed, something new" approach. It was based on the 106-inch wheelbase Valiant, sharing all sheet metal forward of the firewall and below the car's beltline, but incorporated a striking fastback roofline. This hybrid design approach was a good one; design engineering time and tooling costs were cut in half. As conceived, practically all of the fastback was glass, which wrapped down to the fenderline. Planning and sketching at the Plymouth studio coincided with development of large pieces of automotive glass by Pittsburgh Plate Glass. The result of this collaboration was the largest rear window ever installed on a standard production car up to that time, measuring 14.4 square feet.

The fastback glass design was more than sporty, it was functional. Visibility to the rear and interior volume both increased greatly. However, the consequent greenhouse effect also raised interior temperatures during sunny days. A carpeted, folding security panel separated the interior from the trunk area. By folding the rear seatbacks forward and lowering the security panel, you had an enclosed area seven feet long to carry skis, lumber, or other long cargo. A handsome chrome bar prevented cargo from sliding forward into the front passenger seats.

What powertrain options did the sporty Barracuda have? To keep the base list price to $2,365, the 101-horsepower, 170 cubic-inch six-cylinder was standard. Optional was the 145-horsepower, 225 cubic-inch six and the two-barrel 180-horsepower, 273 cubic-inch V-8. Also optional was Chrysler's new four-speed manual transmission with Hurst linkage; a three-speed manual was standard. The suspension was standard Valiant. No, the Barracuda was no *gran turismo,* but it nevertheless struck a nerve with buyers. Despite its very late model-year introduction, the handsome car sold more than 23,000 units.

There were other changes at Dodge and Plymouth for 1964. Stylistically, both divisions featured sheet metal changes, but as before, that's not what all the talk was about. The big news for '64 was the new street Wedge 426. Chrysler engineers knew they would have to turn up the heat and had been development-testing the 426 in its dynamometer cells. The result was high-performance 426 for the street—the Plymouth Commando 426, and the Dodge High-Performance 426 V-8. With single four-barrel carb and 10.3:1 compression ratio, the engine developed 365 horsepower at 4,800 rpm with 470 foot-pounds of torque at 3,200 rpm. One magazine tested a Plymouth Sport Fury powered with this engine, reaching 60 miles per hour in 6.8 seconds and covering the quarter-mile in 15.2 seconds. There were still 413s and 383s to select from if maximum street performance was not what the customer wanted.

The buzz among enthusiast circles, however, was a completely new engine rumored to have hemispherical combustion chamber cylinder heads with a radical valvetrain hidden under huge valve covers. That engine, of course, was the 426 Hemi. It was strictly for racing, everyone was told. (The complete story of the 426 Hemi is in Chapter Five.) Magazine editors kicked around the wild notion of future street cars powered by this engine. "Can you imagine a 426 Hemi on the street? Wow!" Well, it would turn out to be not such a wild notion, after all, but that would have to wait for 1966.

If there was any complaint that could be leveled at Dodge and Plymouth performance cars in 1964, it was this: there was no specific car with a performance identity. This might not have even come up, if it had not been for the new Pontiac GTO.

Amazing what just three letters can do for a car. The GTO was a Tempest with a high-performance 389 stuffed under the hood, and those letters that would make the car immortal. It took the market by storm. Still, Dodge and Plymouth management reasoned, there was no substitute for cubic inches, and Chrysler Corporation offered that in *spades.* Soon, the market would be awash with performance cars with identifiable names: Oldsmobile 442, Buick GS, Chevrolet SS, Mustang GT, and so on. Dodge and Plymouth would soon respond with performance-specific models of their own.

The Roaring '65s

Because new models are typically introduced in the fall, no sooner had the 1964 Barracuda been launched, it seemed, than Plymouth issued literature for the 1965 model. There were subtle cosmetic changes reflected in the new brochure, but these were so slight the two brochures were almost identical. Plymouth wanted to establish the Barracuda as a distinct model. Consequently, the Valiant chrome script that appeared on the '64 model's trunk lid was deleted for 1965. The standard engines were now the 225 cubic-inch six and—yes—the 273 cubic-inch V-8. That's because there was a new high-performance V-8 on the options list. That engine was the Commando 273 V-8, which pumped out a respectable 235 horsepower, with the aid of a four-barrel carb, and cost just under a century note.

To make the performance Barracuda buyer's decision a lot easier, Plymouth introduced the Formula S. This included the Commando 273 V-8, Rallye Pack suspension, wide-rim 14-inch wheels mounted with Goodyear Blue Streak tires, 6,000 rpm tachometer, and other goodies. A Formula S medallion on the left and right front fenders identified the car.

Road & Track tested the 1965 Barracuda Formula S with the optional four-speed manual transmission. The car reached 60 miles per hour in 8.2 seconds and covered the quarter-mile in 15.9 seconds doing 85 miles per hour through the lights. For such a small V-8, this performance was impressive. The editors wrote, "For those people who enjoy sports car driving but, for reasons of family or business need four seats and adequate baggage space, the Barracuda would certainly make an excellent compromise." Plymouth had hit the nail squarely on the head and sales figures proved it: more than 60,000 Barracudas were sold in 1965.

The 1965 Barracuda was just one of "The Roaring '65s," Plymouth's ad campaign promoting performance in its car line. Plymouth was just responding to market demand—and competition. The Pontiac GTO had taken the market by storm, and was back even stronger for 1965. Plymouth responded using the basic numbers approach. To promote the new top-of-the-line Belvedere, the Satellite, Plymouth ran an ad with a

To lower the cost of high performance, Dodge introduced the Coronet R/T in 1967. Powered by the new 375-horsepower 440 Magnum V-8, it offered near-Hemi-like performance at a fraction of the cost. Nonfunctional hood louvers and R/T badging identified the car.

white Satellite at speed with a youthful driver behind the wheel. In bold text below the photo were the words, "Torque, 470 foot-pounds at 3,200 rpm. Not exactly sulky." The first ad line read, "For a street machine, Plymouth Belvedere Satellite's acceleration curve reads like something out of science fiction." No question, torque was what mattered on the street, and the high-performance 426 street Wedge V-8 did not disappoint. The Plymouth line definitely benefited from the division's winning way on drag strips and circle tracks. 426 Hemi-powered Belvederes had taken 13 firsts out of 18 stock car events sanctioned by the United States Auto Club (USAC), to give Plymouth the undisputed Manufacturers' Championship title in

1965. Norm Nelson was the top driver in USAC point standings. However, due to NASCAR's temporary ban on the 426 Hemi during half of 1965, Richard Petty wasn't able to repeat winning the Grand National title as he had in 1964. Instead, he went drag racing! He helped to engineer a specially modified Barracuda with a 426 Hemi set back through the firewall, which pushed the driving position back considerably. The car was titled "Outlawed" and carried the number 43/Jr.

NASCAR had let the 426 Hemi compete during 1964, but put the hammer down in 1965, because the engine was not offered in street-driven passenger cars off the assembly line. That, of course, proved a momentous decision, forcing Chrysler's hand to certify the awesome

The 1967 Coronet R/T was offered both as a two-door hardtop and as a convertible. R/T badging appeared also on the rear quarter panels and on the taillight fascia.

Hemi for the street. Chrysler engineers immediately got to work to civilize the racing engine for street cars, both Dodges and Plymouths. Racing, especially stock car racing, was vital to the corporation's interests, and it was not going to be left out in the cold. Chrysler wanted its Dodges and Plymouths in the winner's circle.

To correspond with Plymouth's new Satellite, Dodge offered the new Coronet for 1965. The intermediate-size Coronet was the basis of much of Dodge's performance efforts for the rest of the decade. There was no Coronet performance model yet, like the GTO, but the engines were there to smoke the competition—including the GTO—on the street. The 225 cubic-inch six was standard in the Coronet, to keep the price as low as possible,

but there were many optional V-8s, including the 273, 318 and 361 cubic-inch V-8s. Serious street work required the 330-horsepower, four-barrel 383. The top performance engine was the 365-horsepower 426 Wedge.

How did the 365-horsepower 426 Wedge in the Coronet stack up against its competition at Ford and GM? *Motor Trend* tested a Coronet 500 with this engine and the four-speed manual transmission. The car reached 60 miles per hour in 7.7 seconds and covered the quarter-mile in 15.7 seconds at 89 miles per hour. A low numerical axle ratio may have been behind these numbers.

Although Dodge wouldn't announce the availability of the 426 street Hemi until the 1966 model year, it did advertise the availability of the race Hemi in the 1965 Coronet. The ad appeared in the December 1964 *Hot Rod*, with the tag line, "Our new 426 Coronet ought to have its head examined." The ad left no doubt the Hemi was available in the Coronet, at one point asking, "Why not drop a Hemi in the new Coronet 500?" Clearly, the implication was you could drive a Hemi Coronet on the street, but the ad failed to tell you one

The Coronet R/T featured bucket seats with shifter console. The original owner of this car chose Chrysler's superb TorqueFlight automatic transmission to harness the 440 Magnum's torque and get it to the pavement.

Despite the big-block Wedge's size, there was still plenty of room under the hood of the Coronet R/T. That room was needed when the optional 426 Hemi was ordered.

thing: This was a race Hemi, and ran with a 12.5:1 compression ratio. Dodge was more than happy to build you a 426 Hemi Coronet at its Lynch Road assembly plant. These assembly line drag cars were giving Ford and GM fits at drag strips from New York to California. The Plymouth Golden Commandos and Dodge Ramchargers drove the Hemis with superb racing success.

The Dodge Rebellion

In 1966, Chrysler hit the automotive world with a double whammy. It introduced the sleek, new Dodge Charger, and it introduced the 426 street-Hemi V-8 in Dodges and Plymouths. With them came what would become one of the most famous corporate division ad campaigns. "The Dodge Rebellion wants you!" These were the words of beautiful blonde Pam Austin, heard in millions of living rooms across America during 1966. Miss Austin was the first in a series of eye-catching representatives for Dodge cars into the early 1970s. Dodge indeed was rebelling from its market perception of offering powerful cars with rather staid styling.

The Dodge Charger of 1966 was tangible evidence of this new thinking. Its styling was the embodiment of that exciting new image. Dodge christened the Charger "The Leader of the Dodge Rebellion"—its performance flagship. The Charger and Coronet shared the same platform and, hence, the same dimensions. As a whole, the Charger's styling and that of the Coronet shared side and front-end sheetmetal, but the addition of the fastback totally altered the Charger's overall look and character. The Charger "wowed" visitors to the big three auto shows around America: New York, Chicago, and Los Angeles.

The interior of the Charger was one of the most exciting and well thought-out designs of the 1960s. There were four padded, stitched-vinyl bucket seats. A full-length console separated the front and rear seats. Courtesy lights were positioned on the console forward of the front seats. A padded armrest was mounted to the console for the driver and passenger. The rear seating borrowed a concept from the 1964 Barracuda. The rear seatbacks and armrest separating them could be folded forward; dropping the hinged trunk panel separating the trunk from the interior, and opening the trunk lid, you then had an area four-by-seven-and-a-half feet. It is one of the best examples of space utilization to come out of Detroit. Complementing the interior appointments was a tasteful blend of brushed aluminum and chrome trim on the console, doors, and rear quarter panels.

Standard engine in the Charger was the two-barrel, 230-horsepower, 318 cubic-inch V-8. Optional were the 265-horsepower 361, four-barrel 325-horsepower 383, and the new dual-quad 425-horsepower 426 Hemi V-8. The TorqueFlight automatic transmission behind the 426 Hemi made an awesome street combination. However, the power and prestige of having a 426 Hemi under the hood came with a price. The option was more than $500 in the Charger, Coronet, Belvedere, or Satellite. This covered much more than just the engine. Heavy-duty suspension, brakes, and driveline components were part of the package.

Like the Dodge Coronet and Charger, the Plymouth Belvedere, and Satellite were also re-skinned with new sheet metal. Plymouth, however, did not get a flashy fastback of its own. Chrysler did not want to double its tooling cost for Plymouth to have a similar model, and the corporation was interested in seeing how Dodge's new car would do in the market. However, performance models were being made ready at

Dodge and Plymouth. For 1967, Plymouth introduced the GTX and Dodge introduced the Coronet R/T. (For the GTX story, see Chapter Three.)

In November 1966, two-page color ads appeared in enthusiast magazines, with the bold copy: "Enter the Big Bore Hunter." The ad copy read in part, "Drag fans, here's your car. Coronet R/T packs 440 cubic inches of go. The big-inch, deep-breathing 440-Magnum sports a special 4-barrel carburetor, larger exhaust valves, longer duration cam and low-restriction dual exhaust." The R/T quite clearly marked the car as a dual-purpose machine—for both road and track. The Coronet R/T's appearance differed from other Coronets by having a unique grill that resembled the Charger's, but with exposed headlights. R/T badges appeared on the front grille, on the sides above and forward of the rear wheels, and near the right rear taillight. Nonfunction hoodscoops also marked the car as an R/T. That R/T meant 375 horsepower with 480 foot-pounds of torque. Backing up the 440 Magnum was either the four-speed manual transmission or Torque-Flight automatic as standard equipment. The Coronet R/T was available as either a hardtop or convertible. The hardtop listed for $3,199 and the ragtop for $3,438. How did the Coronet R/T stack up against the 426 Hemi Coronet the year before? The numbers were virtually identical, with the R/T reaching 60 miles per hour in 7.2 seconds and covering the quarter-mile in just over 14 seconds.

Dodge ran several different ads for the 1967 Coronet R/T. In the April 1967 issue of *Car & Driver* there appeared a very curious ad. A photomontage of the car and its specific features was set off by two bold words in lower-case letters: "road runner." How could these words appear in a Dodge ad only months before Plymouth announced its Belvedere Road Runner? Certainly, it was no secret among Chrysler product planners and management that a car called the Road Runner was nearing production for 1968. Consequently, it is odd that Dodge would take the liberty of using the words, even though the division didn't use the term as a vehicle name.

Chrysler was now coming out with cars having the visual impact to match their tire-melting power. Dodges and Plymouths were winning handsomely in NASCAR, NHRA, AHRA, and USAC. And it was no secret these mighty Mopars were winning on the street as well. The cars coming out of Dodge and Plymouth were great, but even greater cars were destined to come.

road runner

R/T the newest hot one from Dodge

It speaks softly, but carries a big kick. Dodge Coronet R/T. Just about the hottest thing going since the cast-iron stove. Witness these credentials: a rampaging 440-cubic-inch Magnum V8 that deals out **375 bhp** and **480 lbs.-ft. of torque**. 4-barrel carb . . . long duration cam . . . chrome engine dress-up . . . low-restriction dual exhaust . . . heavy-duty brakes and suspension . . . high-performance Red Streak tires . . . special air scoop design. With this standard getup, R/T is described by Super Stock magazine as "one of the best all-around performance packages being offered . . . as much or more performance per dollar than any other car currently available." If you wish, you can have the optional Hemi. And a tach. And mag-type wheel covers. And a lower-body paint stripe available through your Dealer. Check out R/T at your nearby Dodge Dealer's now.

 CHRYSLER MOTORS CORPORATION

MOTOR TREND / JUNE 1967

Dodge ran several different ads announcing its new high-performance Coronet R/T in 1967. This ad, which appeared in the June issue of *Motor Trend*, however, is most curious. It would be several months before Plymouth would announce its entry-level performance car, the Road Runner. Just a coincidence?

CHAPTER TWO

The Dodge Scat Pack

While the Dodge Rebellion was one of the best advertising campaigns of the 1960s, helping Chrysler stamp a performance image on its cars, stylistically the cars were relatively unchanged from the bread-and-butter models. The high-performance Dodges of the mid-1960s were real sleepers. Stoplight knights looking for a joust often didn't know whether that Coronet next to them had a 318 or a 440 Magnum. There was one exception, the Dodge Charger of 1966-67. No question, this car was a head-turner, from its vacuum-operated concealed headlights to the trailing edge of its sweeping fastback. It was the shot fired over the bows, so to speak, of Ford and General Motors. But even sleeker and more muscular cars were taking shape in the Dodge styling studios.

To tie together the new models to be introduced for 1968, Dodge's advertising agency came up with Dodge Fever. Dodge succeeded in raising your body temperature by creating, for 1968, the Dodge Scat Pack, a fleet of high-performance cars based on the Charger, Coronet, and the Dart. These three were the Charger R/T, the Coronet R/T, and the Dart GTS. The cars of the Scat Pack were identified as "The Cars with the Bumblebee Stripes." These stripes were appropriately wrapped around the tail end of the cars. The cars of the Dodge Scat Pack were introduced to the world through a full-color brochure insert in a number of enthusiast magazines in the fall of 1967, most notably the issue of *Car & Driver*. However, the car that was destined to get the most automotive press coverage was the striking new Charger. It was then, and remains to this day, one of the finest examples of performance styling to emerge from Detroit during the musclecar era. It served as the basis of even more aerodynamic cars to emerge from Dodge in its pursuit of the checkered flag in NASCAR.

The 1968 Charger

Bill Brownlie was chief of design of the Dodge studio at the time for the second-generation Charger's gestation. "I wanted to launch into something much more sporty and extremely aerodynamic in image and function than the 1967 model," Brownlie says, "something extremely masculine that looked like it had just come off the track at Daytona." Due to its tremendous success in NASCAR racing, Chrysler had the desire to design and market a full-size, four-passenger, two-door coupe that visually embodied this racing success. The Charger was the logical choice on which to focus this performance styling effort.

Brownlie put his styling studio to a contest, using one-eighth-scale models to visualize the concept. He had one major stipulation: "I wanted the car to look like the cab sitting on top of the lower body shell, a cockpit-type appearance in conjunction with a tapering down in

Dodge launched the Scat Pack in 1968. One of the Pack was the Coronet Super Bee. Powered by the high-performance 335-horsepower 383 ci V-8 with a list price just over $3,000, it was an entry-level musclecar aimed at the youth market.

front, the swelling of the sheet metal over the front wheels, the pinching of the waist, and the rapid swelling over the rear wheels, both in plan view and side view." Although Dodge had no full-size wind tunnel, aerodynamic engineers on the staff made necessary recommendations to the styling team. The final design, chosen by Brownlie and Charles Mitchell (in charge of pulling the Charger program together), was created by Richard Sias.

The body itself was a direct interpretation of the stated design stipulation. The bulges at the front and rear wheels gave physical meaning to the word muscle-car, which originally referred only to a car's horsepower. The most notable things about the body were the sharp edges and the subtle transition of these bulges that made it look as if it were machined out of one block of steel.

The cab that Brownlie spoke of was instrumental in the achievement of an aerodynamic look. As with the body, the roof of a car in the design development stage can consist of infinitely variable compound curves. This was critical with the Charger because of its inherent design concept. In the end, a designer has to choose which combination of curves will be used. Often it is strictly intuitive—what the designer personally feels is visually correct. On the 1968 Charger, the rear roof pillars swept back in a flying buttress configuration with a sharp trailing edge that beautifully set off the flat rear window. The line interface between the windows and the roof broke slightly at the vertical door line before running down to the body. This Charger was one of the few designs where a vinyl roof enhanced the appearance. It was most dramatic when a black vinyl roof was ordered with brilliant red or yellow paint. A white vinyl roof contrasted best with dark body colors.

Certain details contributed to the 1968 Charger's racetrack appearance. The concealed headlights were carried over from the previous model, and the entire grille was blacked out to resemble the taped-over headlights of stock cars. Another race-bred detail was the quick-fill gas cap on the driver side. It was originally conceived for both sides, using a saddle-type gas tank to facilitate fill-up regardless of which side of the bump the driver pulled up on. This idea was scrapped to save on costs. The large hood scallops were a prominent stylistic feature that could accept optional turn indicators. This scallop detail was repeated on the doors.

The result of this unbridled enthusiasm and attention to detail was and still is an aesthetic triumph. It was successful because the original design platform was adhered to. There were no abrupt changes in the sheet metal. It was literally smooth and consistent from nose to tail. *Car & Driver* had this to say about the new Charger: "The new Charger is beautiful. It looks like a real racer, it's all guts and purpose, and—unlike the Mako Shark-inspired Corvette, it's completely fresh and unexpected." Bill Brownlie was right on the money.

The Bumble Bee stripes were standard on the Super Bee and helped to distinguish the car on the street. The small Bumble Bee logo also appeared on the taillight panel.

If any of the cars of the Dodge Scat Pack could produce Dodge Fever, it was the new Charger. As one of the brochures put it: "Down the road slips a new low shape, and you can feel the Fever setting in. The more you look, the harder you fall. For Charger. Every man's dream. Wearing the shape of tomorrow and a price tag that means you can have it today. Watch it, you're getting Dodge Fever . . . and there's only one cure. Charger." Enthusiasts may recall the mini-skirted vivacious brunette in the Dodge Fever ads. Her name was Joan Parker.

The interior of the new Charger was more subdued than earlier models. The front and rear seats were flat, almost plain, with only a "split hide" detail on the seat faces. Dodge erroneously called them bucket seats, but there was no lumbar support to speak of to hold you during handling maneuvers. The doors featured map pockets for various odds and ends. The new padded dash was a vast improvement with an efficient, no-nonsense appearance, like that of an aircraft cockpit. The instrument panel was matte-black with six instruments tastefully trimmed with chrome: clock, speedometer, fuel gauge, temperature gauge, oil pressure, and alternator. A clock/tachometer was optional. The rest of the controls were handsome chrome rocker or thumb-wheel switches. The slide controls for the optional air conditioning were integrated with the heater controls to the right of the steering column underneath the instrument panel. A new cruise control located on the end of the turn signal lever was optional.

With its exciting new shape and all the standard features buyers had come to expect in a Charger, you got a lot of car for the base list price of $3,014. The 230-horsepower, two-barrel 318 cubic-inch V-8 was the standard engine. Invariably, prospective buyers really caught Dodge Fever and heavily optioned their Chargers. Many simply cut to the chase and checked off the R/T option for the Charger and waited to take delivery or drove one right off the dealer's lot. Included in the $3,480 R/T package was the 375-horsepower 440 Magnum V-8, TorqueFlight automatic transmission, heavy-duty manually adjusted brakes, F70x14 Goodyear Red Streak tires, R/T handling package with larger-diameter front torsion bars, extra-heavy-duty rear springs (with an extra half-leaf in the right rear to control torque steer), heavy-duty shocks, and the standard front sway bar. Bumblebee stripes in black or white encircled the rear end; these stripes could be deleted if you wished.

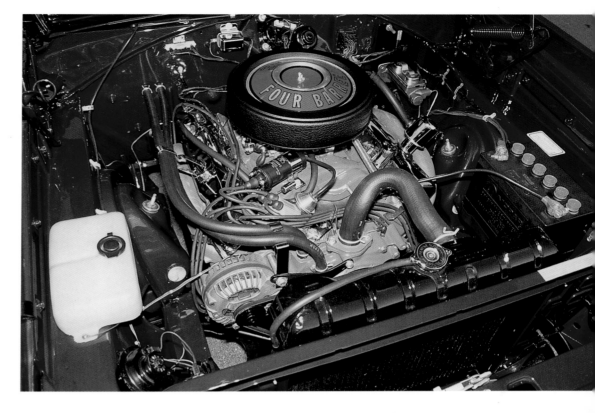

R/T medallions were mounted in the grille and taillight recess. The four-speed manual transmission was, of course, optional. If you wanted the final word in magnificent excess, the 426 Hemi could be ordered, but it was only available on the Charger R/T, not the standard Charger. The Charger R/T was a stunning performer. With a power-to-weight ratio of 10.1 pounds per horsepower, it did 0-60 miles per hour in 6.5 seconds and the quarter-mile in the low 14-second range.

If you didn't want quite so much power under your right foot, you could order the Charger with the 290-horsepower, two-barrel 383 or the newly improved 330-horsepower, four-barrel 383. Chrysler engineers had redesigned the cylinder heads and intake manifold with 10 percent larger intakes, un-silenced dual-snorkle air cleaner, and low-restriction dual exhaust. This produced 425 foot-pounds of torque at a useful 3,200 rpm. It was an excellent powerplant, and for only $137.55 over the standard 318, it was a veritable bargain.

The 1968 Charger had even more show to match its go. Striking color combinations could be had with 16 standard exterior colors (Silver Metallic was an extra cost option) and Optional Black, Antique White, or Antique Green vinyl roof. Two optional wheel covers were available

The 335-horsepower 383 V-8 in the Super Bee used the high-flow cylinder heads and intake manifold from the 375-horsepower 440 V-8 offered in the Coronet R/T and Charger R/T. Meticulous restoration of this Super Bee is evident throughout the engine compartment.

Announcing: CORONET "SUPER BEE"
Scat Pack performance at a new low price.

Run with the Dodge Scat Pack

Beware the hot cammed, four-barreled 383 mill in the light coupe body. Beware the muscled hood, the snick of close coupled four-speed, the surefootedness of Red Lines, Rallye-rated springs and shocks, sway bar and competent eleven-inch drums. Beware the Super Bee. Proof you can't tell a runner by the size of his bankroll.

These specifications are published for the uncommon interest:

POWERPLANT: Standard: 383 CID V8. Carb: 4-bbl. Compression ratio: 10:1. Special camshaft: Lift (Intake, .450; Exhaust, .465). Duration (Intake, 268°; Exhaust, 284°). Overlap: 46°. Valves, hydraulic (Intake, 2.08 head dia.; Exhaust, 1.74). Intake manifold: Equal length four branch low-restriction type. Exhaust: Dual. Horsepower: 335 at 5200 RPM. Torque: 425 lbs.-ft. at 3400 RPM. 10.2 pounds per horsepower. (Dry.) Air cleaner, unsilenced, both standard and optional V8.

Optional: Hemi 426 CID V8. Hemispherical combustion chambers. Carb: dual, 4-bbl. Compression ratio: 10.25:1. Camshaft lift (Intake, .490; Exhaust, .480). Duration (Intake, 284°; Exhaust, 284°). Valves (Intake, 2.25 head dia.; Exhaust, 1.94). Intake manifold: Cast aluminum dual level with heat shield. Exhaust manifold: Special cast-iron low-restriction exhaust headers. Horsepower: 425 at 5000 RPM. Torque: 490 lbs.-ft. at 4000 RPM.

TRANSMISSION: Four-speed full synchromesh manual. Ring block synchromesh. Floor-mounted shift. Gear ratios with std. eng.: 1st, 2.66; 2nd, 1.91; 3rd, 1.39; 4th, 1.00.

Optional: TorqueFlite Automatic three-speed. Column-mounted shift. Gear ratios: 1st, 2.45; 2nd, 1.45; 3rd, 1.00.

SUSPENSION: Heavy-duty springs and shocks, all four wheels. .94-inch dia. sway bar standard.

BRAKES: Heavy-duty standard on all four wheels. 11-inch drums, cast iron. Shoes: 11"x3", front; 11"x2½", rear. Lining area: 234.1 sq. in. Front discs optional. Self-adjusting Bendix type. Swept area, 387.8 sq. in.

ADDITIONAL OPTIONS: High-performance axle package consisting of 3.55 axle ratio with Sure Grip. High-capacity radiator, 7-blade slip-drive fan with shroud.

INSTRUMENTATION AND APPOINTMENTS: Padded Rallye-type dash standard, matte black, includes circular speedometer, oil and temperature gauges, electric clock. Matching tach optional. Matte black grille, power hood, Red Line wide-tread tires, seat belts, front shoulder belts, carpeting, foam seats, bumblebee striping and special ornamentation standard. Vinyl roof optional.

RACING JACKET OFFER Show your stripes right away. Order your special all-nylon, red Scat Pack racing jacket. Comes in sizes for everyone! Men: S-M-L-XL-XXL. Women: S-M-L. Children: 6-8-10-12-14-16. Send $9.95 for each jacket (check or M.O.) to Hughes-Hatcher-Suffrin, Shelby at State, Detroit, Michigan 48226.

SPECIAL OFFER Write: Dodge Scat Pack HQ, Dept. D, PO Box 604, Detroit, Michigan 48221. Send me the Scat Pack decals, lapel badges and catalog of goodies. Here's my quarter.

Name _____

Address _____

City _____ State _____ Zip _____

Car Owned: Make _____ Model _____ Year _____

Dodge heavily advertised and promoted the Coronet Super Bee. This ad was one of several run by Dodge in 1968. It included order forms for Scat Pack goodies, even a Scat Pack racing jacket.

as well as the ever-handsome, deep-dish chromed mag-type road wheels. With looks like this, the Charger R/T was a scene-stealer, but it was only one of the cars in the potent Scat Pack.

The Coronet R/T and Super Bee

The Coronet was completely redesigned for 1968 and the styling, a product of Brownlie's studio, was clean and handsome. The high-performance R/T option was carried over for 1968. The advantage of the Coronet R/T was its availability as a convertible as well as a two-door hardtop. The 1968 Coronet R/T convertible was a rare bird—only 569 were built that year. Far more plentiful was the hardtop R/T with 9,989 cars built. Since the Coronet R/T was equipped comparably to the Charger R/T, the price was only slightly less at $3,353. The Coronet R/T convertible was $3,613.

A power bulge in the hood and the bumblebee stripes in the rear distinguished the exterior of the Coronet R/T. The interior took styling cues from the Charger R/T, with bucket seats standard and the dressy console optional. In fact, Dodge was able to keep the price of the Coronet R/T under $4,000 by making so many desirable features optional. Add air conditioning for $342.85, Sure-Grip differential for $138.90, solid-state AM radio with stereo tape player for $196.25, power brakes for $41.75, power steering for $94.85, power windows for $100.25, that spiffy-looking console for $52.85, tinted glass for $39.50, left and right head restraints at $21.95 each, those stylish chrome road wheels at $97.30, and top it all off with a vinyl roof for $81.60, and the grand total was nearly $4,600. Nevertheless, that was a lot of show and go for the buck.

Another member of the Dodge Scat Pack made its appearance later on in the 1968 model year. That car was Super Bee. The Plymouth Road Runner was getting a great deal of press when it was introduced for 1968, and the Dodge Coronet Super Bee was somewhat overshadowed by Plymouth's economy performance car. But, the Super Bee was conceived to be the most bang for the buck from Chrysler's Dodge division. The Super Bee began life as a Coronet 440 two-door coupe. The Super Bee achieved a low price tag by deleting certain nonessential items. Roll-down rear windows were nixed in favor of more economical pop-out windows, which necessitated the use of a center pillar. It came without a vinyl roof. The interior was the base version with a bench-type front seat. Actually, that was a plus in a car designed for cruising with your sweetheart right next to you. Interior and exterior trim were minimal to pare down costs.

Standard on the Super Bee was a 335-horsepower version of the four-barrel 383 V-8. The engine had the high-performance cylinder heads off the high-perform-ance 440 V-8. Everything was high performance on the Super Bee, including the exhaust system, which had 2-1/4-inch exhaust pipes and tuned mufflers, and 2-1/4 inch tailpipes. The standard transmission was a heavy-duty four-speed manual with Hurst Competition-Plus floor shift. The shifter came with a simulated woodgrain knob and reverse-engagement warning light. The Torque-Flight automatic transmission was optional for less than $50. Heavy-duty driveshaft, rear axle, and U-joints pro-vided driveline insurance. The 426 Hemi engine was also optional, but at considerably greater expense.

The Super Bee suspension was heavy duty all the way around. Front torsion bars measured 0.90-inch in diameter. The number of rear leaf springs was increased to six. To limit sway in the corners, there was a 0.94-inch diameter front stabilizer bar. The shock absorbers and drum brakes were heavy duty as well. Power front disc brakes were optional. The Super Bee rode on Goodyear Red Streak wide-tread F70x14 tires mounted on wide-rim wheels. Other equipment not directly tied to per-formance included a hood with power bulge, but this was nonfunctional. The Super Bee's bumblebee stripes announced this was no ordinary Coronet.

The Super Bee went on sale in February 1968. Prior to introduction, Dodge sent descriptive brochures on the car to all its dealers. The copy was typical of its day, yet it is almost alien to today's car buyer: "It's the super car for the guy who doesn't want to shy away from GTOs . . . only their higher prices. Super Bee's for the guy who wants a low-priced performance car that he can drive daily . . . but still take to the track on weekends. One that commands respect when the Christmas tree lights up. The Super Bee's the car he's been looking for. It's a gutsy road car with all the goodies to make it a true perform-ance car. If your customer doesn't believe it, tell him you'll meet him with a Super Bee at the local drag strip."

To let performance buffs know the Super Bee was coming, Dodge saturated the performance magazines with full-color, full-page ads. The magazines included *Hot Rod*, *Car and Driver*, *Super Stock & Drag Illustrated*, *Motor Trend*, *Popular Hot Rodding*, *Road & Track*, *Car Life*, *Drag Strip*, *Auto Racing*, *Car Craft*, and *Cars*. In

The 1968 Dodge Charger was a flawless performance styling statement. For all its sleek good looks, it was also quite affordable. Who wouldn't like to turn back the hands of time so he could walk into a Dodge showroom and order one today?

The 1968 Charger looked perfect from any angle. The tunnel backlight caused turbulence and drag on the NASCAR super speedways, but this was corrected later with the Charger 500.

addition, Dodge placed black-and-white ads in almost 250 college newspapers. Talk about a new model rollout!

The Super Bee's performance was comparable to that of the Road Runner. According to Dodge tests, the Super Bee accelerated to 60 miles per hour in 6.8 seconds, and covered the quarter-mile in 15 seconds. The optional Hemi propelled the Super Bee to 60 miles per hour in 6.6 seconds and cut the quarter-mile time by nearly a second. Much of the Hemi's awesome power was wasted literally spinning its wheels leaving the staging lane. These times were confirmed by published road tests. The Super Bee was not as big a seller as the Road Runner, but it still hit the bull's-eye in the market.

The smallest member of the Dodge Scat Pack was the Dart GTS. However, its size was not a metaphor for its performance. Dodge had been hard at work to make the Dart as fast as other cars in the Scat Pack.

The Dart GTS

The hottest compact car you could buy in the 1967 Dodge line was the Dart GT. That was the year the car received a completely new, crisp body style. The most powerful V-8 offered as an option in the GT that year was the 235-horsepower, four-barrel 273. It was a good performer, but Dodge had something much more dramatic planned for 1968.

As the smallest member of the Scat Pack for 1968, the Dart GTS gave new meaning to power-to-weight ratio. The GTS was the top of the Dart line, and was the fastest production Dart Dodge had built, including the longhorn, cross-ram 383 Darts of the early 1960s. The standard V-8 was the 275-horsepower, four-barrel, 340 cubic-inch V-8. But the big news was just that— the GTS was available with a big-block Wedge! Optional in the GTS was a 300-horsepower, four-barrel 383 V-8. This engine turned the car into a screamer. Output was aided by a high-performance dual exhaust system with 2-1/4-inch pipes from the exhaust manifolds to the tailpipes. The tuned mufflers gave the big-block Wedge a really sweet sound on the street. The standard transmission in the GTS was a three-speed manual column shift. This entry-level transmission was out of keeping with the character of the car, and most GTS buyers opted for either the TorqueFlight automatic or the four-speed manual transmission with Hurst Competition-Plus floor shift with simulated woodgrain knob and reverse-engagement warning light.

With the 275-horsepower 340 V-8, the GTS could reach 60 miles per hour in 6 seconds and cover the quarter-mile in just over 15 seconds. The optional 300-horsepower 383 pushed the performance envelope for compact cars to a level not seen in a Mopar of that size.

While the heavier big block impacted the car's handling somewhat, the GTS was really conceived as a straight-line machine. After all, this was the car Dick Maxwell chose, along with the 1968 Barracuda, to build around the 426 Hemi for Super Stock competition.

Nevertheless, the Chrysler engineers made sure the GTS has the best suspension for high-performance all-around use. This meant heavy-duty torsion bars (0.88-inch diameter for the 340 GTS, and 0.94-inch diameter for the 383 GTS), heavy-duty ball joints, and anti-sway bar. Also standard on the GTS were E70x14 Red Streak tires mounted on 14x5.5J wide-rim wheels. With these wheels and tires, the GTS had a slightly wider track than that of the other Dart models. The deep-dish simulated "mag" wheel covers were standard on the GTS and optional on other Dart models if ordered with the 5.5J wide-rim wheels.

Among the rarest of all Dodges was a very special Dart built in 1968. Chrysler contracted Hurst Performance to build its Hemi-powered Super Stock Barracudas and Darts (see Chapter Five). The 383 was a big-block Wedge, so it wasn't a big deal to put a 440 in there. But Chrysler did not want to incur the wrath of Washington and provoke the insurance lobby, so a pilot run of 50 Darts powered by the 440 were built and targeted as special drag racing vehicles. For 1969, the 440 Dart program was expanded. According to Chrysler's Larry Shepard, "In 1969 we built over 600 440-powered Darts, basically the same as the 383 GTS, except for the engine."

Improving the Breed

For 1969, the winning formula for the Dodge Scat Pack remained the same. The changes to the Scat Pack were subtle. A new high-performance Charger model was added in 1969—the Charger 500. Its design and development is recorded in Chapter Five. The 1969 Charger received some cosmetic work. Car spotters could distinguish a '69 from a '68 by the new louvered grille divider. The four round taillights were superseded by two rectangular recessed bezel taillights. The side marker lights were also new. On R/Ts, the bumblebee stripe was now one band instead of two.

Nearly 20,000 Charger R/Ts were built in 1969.

There was a new option available on the Charger—the SE, for Special Edition. This included genuine leather seat facing on the front bucket seats, simulated woodgrain steering wheel, deep-dish wheel covers,

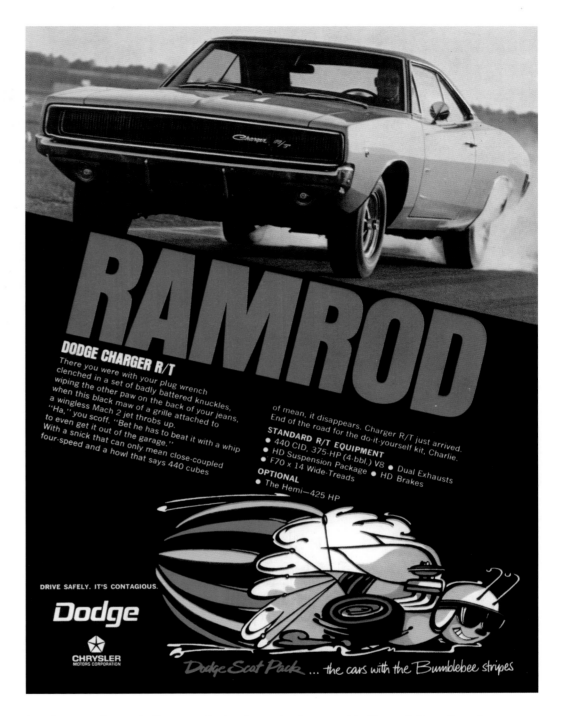

hood-mounted turn indicators, simulated woodgrain-finish instrument panel, and an extensive Light Group. The $161.85 SE package could be ordered on the R/T, but not with the 426 Hemi option.

Changes to the Coronet R/T and Super Bee were also cosmetic, but Dodge added some exciting performance options in 1969. The Super Bee coupe was joined

The Charger R/T was the performance flagship of the 1968 Dodge Scat Pack. This RAMROD ad for the Charger R/T was the only one depicting a smoky burnout. The ad copy in this advertisement says pure performance.

The Dart GT Sport, or GTS, was the compact member of the Scat Pack. It came standard with a 275-horsepower 340 ci small-block Wedge V-8. Optional was the big-block 383.

by a hardtop model, but a Super Bee convertible was still not available. Cosmetically, the only visible difference between the 1968 and 1969 models was a switch to the single broad bumblebee stripe like that on the Charger, and the addition of a Scat Pack bumblebee medallion on the front grille and on the trunk lid. A small decal giving engine displacement appeared on the side of the front fenders. Performance specifications remained unchanged for the Super Bee.

Likewise, the Coronet R/T was little changed in appearance or performance—and that was good. The R/T medallion on the front fenders was eliminated and, in somewhat larger form, appeared as part of the bumblebee stripe. The brochure for the 1969 Coronets showed color renderings of the R/T with two simulated air scoops on the rear quarter panels; this was a $35.80 option. This was also optional on the Super Bee.

At the same time, several performance-enhancing options were newly available. Both the Super Bee and the R/T could be ordered with the new Ramcharger fresh-air induction system, costing only $73.30. It was identical in function to the Air Grabber fresh-air induction system offered on the Plymouth Road Runner and GTX. The Ramcharger system differed by having two large functional hood scoops that fed the fiberglass plenum bolted to the underside of the hood, which surrounded the oval air cleaner when the hood was closed. You could get cool outside air or warm under-hood air by the switch of a lever beneath the dash. Most owners of Super Bees or R/Ts with the Ramcharger option left the scoops open. The Ramcharger was standard on Hemi-equipped Coronets.

Another option that had a more direct effect on performance was a wider selection of rear axle ratios for

1969. Dodge essentially had the same axle ratios as Plymouth that year. Depending on the standard or optional engine and transmission, you could improve on the standard axle ratio of 3.23:1 by ordering a 3.54:1, 3.55:1, 3.91:1, or 4.10:1 Performance Axle Package. Other heavy-duty equipment, such as radiators, fan shrouds, even whole suspensions were sometimes part of the package. There was something for every taste and need.

Coronet Super Bee Six Pack

The real excitement for 1969 was the addition of a new model to the Scat Pack. That car was the Coronet Super Bee Six Pack. In both name and concept, it was one of the wildest musclecars of the sixties. This car was, in fact, what Chrysler had come to refer to as a Package Car—a specially built vehicle for a particular niche in the market.

This car, in fact, was designed and built around a new big-block Wedge V-8 , the six-barrel 440. The baseline for this engine was the high-performance 440 introduced in 1967 and installed in the Dodge R/T and the Plymouth GTX. That engine was rated at 375 horsepower. Chrysler saw a window of opportunity to offer a 440 V-8 with three dual-barrel carburetors, placing it between the four-barrel high-performance 440 and the

The 1969 Dodge Charger displayed only subtle changes from the previous year. The center grill divider and different taillights were the only outward signs of change. That suited Charger lovers just fine.

dual four-barrel 426 street Hemi. The logic was to offer a big-block Wedge with torque and horsepower ratings within reach of the 426 Hemi without the steep cost.

Chrysler did not simply come up with a 3x2-barrel intake manifold and bolt on three deuces. Chrysler thoroughly engineered each engine it built, and this one was no different. The six-barrel 440 went through the same rigorous research and development program as all other engines. The purpose of this engine was to surpass all other big-block Wedges while still being streetable and affordable. The engine would go into the low-cost Super Bee as a means of offering maximum performance at the minimum possible cost. The car would achieve a unique appearance by having a special flat-black fiberglass hood with large scoop held in place with hood pins. There would be no wheel covers or fancy mags—

only five chrome lug nuts. When the prototype car was shown to Chrysler insiders, there was grinning from ear to ear. Chevrolet and Ford had nothing like it, and that was precisely the idea.

The key to the car, of course, was the engine. The success of the 375-horsepower, four-barrel, high-performance 440 offered a sound basis for the 440 Six Pack. This engine was conceived to operate on both street and strip, and the majority of the development work was concentrated on the induction system. Garry Congdon was an account engineer with Holley working at Chrysler's Highland Park headquarters and was closely involved with the engine program.

"When Chrysler decided to do this program," Congdon remembers, "the 3x2-barrel 427 Corvette was already in production. Chrysler said, 'Let's start with the

Many second-generation Chargers were ordered with contrasting vinyl roofs. This worked particularly well on the Charger. The standard 375-horsepower 440 Magnum in the Charger R/T could be superseded only by the 425-horsepower 426 Hemi.

Corvette-sized carburetors.' From there we went to larger outboard carburetors than those on the Corvette to get more performance. We worked on the fuel/air distribution. We used different carbs front and rear with different jets for optimum fuel distribution, which is why they had different part numbers. There wasn't room to package all the carbs using metering blocks, so the front and rear carbs used metering plates."

Chrysler engineers chose to use the three two-barrel carburetors on a dual-plane intake manifold to offer the best balance of street and strip performance. The center carb would handle around town and highway duties using a mechanical linkage. The fore and aft carburetors were actuated using vacuum diaphragms to allow supply to meet demand. This setup was nothing new in the automotive world, but the six-barrel 440 brought it to a new level of performance and refinement.

Wind tunnel testing revealed turbulence and drag generated in the recessed front grill area and tunnel backlight of the Dodge Charger (below). The Charger 500 (above) was the answer. 1969 Chargers were shipped to Creative Industries for aerodynamic modifications. With its flush grill and backlight, the Charger 500's top speed on NASCAR super speedways was effectively increased.

A new member of the Dodge Scat Pack in 1969 was the Super Bee Six Pack. The six-barrel 440 under the fiberglass hood generated 390 horsepower and 490 foot-pounds of torque. Acceleration times rivaled those of the 426 Hemi. These truly were the glory days of Mopar performance.

Chrysler performed the intake manifold design and development, but production was outsourced to Edelbrock. Manifolds made for the 1969 engines were aluminum, but as the 440 Six Pack was expanded to other Dodges in 1970, Chrysler also cast the manifold in iron. Thus, there was a mix of both iron and aluminum intake manifolds on this engine during 1970 and 1971.

As good as the high-performance 440 was, this new engine would see serious drag strip conditions and Chrysler wanted no failures of any kind. Durability testing was as exhaustive on this engine as it had been on the original high-performance 440. The new pieces to go into the six-barrel 440 included the crankshaft, crank sprocket,

camshaft, tappets, cam sprocket and screws, timing chain, connecting rods, pistons, piston rings, intake and exhaust valves, and finally, special rocker arms.

A team of development engineers and dyno operators was placed on the 440 Six-Pack program. Among them were Tom Hoover, Joe Volpe, Ed Poplawski, Andy Thomas, Rich Hoard, Joe Nunez, Pete Haganbuch, and Chuck Willits. One dyno test involved wide-open throttle with no load. The point of the test was to see how long the engine could hold together while screaming along at 6,000 rpm-plus. Even the Max Wedge 413 and 426 engines were not to be operated at maximum rpm under load beyond 15 seconds according to the owners manual. After several minutes the engine began to lose rpm and finally it stopped.

"They pulled the heads off," Thomas recalls. "The valves were bent and the pistons were nicked. They put new valves in it, put it all back together, and it fired right up! The laboratory gross horsepower for the A134 (high-performance four-barrel 440) would run right around 375 horsepower. The six-barrel was another 15 horsepower. The 390 horsepower rating was a good number."

With successful completion of the engine development program, vehicle production moved forward. On January 28, 1969, D. R. Hubbs in Product Planning Technical Services Fleet Engineering at Chrysler's Lynch Road assembly plant issued the production order on the subject: "Special Order Group Release E-101 For Plymouth Road Runner And Dodge Super Bee Cars With A Special 440-CID Engine With Three Two-Barrel Carburetors." It also outlined the vehicle rework necessary to accommodate the fiberglass hood, to be held in place with four hood pins, as well as other modifications and specific part installation. The six-barrel 440 V-8 itself was assembled at Chrysler's Trenton, Michigan, engine plant.

The six-barrel 440 appeared as a mid-year offering as option code A12 on the 1969 Dodge Coronet Super Bee for $468.80. The black fiberglass hood with huge hood scoop and stark wheels adorned with only chrome lug nuts was the gutsiest display of street power projection Detroit had ever seen. The true success of these cars was spelled with one word: performance. *Motorcade* magazine did a test of the Super Bee Six Pack in its July 1969 issue. Weighing 3,790 pounds and equipped with the Torque-Flite automatic transmission, the car did 0-60 miles per hour in 6.6 seconds and covered the quarter-mile in 13.65 seconds at 105.14 miles per hour at the Orange

County International Raceway. Chrysler engineers had indeed succeeded in building a budget street racer with Hemi-like performance.

Almost lost in all the mid-size performance hoopla of the Scat Pack for 1969 was the compact Dart. However, it was by no means at the bottom of the performance food chain. While the GTS was the member of the Scat Pack, budget-minded enthusiasts also looked over the Dart GT and a new member of the Dodge Scat Pack—the Dart Swinger 340. This new car was designed to offer you the most for your performance compact dollar. It had less luxury than the GTS but just as much scat. It came standard with the 340 cubic-inch four-barrel V-8, four-speed manual transmission with Hurst shifter, three-spoke steering wheel with padded bug, Rallye suspension, bumblebee stripes with the word "Swinger," performance hood, and D70x14 wide tread tires on 5.5J wheel. List price for the Swinger 340 hardtop was less than $2,900. By comparison, the GTS

In 1970, Dodge introduced the Challenger, and the Challenger R/T was added to the 1970 Scat Pack. The R/T was available as a hardtop and convertible, but fewer than 1,000 R/T ragtops were built that year. The performance hood was standard, but the blackout hood paint was optional. The Sub Lime paint color was one of the High Impact optional exterior colors.

hardtop cost $3,226 with the same standard engine. The GTS convertible cost $3,419.

Without question, the sleeper of the 1969 Dodge Scat Pack was the Dart GTS equipped with the optional 383 four-barrel V-8. This engine had received a boost in performance and was now rated at 330 horsepower, just five less than the 383 installed in the heavier Coronet Super Bee. Performance of the GTS could be further improved by bumping the axle ratio from the standard 3.23:1 to 3.55:1 or even the 3.91:1 optional ratios. These higher numerical axle ratios were available at no extra cost if you also ordered the Sure-Grip differential.

As the 1960s came to a close, Dodge was riding on a performance wave that couldn't be stopped. The Chrysler division was offering some of the most striking cars on the street and the cars of the Scat Pack were among the fastest on the street and strip. Dodge was on a roll, and had been secretly working on a new car to compete with the Chevrolet Camaro and Ford Mustang.

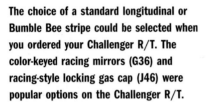

The choice of a standard longitudinal or Bumble Bee stripe could be selected when you ordered your Challenger R/T. The color-keyed racing mirrors (G36) and racing-style locking gas cap (J46) were popular options on the Challenger R/T.

Creating the Challenger

In the fall of 1966, Chrysler product planners decided to develop a new car to compete with the newly introduced Mercury Cougar, a sporty, personal luxury car. Dodge was given the job and the program was headed by Harry Cheeseborough, Senior Vice President of Styling and Product Planning. The task of coming up with the all-important body design belonged to Bill Brownlie, then chief of design in the Dodge studio.

By the early part of 1967, a full-size finished clay model was produced to allow the young stylists a chance to gain a basic concept of the new car's length, height, wheelbase, and interior size. It reflected the long hood, short rear deck design in vogue, typified by the new Chevrolet Camaro. Brownlie turned his stylists loose to come up with drawings incorporating their ideas for the unnamed car. In numerous meetings, ideas were kicked around and the first styling clay model using their ideas took shape. A total of four full-size clay bucks were

The standard mill in the Challenger R/T was the 383 Magnum big-block V-8. The optional engines available in the Challenger R/T included the 440 Six Pack and the dual four-barrel 426 Hemi.

made with the right and left sides of each shaped differently to offer eight separate concepts. Things did not go smoothly, however. There were still differing opinions on how the car should look, and the time for presenting the design to top management was drawing near.

"I felt I should back up the styling studio," says Brownlie, "so I came up with some sketches the weekend prior to the meeting, and had models made from the sketches as I conceived the car, ready for the meeting."

After the dust had settled and the various designs were evaluated, it was Brownlie's design that was chosen, and it remained virtually unaltered for production. Subsequent detail to the extreme front and rear ends was handled by the styling studio. His suggestion for the name Challenger was also adopted because of its association with the Charger. Performance enthusiasm had surged to such an extent in 1968 and 1969 that it was decided to market the 1970 Challenger predominantly as a performance car. This decision was also influenced by Sportscar Club of America (SCCA) Trans-Am competition where Ford Mustangs, Chevrolet Camaros, and even American Motors were competing with their pony cars.

Dodge was the last of the car manufacturers to join the pony-car race, so the Challenger, introduced in the fall of 1969, was an appropriate name. Unlike its brother, the Barracuda, the Challenger had no ancestry. Nevertheless, when it hit the showrooms, Mopar fans were understandably excited by the newest addition to the Dodge Scat Pack.

Although the Challenger shared all window glass with the 1970 Barracuda, it had a strikingly different look. Its contours were more sculpted, and it featured a prominent S-bend beltline crease. The Challenger had a four-headlight arrangement in contrast to the Barracuda's two headlights. It also differed dimensionally. Both cars had the same front and rear track of 59.7 inches and 60.7 inches respectively, but the Challenger had a 110-inch wheelbase, 2 inches longer than the Barracuda.

There were six distinct Challenger models offered in its debut year: a hardtop for $2,851, a convertible for $3,120, and the SE (for Special Edition) hardtop for $3,083; these three models came standard with the trusty 145-horsepower, 225 cubic-inch slant six or 230-horsepower, 318 cubic-inch V-8. Rounding out the Challenger lineup were the three R/T models: the R/T hardtop for $3,266, the R/T convertible for $3,498, and the R/T SE for 3,498. Adding the convertibles to the Challenger line was a very smart move on Dodge's part. It gave the prospective pony car buyer a broader selection than did the competition. By 1970, the Pontiac Firebird and Chevrolet Camaro no longer were offered in a convertible. American Motors never offered the Javelin or AMX in convertible form. The Ford Mustang was available as a convertible but not in a distinct performance model—there was no Mach 1 Mustang convertible. Thus, if you wanted a powerful ragtop pony car, the Challenger R/T convertible, and its corporate sister, the 'Cuda convertible, were the only ways to go.

Just what did the R/T designation get you? A whole lot of Mopar, that's what. The Challenger R/T came standard with the 335-horsepower, four-barrel 383 Magnum V-8, three-on-the-floor synchromesh manual transmission, heavy-duty Rallye suspension, heavy-duty drum brakes, Rallye Instrument Cluster (which included a 150 mile per hour speedometer, oil pressure gauge and 8,000 rpm (!) tachometer, and a performance hood with two hoodscoops. These hoodscoops were open to the engine

bay but did not feed directly to the air cleaner. You could specify a longitudinal or a rear-end bumblebee tape stripe at no extra cost. The three optional engines in the Challenger R/T were the 375-horsepower, four-barrel 440 Magnum; the 390-horsepower, six-barrel 440 Six Pack (with three two-barrel Holley carburetors); and the 425-horsepower, dual four-barrel 426 Hemi. An extra-heavy-duty suspension came standard with these engines, as well as bigger drum brakes to haul the R/T down from the higher anticipated speeds.

The Challenger R/T was identified on the front fenders, front grill, and trunk lid. Engine displacement was proudly announced on the side of the performance hoodscoops.

Dodge leaned heavily on the Challenger's performance image and backed it up with substance. The second page of the 1970 brochure read: "The Six Pack. It snarls, it quivers, it leaps vast prairies at a single bound." This sounds outrageous today, but in 1970, the youthful buyers believed it without blinking, because it wasn't far from the truth. The 440 Six Pack Challenger R/T had a snarling exhaust note, the optional "shaker" hoodscoop did quiver at idle, and when you floored the beast, its acceleration was almost frightening.

These optional engines were just the beginning of a long list of available options on the Challenger. In fact, this was truly the era of freedom of choice. Today, cars usually come with one engine and one engine only and there are no optional axle ratios. But in 1970, car companies pretty much were able to sell whatever they could engineer and felt the market wanted. One very special option available on the Challenger wasn't an engine but was actually an entire vehicle—the Challenger T/A. This car is covered in detail in Chapter

The Coronet received front and rear end restyling for 1970. This was the last year for the Coronet R/T. The nonfunctional side scoops were standard. The functional hoodscoops were part of the Ramcharger option, which was standard when the 426 Hemi was ordered.

Vitamin C was one of the High Impact colors offered for 1970. The Coronet R/T came standard with either black or white Bumble Bee stripes. This R/T was ordered with the optional J81 rear spoiler.

Five. The specially designed hood scoop on the Challenger T/A wasn't limited to that model alone in 1970. Chrysler's Larry Shepard explains:

"Some of the Challengers with 340, 383, 440, and Hemi engines also used the 1970 T/A fiberglass hood in 1970," Shepard says. "This was caused by a production shortage of the shakers so that the T/A fiberglass hood was used in place of the shaker on the engines with the fresh-air option. In 1971, they only used the shaker."

The Challenger was available in 18 exterior colors. Five of these were optional High-Impact colors: Plum Crazy, Sub Lime, Go-Mango, Hemi Orange, and Top Banana; later these were joined by Panther Pink and Green-Go. You could order these colors on your Challenger and get away with it because they looked so absolutely right on the car. As if these were not enough, you could specify horizontal iridescent body striping, color-keyed to Panther Pink or Green-Go on R/T models at no extra cost.

Many Challengers were ordered with an optional contrasting vinyl roof in black, white, green, or Gator Grain. The vinyl roof came standard on the SE and the R/T SE models, which also included an overhead interior consolette with a seat belt warning light and indicator lights reading "door ajar" and "low fuel." With such a handsome body, striking colors, and a plethora of available models, engines, and other options, it is no wonder the Challenger sold 76,935 units. But 1970 was a good year for the other cars of the Scat Pack as well.

Scat City–1970s Style

The superb styling of the Charger continued for 1970 with subtle enhancements. Most notable among the stylistic changes was the chrome loop front bumper and redesigned front grille, retaining the concealed headlights. Dodge was also making a push to lower the price of the Charger. It succeeded in reducing the base list price of the six-cylinder Charger to $3,001 by substituting a bench seat for the more expensive buckets (which were not optional), eliminating the door pockets, using simpler window moldings, and making the electric clock optional. According to the *Dodge & Plymouth Muscle Car Red Book* (Motorbooks International, 1991), only 29 units of this car were built! The 1970 Charger shared some of the optional exterior colors available on the Challenger. These included Plum Crazy, Sub Lime, Go-Mango, Hemi Orange, and Banana.

R/T badging was prominently displayed on the sidescoops on the Coronet R/T. It was performance styling cues like this that helped to distinguish Mopar musclecars from the standard offerings. There definitely was go to back up the show.

The Ramcharger fresh-air performance hood (option code N96) was a desirable option to order with the standard 375-horsepower 440 Magnum in the Coronet R/T. This was a formidable street machine and the big-block Wedge took many victims at stoplights all across America.

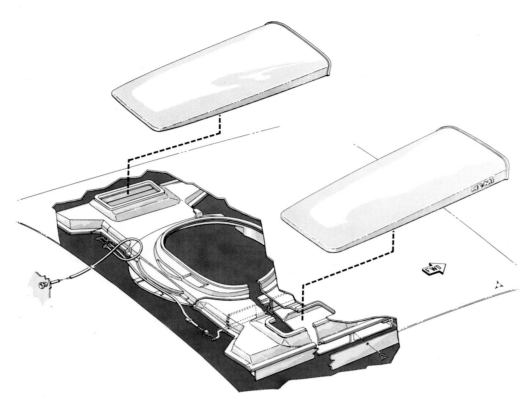

This cutaway illustration shows the method of operation for the Ramcharger fresh air hood. Trap doors in the underhood plenums could be opened by a cable mounted underneath the dash. In heavy rain or snow, the doors could be closed and the engine would get air via the air cleaner.

Dodge did some model name reshuffling for 1970. The 1969 Charger 500 was not carried over for 1970, having fulfilled the production requirement set by NASCAR and having been effectively replaced by the Daytona. Wanting to capitalize on its racing heritage, Dodge offered a Charger 500 powered by the same slant six, but with all the items deleted from the base model. The six-cylinder Charger 500 is among the rarest of all Chargers—only 182 were built. Naturally, the Charger screamed for a muscular V-8.

Why did Dodge even bother to build a six-cylinder Charger? To attract buyers with the low price. In fact, a full-color ad was run on the back of *Car & Driver* for the 1970 Charger shown wearing Plum Crazy. Naturally, when prospective customers were lured to the showroom with this ad in hand, the salesmen steered them toward the V-8 models.

The Charger most likely to be the center of showroom attention was the Charger R/T. With nearly 20,000 sold in 1969, the R/T proved to be a great magnet for showroom traffic, even if prospective buyers were interested in something just a little less potent. The most distinguishing feature of the 1970 Charger R/T was the flat, reverse-facing scoop over the scallops on the doors. Beyond the cosmetic, the big news for 1970 was the

availability of a new optional engine—the 440 Six Pack. The E87 option code for the 440 Six Pack was only $119.05. This was a fraction of the cost compared to the 426 Hemi, which cost $648.25. In terms of performance, the 440 Six Pack ran neck and neck with the 426 Hemi. The price of the Charger R/T with standard 440 was bumped to $3,711. In all other respects, the 1970 Charger was the same car that had earned the respect of enthusiasts for the previous two years—the literal embodiment of performance and musclecar aesthetics.

Sales of the Charger were way down for 1970, however. Total production dropped to 46,315 units, nearly half the previous year's production. It is difficult to determine how much of the drop was attributable to the dramatic rise in insurance premiums on musclecars and how much of an effect the new Challenger had on Charger sales; it is likely that both had a dramatic effect. For 1970, the Coronet received all new front-end sheet metal. The redesign was not entirely successful, drawing criticism from the automotive press for its oddly shaped split grille. The Coronet Super Bee and Coronet R/T both returned for 1970, but the Super Bee Six Pack model was not continued. However, the 440 Six Pack was optional in both cars.

On the Super Bee and R/T was a new power bulge hoodscoop with two formidable razor-edged scoops, but these were nonfunctional. That could be fixed by ordering the Ramcharger fresh-air hood, which remained unchanged from 1969. Performance specifications remained unchanged for 1970 in the Super Bee and R/T.

In fact, the embarrassment of performance riches made for some curious combinations. For example, Super Bees with a base list of $3,074 for the two-door hardtop were ordered with the optional 440 Six Pack for an additional $249.55, bringing the total to $3,323.55—a car with more performance than the Coronet R/T, and with a lower sticker price. Or you could order the same 440 Six Pack in the Coronet R/T for only $119.05. In fact, it is a tantalizing thought to consider the kind of musclecar collection you could have put together back then. The "earthmovers" sitting in Dodge dealers' lots with big-block Wedges and Hemis would disappear in less than two years, but few enthusiasts realized this. Having the luxury of hindsight today of the production figures for 1970, it would have been easy to put together a collection that would have outstripped the performance of any stock portfolio. Take, for example, the Coronet R/T convertible. Only

236 were built. Most had the standard 440 Magnum V-8, but how many were ordered with the 440 Six Pack, and how many were ordered with the 426 Hemi? The Ramcharger fresh-air hood came standard on the Coronets ordered with the Hemi, but how many of the Six Pack 440 Coronet convertibles were ordered with the optional Ramcharger fresh-air hood? The figure is probably somewhere in the single digits.

Good Times and Bad

For fans of the Scat Pack cars, 1970 was the best of times and the worst of times. Unprecedented high performance could be had at a price that could not be beat. But the insurance companies were really socking it to the buyers, which dramatically impacted sales. Sales of the Coronet Super Bee dropped nearly 50 percent to only 14,254 units, while sales of the Coronet R/T totaled only 2,408.

Seeing the handwriting on the wall, Dodge planned to totally de-emphasize the big-block Wedge in its compact Dart for 1970. The GT two-door hardtop and convertible, as well as the GTS two-door hardtop and convertible, were dropped. Only the Swinger two-door hardtop for $2,261 and the Swinger 340 for $2,631

1970 was also the last year for the Coronet Super Bee. In 1971, the Super Bee and R/T would be options on the Charger. This ad for the 1970 Super Bee was designed to appeal to the weekend racers on a budget. The nonfunctional performance hood was standard.

Dick Landy tests '70 Super Bee SixPack: Won't give it back.

Cigar chompin' Dick Landy is a national super stock drag racing champion, driving Darts and Chargers. Holder of Super Stock/F national record and countless track records.

"Let's get one thing straight first. The '70 Dodge Super Bee was designed to provide a full-sized car with a lot of performance and a minimum of gingerbread. To provide it with stuff that only effects performance. And that's why Super Bee's standard engine is the husky 383-cubic-inch V8 with heads right off the big 440 Magnum which has got to be the hot set up!

"Super Bee is truly the budget supercar for the man who wants a big car performance without spending a bundle for it.

"The Super Bee I tested had the swingin' SixPack setup . . . three mind-blowing two-barrel Holley carbs on a new high-rise manifold . . . all bolted on the 440 Magnum engine. Biggest problem was getting off the line without smoking it. Feather foot definitely required. The engine, by the way, has had some extra care applied. Optional special cams, mains, and crank. It can take it. The hood has hinges this year, nice when you check the oil, and the scoops feed directly into the Holleys. If the marine-like exhaust rumble doesn't tell you the engine's running, the optional tach will. By the way, I'm not going to give this Super Bee SixPack back to the factory. I'm buying it for my wife. She doesn't care if its clutch-pedal pressure is a little high. She loves the optional, full-synchro, four-speed manual. I told her so."

1970 Dodge Coronet Super Bee DIMENSIONS

WIDTH
Track, front 59.7
Track, rear 59.2
Maximum overall car width 76.7

LENGTH
Wheelbase 117
Overall car length 209.7

HEIGHT
Overall height 53.0

FRONT COMPARTMENT
Effective headroom 37.3
Maximum legroom 41.8
Shoulder room 58.1
Hiproom 60.6

REAR COMPARTMENT
Effective headroom 36.7
Minimum legroom 31.1
Rear comp. room 25.2
Shoulder room 58.1
Hiproom 60.6

CAPACITIES
No. of passengers 6
Fuel tank, gal. 19
Crankcase, qt. . . 4 (5 when replacing oil filter)

CHASSIS/SUSPENSION
Body/frame type .... unitized
Front suspension .... torsion bars
Rear suspension . . asymmetrical leaf springs
Steering system ...... recirculation ball gear

BRAKES—DRUM
Heavy-duty drum brakes—standard
Front automatic adjusting ....11 x 3
Rear automatic adjusting ....11 x 2½

WHEELS/TIRES
Wheels ....14 x 6.0JJ
Sta. tires ....F70 x 14 whitewalls

ENGINE
Type and no. of cyls. V8
Bore and stroke ....4.25 x 3.38
Displacement, cu.-in. 383
Compression ratio 9.5:1
Fuel req. ....premium
Rated BHP @ RPM ....335 @ 5200
Rated torque (lbs./ft. @ RPM)....425 @ 3400
Carburetion ....4-barrel Holley
Valve train .... Hydraulic lifters, pushrods and overhead rocker arms
Cam timing
  Intake duration ....268°
  Exhaust duration ....284°

DRIVE TRAIN
Transmission type ....3-speed floor shift standard
Gear ratio ....3rd direct 1:1
2nd 1.49:1
1st 2.55:1
Rev. 3.34:1

Dick Landy's Super Bee SixPack test car had the following additional items of extra-cost optional equipment: vinyl top, hood scoops, rocker and sill mouldings, bumper guards, road wheels, front bucket seats, center console, TorqueFlite automatic transmission, and rearview mirror on passenger's side.

The 1970 Scat Pack brochure featured evaluations by great names in auto racing. Dick Landy was called on to test the Coronet Super Bee Six Pack. The 440 six-barrel option was also available on the Challenger R/T but not on the Charger R/T.

were carried over from 1969. Some solace could be had in the $200 lower price tags. Dodge achieved the lower price by using a fully synchronized three-speed manual transmission with floor shifter. The four-speed manual was now optional. The Swinger 340 was the only car in the 1970 Scat Pack to have front disc brakes standard.

In its 1970 performance brochure, "Big News from Scat City," Dodge stated that the four-barrel 340 V-8 in the Swinger 340 came with an 8.8:1 compression ratio. This was probably an error because the engine was still rated at 275 horsepower and still required premium fuel. Other sources listed the engine as having a 10.5:1 compression ratio, and Plymouth's equivalent engine did have a 10.5:1 compression ratio.

The Swinger 340 came with nonfunctional hood-scoops with 340 on the sides. These scoops were the same as those used on the Coronet Super Bee when the Ramcharger fresh-air performance hood was ordered, but the fresh-air induction system was not available on Dodge's performance compact. With the optional rear-axle ratios and four-speed manual transmission available, the Swinger 340 could be made into a real performer. This car became increasingly attractive to buyers put off by climbing insurance rates.

Chrysler was attuned to the changes that had been taking place on the emissions front and the depressing effect insurance premiums were having on the sales of its musclecars. With sales of big-block Wedge and Hemi V-8s falling and the specter of tough future emissions requirements looming, Dodge product planners were able to see the beginning of the end of the Dodge Scat Pack. It had become apparent that catalytic converters would eventually be required in order to meet the emissions levels proposed by the 1970 Clean Air Act, and permissible emissions levels were to be ramped down almost annually during the first half of the decade. Crash-test standards and five-mile-per-hour bumper standards were also on the way. Chrysler was going to be more committed to meeting government regulations than satiating the market desire for performance. Still, that was several years down the road, and there were performance cars to build!

In the 1971 Scat Pack brochure, the Mopar enthusiast was urged to join the Dodge Scat Pack Club. For only $5.95, membership included an illustrated tune-up tips folder, a Hustle Stuff parts catalog, a Pocket Pack, all-weather racing jacket, an official club blazer patch, a "Scat Packers Unite!" bumper sticker, an official club identifier folder with four pages of Dodge Scat Pack Club outside/inside car decals, a wallet-size membership card, *Scat Speaks*, an illustrated quarterly featuring club news, service and tuning tips and other articles and features, a 1971 Auto Racing Guide and, finally, *Dodge Performance News*, a monthly four-page flyer about Dodge racing activity across the country. Membership in the Dodge Scat Pack Club was a bargain, to be sure!

The Scat Pack Scoots

The consolidation of the Dodge Scat Pack began to take place in 1971. The Coronet R/T and Super Bee production was halted at the end of the 1970 model year. The Super Bee name and concept reappeared in the Charger line and the Charger itself was re-skinned for 1971. While it did not have the "machined steel" look of the previous generation, it retained enough of the styling to bear a resemblance. The wheelbase was shortened from 117 to 115 inches. The windshield wipers were now concealed, with an articulated blade on the driver side. The windows were now ventless. The 1971 Charger featured a semi-fastback roofline with flush rear window, and an integral rear deck spoiler more pronounced than on the previous Charger.

The Charger Super Bee was offered with a slightly de-tuned high-performance 383, having compression lowered to 8.7:1 to run on regular fuel and improve emissions. Gross horsepower was still a respectable 300, but this amounted to a more than 10 percent drop in output. The transmission was a three-on-the-floor manual. The Super Bee had the same basic interior appointments of the Charger 500, with the substitution of a full-width bench front seat. Outside, the Charger Super Bee had a prominent power bulge on the hood; the top of the bulge was blacked-out and brandished a Super Bee decal. A color-keyed bumper group could be ordered, and this made the Super Bee look even more imposing.

For the first time, the Ramcharger fresh-air hoodscoop was available on the Charger; it was optional on the Super Bee. Instead of the two fixed hoodscoops used on the Coronet the previous year, the Ramcharger featured a vacuum-operated hoodscoop that popped up when the accelerator was mashed. In the fresh-air sweepstakes, image counted for everything, and the

When Dodge redesigned its compact line for 1971, it did away with the Dart name as well. The Demon was the new name and Demon 340 was the new performance model. Sheet metal was essentially the same as the Plymouth Duster. This one has the optional hoodscoops and blackout hood treatment.

Plum Crazy enhanced the good looks of Dodge's redesigned compact. The Demon 340 received a black taillight panel with Demon 340 logo.

Equipped with TorqueFlight automatic transmission, the Demon 340 was a sleeper on the street, with the ability for the driver to manually shift to extract maximum performance from the small-block Wedge V-8.

Ramcharger system for 1971 delivered. Whether it actually boosted performance or not was almost moot!

Performance could be boosted considerably in the Super Bee by ordering the optional 440 Six Pack or 426 Hemi. The 440 Six Pack was rated at 385 horsepower, down five ponies as a result of a minuscule 0.2 percentage point drop in compression to 10.3:1. The 426 Hemi remained unscathed, still churning out 425 horsepower. In the Super Bee the 440 Six Pack V-8 cost $262.15, while the Hemi cost a whopping $883.55. With a base list price of $3,271, however, the Charger Super Bee was a performance bargain.

The next rung in the Dodge Charger performance ladder was, of course, the R/T, with a list price roughly $1,000 more than the Super Bee. The standard mill was again the four-barrel 440 Magnum, still having 375 horsepower. The R/T came standard with the pop-up Ramcharger fresh-air hoodscoop. The bulletproof TorqueFlight automatic transmission was standard and ideally suited to the torque curve of the 440 Magnum. The interior of the R/T differed from the Super Bee only in the use of front bucket seats.

Cars have always been essential props in movies, and car chases have been key action scenes in films from the gangster era to the present. Despite the abundance of musclecars in the late sixties, it wasn't until *Bullitt*, released in 1968, that cars played such a memorable role in the movie's plot. In this fast-paced film, Steve McQueen portrayed Frank Bullitt, very much an independent-minded San Francisco cop. When a Mafia informant awaiting jury testimony is rubbed out by two hit men, Bullitt gives chase—and what a chase it is! It starts as a cat and mouse encounter as the hit men, in a black 1968 Charger R/T, do their best in avoiding Bullitt, driving a Mustang GT. When Bullitt gets just a little too close, the hit men make a break for it, lighting up the R/T's rear tires, the signal Bullitt needs to downshift and accelerate in hot pursuit. The chase scene that follows over San Francisco's roller coaster streets is acknowledged as one of the best ever put on film.

In order for the cars to withstand the severe punishment of repeatedly leaping into the air and hard landings, the suspension components had to be modified. Koni shocks were installed on both cars. The Charger spring rates were increased. Many parts of both cars were magnafluxed to detect any hairline cracks, which could prove disastrous. The Charger R/T was driven by veteran stuntman Bill Hickman, who also played the role of one of the hit men. McQueen did most of the driving in the Mustang, but the really dangerous scenes, such as the leaps, were done by Bud Ekins. The firey crash of the Charger that climaxes the fender-bashing chase scene was accomplished by hooking up the Charger alongside the Mustang with a connecting bar and release pin pulled from the Mustang's driver's seat. The Charger, with dummies strapped in, had rigged explosives and impact switches so it would blow up and be engulfed in flames upon hitting the gasoline pumps. Moviegoers who watched *Bullitt* at drive-in theaters received the heightened effect of "being there" during the hair-raising chase.

Trivia buffs will be interested in knowing Bullitt was nominated for an Oscar in the category of Best Sound, and it won the Oscar for Best Film Editing at the 1969 Oscar ceremonies. On the light-hearted side, there were numerous goofs in the film that sharp-eyed viewers took pleasure in spotting. The same green Volkswagen keeps reappearing in several different scenes during the chase, the front fender of the Charger is damaged when it scrapes a retaining wall, but in subsequent scenes it's as good as new, and the Charger loses three hubcaps during the chase, then another three when it careens off the highway into the gas pumps, to name but a few. Still, the action is so fast-paced, these details were missed by the majority of moviegoers.

If any movie can rival *Bullitt* for the title of ultimate automotive cult classic, that movie would have to be *Vanishing Point*, released in 1971.

As every Mopar enthusiast knows, the automotive focus of the movie was the Alpine White Dodge Challenger R/T, driven by actor Barry Newman. The plotline involves a car delivery driver by the name of Kowalski, played by Newman, who bets he can get the car from Denver, Colorado, to San Francisco, California, in 18 hours. Frequently seeing the far side of the double nickle, Kowalski attracts an ever-growing police dragnet as he races toward his goal. The antihero, existential theme of the film resulted in the film slowly becoming a cult classic in the seventies.

There were five white Challengers used for the film. Four were equipped with 440 Magnums with four-speed transmissions, and the fifth car had a 383 with TorqueFlight transmission. No special equipment was added to the cars, with the exception of heavier-duty shocks installed on the Challenger that jumped No Name Creek. The cars were checked out and maintained throughout filming by Max Balchowsky, who performed similar duties on the Charger and Mustang in *Bullitt*. The stunt sequences were choreographed by Hollywood veteran Carey Loftin.

In an interview for the March 1986 issue of Muscle Car Review, Newman says of the cars, "I remember the cars had 440 engines and had a tremendous amount of power. It was almost as if there was too much power for the body. You'd put it in first and it would almost rear back! They had a four-speed and there was also an automatic car. That was a 383. I think we used that one as the camera car on the straight runs."

Desperate to stop Kowalski from evading them any longer, police bring in two massive Caterpillar bulldozers, which are angled blade to blade to bring the renegade driver to a stop. As viewers know, Kowalski met his end in the blades of those Cats in spectacular fashion. However, since the Challengers were on loan from Chrysler to the production company and had to be returned in reasonable condition, a derelict 1967 Camaro was located to act as the stand-in. Balchowsky removed the drivetrain and had the car painted a matching white. Loftin used the 383 automatic Challenger as the tow vehicle to get the Camaro up to speed, a method Loftin had successfully used in many films. The Camaro was rigged with explosives to detonate when the car hit the dozers. The last scene of Kowalski shows him smiling, determined to remain free and never be captured. The light between the blades of those bulldozers was his vanishing point.

"At the time it was made," Newman says in the interview, "we were still living in the sixties, with the individual against the institutions—the establishment. The individual, the loner, the antihero was very, very popular then, and it was a very moving thing when the guy killed himself. When he died, it stayed with people. They came back and saw the film over and over again. I was never aware of the impact of the film while I was making it."

The Scat Pack in the Movies

Although power-robbing emissions controls were looming over the next few years, the high-performance 340 in 1971 still provided the punch to make the Demon 340 a satisfying car to drive on the street and the strip. It was a viable alternative to the high premiums levied against the 440 and 426 Hemi Mopars.

As in previous years, the R/T's suspension components were extra heavy duty, using high-rate torsion bars, heavy-duty shocks, extra-heavy-duty rear springs with special right rear spring, and front anti-sway bar. This same suspension was included in the engine package for Hemi and 440 Six Pack-equipped Chargers. Owner of Chargers so equipped who intended weekend drag racing were smart to order the Super Trak Pak which included the limited-slip Dana 4.10 rear axle to handle the torque, a manual four-speed tranny with Hurst pistol-grip shifter, dual-breaker distributor, a bigger radiator, and a seven-blade fan—all costing $219.30. Externally, the R/T was identified using the same blackout hood, with a longitudinal tape stripe running from the blackout area of the hood all the way to the rear trunk lid. The R/T logo appeared on the hood and rear trunk lid, and R/T medallions on the front fenders. In addition, the R/T had two curved tape stripes on the doors, simulating vents. New on the option list and of interest to Mopar enthusiasts were front and rear spoilers. The rear spoiler was similar in design and function to the one used on the 1969 Pontiac GTO Judge. Few buyers chose to order their Chargers with these spoilers, however.

Charger buyers were not disappointed with their car's performance that year. A Super Bee with optional 440 Six Pack could reach 60 miles per hour in 6.9 seconds and do the quarter-mile in 14.0 seconds. A Hemi-equipped Super Bee, weighing almost 100 pounds more, reached 60 miles per hour in 5.7 seconds and covered the quarter-mile in only 13.7 seconds. This set the high-water mark for Dodge Charger performance. Never again would Mopar enthusiasts enjoy the freedom of choice and levels of performance established in 1971. Sales continued to drop and by the end of the model year, only 4,144 Super Bees and 2,659 R/Ts had been sold. A number of enthusiast magazines issued the warning that 1971 would be the last year of the 440 Six Pack and 426 Hemi, and smart buyers would buy one while they still could. Not many followed this sage advice. Only 22 Super Bees were ordered with the 426 Hemi; 13 were equipped with the TorqueFlight and 9 with the manual four-speed. The Hemi was ordered by 63 visionary buyers, 33 having the TorqueFlight and 30 with the four-speed manual.

Challenges for the Challenger

Dodge did not tamper with the winning sales success formula for the Challenger and continued to promote the car's strong performance image for 1971. The major aesthetic change to the Challenger was to the grille, with two distinct openings that altered the car's looks to a degree. Model availability was juggled for 1971. Looking at the entire Challenger line, the R/T SE and the R/T convertible were dropped. Added was a base two-door coupe with fixed rear windows and a lower price tag than the hardtop. Base price for the two-door coupe was $2,727. The two-door hardtop cost $2,848. The six-cylinder Challenger convertible had a base list price of $3,105. The base V-8-equipped Challenger convertible, with the 230-horsepower, 318 cubic-inch V-8, listed for $3,207. This was also the standard engine in the Challenger V-8 coupe for $2,853 and the Challenger V-8 hardtop for $2,950. It is a bit surreal to reflect on these prices today.

The Challenger R/T also went through some changes for 1971 as the Scat Pack lured buyers who missed buying in 1970. The biggest change was under the hood. The 375-horsepower 440 Magnum was dropped as the standard V-8. In its place was the 300-horsepower, four-barrel 383. Optional engines on the R/T included the 385-horsepower 440 Six Pack, and the

425-horsepower 426 Hemi. The net horsepower ratings on these two engines were 330 and 350, respectively. Net ratings were adopted by Chrysler to publish more realistic, rear wheel horsepower. Outside, the Challenger R/T split-grille was painted a flat black, and fake scoops were positioned just in front of the rear wheels.

Only 250 Challenger R/Ts were ordered with the 440 Six Pack, and a mere 71 R/Ts were ordered with the 426 Hemi. Production of the 426 Hemi could not be justified in the face of such production numbers, and the difficulty of meeting emissions in the 1972-1973 time frame only hastened the elephant engine's demise. The 440 Six Pack suffered the same fate for the very same reasons. In a Product Planning Letter dated October 14, 1971, on the subject of "440/6V Engine Availability,"

the epitaph of the engine was written. Under "Description of Change" was the following: "Cancel the 440/6V Engine (Sales Code E87). Certification efforts to date have been unsuccessful. Probable earliest production is now projected as late March 1971. The low balance of the year volume does not warrant the development and tooling costs yet to be spent. (The engine will not be available in 1973 and beyond.)"

"We could have saved the cars with good, aggressive management," Chrysler's Larry Shepard says of the big-block Wedge and Hemi Dodges as well as Plymouths. "The whole industry was to blame for being intimidated by the federal government and the insurance companies."

Nevertheless, the sales numbers were not adding up, and Chrysler had to respond to the market trends.

By 1972, the Charger Super Bee and R/T were also history. The swan song of Charger performance was the 1972 Charger Rallye. The 318 ci V-8 was standard, but big-block Wedge power was available.

Those big-block musclecars were involved in more than the fair share of accident claims. As has been said, "Power corrupts, and absolute power corrupts absolutely." There was no question the 426 Hemi and 440 Wedge engines constituted absolute power. It was intoxicating having all that power under one's right foot, and it was too easy to let that power take over one's adrenal glands. Clearly, the small-block Wedge was going to take on increasing importance in the future.

A Demon Appears

The Dodge Dart Swinger and Swinger 340 were gone from the Dodge lineup in 1971, replaced by new models—the Demon and Demon 340. The compact members of the Scat Pack received new sheet metal, and it was a very successful redesign. It shared the same basic body shell with Plymouth's stylish Duster. The two cars differed primarily in the grille and rear taillight assembly. Dodge chose to call its model the Demon. Some cited the car's name as less than appropriate. Still, it was perhaps a better choice than Beaver—a name Dodge management had considered and, fortunately, dropped. An interesting manufacturing step shared by both the Demon and Duster was the blending of the taillight panel with the rear quarter panels so no seam was visible. This was done by leading, filing, and sanding, then priming the seam so it was invisible. This was a routine operation on the roofs of cars.

The Demon was termed a coupe instead of a hardtop because the rear windows did not roll down; they were hinged to swing out about 2 inches to permit ventilation. This also helped to keep the price tag down. That was reflected in the Demon 340's list price of only $2,721. Under the hood was the 275-horsepower, four-barrel 340 V-8, with dual exhaust. This was backed up by Chrysler's heavy-duty three-speed manual transmission with floor shifter. The Rallye Suspension Pack with heavy-duty front torsion bars, front stabilizer bar, rear springs and shock absorbers improved the car's handling.

There were numerous performance and performance-related options for the Demon 340. A heavy-duty four-speed manual transmission could be ordered, or the high-upshift TorqueFlight automatic. Optional dual hoodscoops and a blacked-out hood paint treatment backed up the Demon 340's performance with looks to match. Hoods pins could lend a racy look. A rear spoiler was available. A 6,000-rpm tachometer was a very

The third generation Charger received all-new sheet metal in 1971 and attempted to blend in the rear window for more aerodynamic efficiency. Some argue the Charger lost its crisp, coherent design theme in the process.

worthwhile option to have in this high-winding small-block Wedge.

How was the Demon 340's performance at the drag strip? With the stock 3.23 rear cogs, the car reached 60 miles per hour in 6.5 seconds and the quarter-mile was covered in a very respectable 14.5 seconds. The car's power-to-weight ratio was almost identical to Dodge's bigger and heavier performance cars. The Demon 340's quarter-mile times were within a few tenths of a second of the Super Bee and Charger.

Dodge performance enthusiasts who voraciously read *Cars, Hot Rod, Car Craft, Motor Trend*, and other magazines got a jolt when the September and October 1971 issues started to hit the stands. They learned the Charger R/T and Super Bee were gone, as was the Challenger R/T. They read in stunned disbelief that the mighty 426 Hemi and 440 Six Pack were history. The Challenger could not even be ordered with a 383 V-8. Things, indeed, looked bleak. However, those who were too late to snap up the high-compression, high-performance Dodges now gone could still get a good performer by carefully perusing the option list for the Dodge of their choice.

The Rallye was the only performance model offered in the 1972 Charger line. Included in the Rallye package was a sculpted dark grille, simulated door louvers with blacked-out treatment, louvered black taillights, and blacked-out power-bulge hood treatment. The Rallye suspension was a bit softer than the R/T suspension, but included front and rear anti-sway bars. Standard in the Rallye was the 318 cubic-inch V-8, but the option list held the key to respectable performance. First up was the 240 (net) horsepower 340 V-8. The 383 was replaced by a new 400 cubic-inch Wedge. The four-barrel 400 V-8 was rated at 255 horsepower. The top engine was the 280-horsepower, four-barrel 440 V-8. However, what really counted on the street was torque. Even with a low 8.20:1 compression ratio, this 440 put out 375 foot-pounds of torque at 3,200 rpm. Add to this the four-speed manual transmission and the still-available Trak Pak Package, and you had a still-impressive performer.

The Challenger also had a Rallye model, and it reflected the new market reality. The brochure describing the Challenger Rallye stated: "The way things are today, maybe what you need is not the world's hottest car. Maybe what you need is a well-balanced, thoroughly instrumented road machine. One with a highly individualized style; a well-proportioned balance between acceleration, road-holding, braking—you know the bit. This is it. Challenger Rallye. Reasonable to buy, to run. About as enjoyable in the legal range as anything its size. And a lot more thoughtfully done."

The Challenger Rallye came with a 240-horsepower, four-barrel 340 V-8, three-on-the-floor synchromesh manual transmission, 3.23:1 axle ratio, and dual exhaust with chrome exhaust tips. Performance could be increased by ordering the optional four-speed

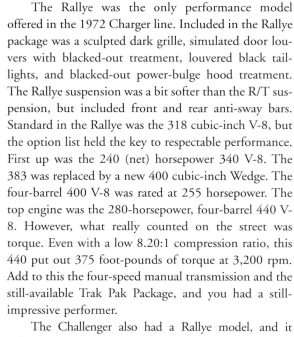

The top optional engine available in the 1972 Charger Rallye was the four-barrel 440 Magnum with 280 net horsepower with 375 foot-pounds of torque, running an 8.2:1 compression ratio in order to run on low-lead gas.

manual transmission and the Performance Axle Package with 3.55:1 heavy-duty axle, Sure-Grip differential, high-performance radiator, fan shroud, and—when power steering was ordered—a power steering oil cooler. The grille was changed on the 1972 Challenger, and the Rallye came with simulated side body louvers with black tape stripes aligned with the louvers. Only two High Impact colors were available to make the Rallye stand out: Hemi Orange and Top Banana.

The Challenger Rallye, with a list price of $3,056, was actually not a bad package. It was a better-balanced, better-handling all-around machine, compared to the Challenger R/T with the 440. The Rallye served the purposes of the majority of Challenger buyers looking for something more than the plain Challenger. If the Dodge enthusiast was looking for something more in the way of straight-line performance, he had to look to the bigger-bodied Charger. Total Challenger Rallye production for 1972 totaled 6,902 units.

There were also changes in the compact end of the Dodge lineup for 1972. The Demon 340 continued for the new year, powered by the same engine in the Challenger Rallye. It was clear looking at the entire Dodge lineup that performance had entered into a full-blown recession. Seeing this undeniable trend, more than a few Mopar enthusiasts began looking for used Chargers, Challengers, and Coronet Super Bees. At this point these cars were not being bought for investment purposes, but merely performance preservation and enjoyment. In the early 1970s, few realized that many of Dodge's most desirable musclecars would one day be worth a considerable amount of money.

The Last Hurrah

There were some bright spots in this somewhat depressing scene. A number of the specialty dealers around America were doing some very interesting conversions in an effort of boost performance. One of them was one of the most famous Dodge dealers in the country—Grand Spaulding Dodge. The president of Grand Spaulding Dodge was Norm Kraus, known to one and all as Mr. Norm. Surveying the declining fortunes of Mopar performance, Mr. Norm engineered a supercharged Demon 340 and offered it for 1972. This car was the Demon GSS. The Paxton supercharger dramatically boosted the output of the 340 V-8. Several high-performance car magazines tested this latest offering from Grand Spaulding, which was always a great way to

get the needed publicity without great advertising expense. The car had so much power the stock tires were all but useless in trying to get good quarter-mile times. However, with a proper set of slicks, the car could run in the upper 12 to low 13 seconds range, doing over 105 miles per hour going through the lights. The price of this pocket rocket was only $3,595. Fewer than 200 were sold in its only year of production.

By 1973, the cars that had once made up the Scat Pack were making the transition to personal luxury-type cars, where performance was not emphasized. Still, Dodge continued to offer Wedge V-8s with the most horsepower they could extract while keeping within the requirements of the EPA. The Challenger in particular still made a striking performance styling statement. The following year, 1974, output for the Wedge V-8s dropped again slightly. Dodge abruptly stopped production of the Challenger after only a few months of production. This was the last year before many manufacturers were forced to adopt catalytic converters on their cars, necessitating a single exhaust system. The performance Dodges from the 1972 to 1974 model years are now being recognized by enthusiasts and collectors as desirable machines—the last hurrah for the dual exhaust, four-speed, Wedge V-8-powered Mopars from Chrysler's Dodge division.

A 440 Magnum was still something to be proud of in 1972. This hood identification was included when the big-block Wedge was ordered.

CHAPTER THREE

The Rapid Transit System

Managers of the Plymouth Division were becoming increasingly aware that they needed a car with a distinct performance image and identity. Pontiac had it with its GTO, Oldsmobile had its 4-4-2, Ford its Shelby Mustang GT-350, to name just a few. The Barracuda, based on the Valiant, was essentially a compact offering only a small-displacement Wedge powerplant. Plymouth's product planners were aware of its musclecar identity crisis and they got to work to build a car that would really put Plymouth on the performance map.

GTX–The Executive Supercar

Plymouth had marketed big-block Wedge cars during the early and mid-1960s in the Belvedere and dressier Satellite line, but there was no identifiable performance model, per se. That was due to change with the introduction of 440 cubic-inch Wedge V-8 in 1966. This engine was, essentially, a 426 Wedge with the same 3.75-inch stroke but a larger 4.32-inch bore. In its standard trim, the 440 with four-barrel Carter AFB pumped out 350 horsepower at 4,400 rpm with 480 foot-pounds of torque at 2,800 rpm. Plymouth Division wanted a high-performance car it could truly call its own, but it needed a high-performance engine to go in it. While Chrysler engineers got to work developing the High Performance 440, Plymouth product planners got to work on what would become the 1967 GTX.

GTX Engine

Shortly after the introduction of the 440 in 1966, work was begun on a high-performance version of that engine. The objectives targeted for this engine were outlined in a technical paper issued by Chrysler's Engineering Office in October 1966 at the time of the 1967 model introductions. It was a paradigm of unembellished engineering-speak: "This engine was developed with the objectives of obtaining high output, tractability under all driving conditions, high durability to allow coverage by the 5-year or 50,000-mile warranty, quiet operation, and suitability for volume production. As a result, performance approaches that of the 426 Hemi, with driveability and general operating characteristics more like those of the normal 383- and 440 cubic-inch engines."

The most efficient and cost-effective means of doing this was to increase the 440's breathing ability in the mid- to upper rpm range without sacrificing low-end torque, and beef up key components that would see repeated high-output applications, such as the local quarter-mile strip. During development work, it was determined the engine block, forged steel crankshaft, lead-base babbitt-on-steel main bearings, and forged-steel connecting rods of the base 440 V-8 were suitable for use in the high-performance engine. The cast-aluminum pistons did receive redesigned rings to improve oil control. The connecting rod bearings were replaced

The GTX was Plymouth's first identifiable musclecar. Introduced in 1967, it boasted a high-performance version of the standard 440 cubic-inch V-8. Based on the Belvedere, it displayed the addition of modest hoodscoops and GTX identification. With a base list price under $3,200, it was a bargain.

Plymouth is out to win you over with Belvedere GTX.

GTX. Plymouth's exciting new Super-car. King of the Belvederes. Standard equipment: the biggest GT engine in the world. Our Super Commando 440 V-8. Optional equipment: the famous Plymouth Hemi.
This Plymouth goes flat out to win you over. And there's nothing hidden about its promise. Check the twin hood scoops up front, twin chrome exhaust megaphones out back.

Note how the GTX sits up on its special suspension. Obviously, this is something special—right down to the new pit-stop gas filler, Red Streak tires, chrome valve covers and custom, no-nonsense grille.
Now, if this Belvedere is a little heady for you, we've got 21 other models—all with varying degrees of devilment—out to win you over.
Be prepared to be persuaded.

Plymouth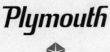

CHRYSLER
MOTORS CORPORATION

Plymouth ran several different ads in 1967 introducing the GTX to enthusiasts. This ad is particularly interesting because the car pictured displays the "Hemi" badge on the lower beltline of the front fender.

with those patterned after the 426 Hemi rods: steel back, copper-lead intermediate layer, and high lead overplate. The bulk of development work on the high-performance 440 revolved around the cylinder heads, camshaft, and induction system.

A completely new camshaft was designed for this engine. Numerous cam profiles were dynoed concurrently with the cylinder head, induction, and exhaust systems. During cam development, the engine proved responsive to increases in the exhaust valve lift and duration. Consequently, the cam lobes on the exhaust side reflected this. The bumpstick that emerged had an intake duration of 268 degrees with .450-inch lift at zero lash and an exhaust duration of 284 degrees with .465-inch lift at zero lash with 46 degrees of overlap.

The cylinder heads received much attention. Both intake and exhaust ports were substantially increased. The intake port was increased to 2.3 square inches—nearly 10 percent—and the port shape modified to improve flow. The exhaust port shape was also changed to take advantage of the larger exhaust valve. The 2.08-inch diameter intake valve was unchanged from the standard 440, but the exhaust valve diameter was increased from 1.60 inches to 1.74 inches. The valve springs themselves were a bit more stout (Chrysler referred to them as "high-load") with flat-wound dampers to ward off valve float during vigorous stoplight high-rpm shifting. The intake manifold was completely new with correspondingly larger passages and was .51 inch taller at the carburetor mounting flange. The Carter AFB four-barrel carburetor came with 1 11/16 primary and secondary bores, with mechanical secondaries; manual transmission-equipped cars used the AFB-4326S, while cars with TorqueFlights used the AFB-4327S. Even the exhaust manifolds received attention, and bore a family resemblance to the wilder exhaust manifolds used on the Max Wedge engines of a few years before. The outlet diameter for these manifolds was 2.38 inches. Chrysler was pleased with the final numbers for the high-performance 440: running a 10.1:1 compression ratio, the engine developed 375 horsepower at 4,600 rpm with 480 foot-pounds of torque at 3,200 rpm.

A Chassis to Handle the Power

The GTX would be based on the Satellite, but the vehicle and chassis engineers working with the prototype at Chrysler's Chelsea, Michigan, proving grounds made sure the car could handle well with the power pouring out of that 440 Wedge. They learned a lot from the 426 Hemi application in Plymouth's B-bodies. The GTX received heavy-duty front torsion bars, heavy-duty six-leaf left rear spring and seven-leaf right rear spring, heavy-duty shocks at all four corners, 0.94 inch-diameter front stabilizer bar, heavy-duty ball-joints, heavy-duty front and rear drum brakes, heavy-duty radiator, heavy-duty drive shaft . . . the list went on and on.

In terms of exterior appearance, GTX medallions appeared on the front fenders and on the right rear portion of the trunk lid. The nonfunctional hoodscoops and quick-filler chrome gas cap were unique to the GTX. The Sport Stripes shown on the GTX in Plymouth brochures and ads for the car were optional, but cost a mere $31 more than the GTX's suggested retail price. You could also order your GTX as a convertible.

Plymouth's Sales Division knew how to write promotional copy for its showroom brochures to lure buyers into test driving a GTX, if not buying one. "GTX: Plymouth's fastest way to win you. The most exciting Supercar to come out of Detroit in years. What lights the GTX flame? That deep-throated roar from under the hood gives you an inkling. It's the Super Commando 440 cubic-inch V-8. Biggest GT engine anywhere. It's standard. And formidable."

The GTX became *the* cover car of the enthusiast magazines for 1967 and helped to launch the Plymouth's performance image—with the horsepower and acceleration numbers to back it up. The advertising emphasis in enthusiast magazines would now be on performance-specific models, like the GTX.

The Fish Gets New Scales

In 1967, Plymouth launched a new ad campaign with the line: "Plymouth is out to win you over" with a red heart having an upturned arrow symbol. To win over prospective Barracuda owners, Plymouth completely redesigned the car and added a hardtop coupe and convertible. The new Barracuda made a complete break from its Valiant roots and all sheet metal was uniquely its own. Plymouth targeted the second-generation Barracuda directly at the youth market, those who admired the Chevrolet Camaro, Ford Mustang, and Pontiac Firebird, but wanted a car built by Chrysler.

The new Barracuda was longer and wider, but not lower. The wheelbase was extended from 106 inches to 108 inches. Front track increased from 55.9 inches to

57.4 inches, while rear track remained the same at 55.6 inches. Overall length increased from 188.2 inches to 192.8 inches and overall width increased from 70.1 to 71.6 inches. In redesigning the fastback Barracuda, named the Sports Barracuda for 1967, Plymouth aimed for an Italian GT look. The stylists came pretty close.

'67 Belvedere GTX A machine of many talents.
Most assuredly it has an engine. A big wedge-head V-8 at that: 440 cubic inches' worth, with 375 hp. and 480 lbs.-ft. of torque as standard equipment.

It also comes with the street Hemi at 426 cubic inches. The Hemi puts out 425 hp. and 490 lbs.-ft. of torque. (And, of course, costs extra.)

But the nicest thing about the GTX is that it isn't *all* engine. Fact is, it's the most well-rounded Supercar to come out of Detroit (or anywhere, for that matter) in a long time.

Heavy-duty suspension is standard and includes stiffer front torsion bars, beefier ball-joints, heavier front stabilizer bar, firmer shocks and rear springs.

Brakes are big 11 in. drum-type units; although front discs are optionally available.

Tires are special Red Streaks, mounted on 5½ in. rims.

Transmission is through a high-upshift TorqueFlite automatic. But a 4-speed is available as an option.

Other standard GTX items include buckets, hood scoops, low-restriction exhaust system and pit-stop gas filler.

The result is a road machine that not only looks and goes, but one that handles. And steers. And stops. And sticks. It'll do everything but bring you your morning coffee. But with a list of eye-openers like this—who needs it? As you may have heard, Plymouth is out to win you over this year.

Cubic inches aren't everything.

PLYMOUTH DIVISION   CHRYSLER MOTORS CORPORATION

Plymouth identified the GTX powerplant as the Super Commando 440. With a single four-barrel Carter on top of the high-flow intake manifold and cylinder heads, it developed 375 horsepower and tree-stump-pulling torque.

tures were retained in the Sports Barracuda. The folding rear seat had a redesigned latch that made it more convenient to lock or release the seat in the up or down position, but the catch bar was eliminated for 1967. All three Barracuda models had full instrumentation.

Four engines were offered. Standard was the slant six or 273 cubic-inch V-8. Optional was the 235-horsepower 273, or the 280-horsepower 383. The three-speed manual transmission was standard; the four-speed manual tranny was the performance choice, but the TorqueFlight automatic could also be ordered. Back in the 1960s you could order your choice of rear axle ratios; if the factory didn't have the precise numbers you wanted, the dealer would be happy to install axle ratios of your choosing. Today we have no such choice; we take what comes with the car.

The top-of-the-line Formula S package was expanded and improved in a number of ways. The aforementioned 383 boosted the car's performance considerably, with the car able to reach 60 miles per hour in 7.4 seconds and tripping the quarter-mile timing lights in 15.9 seconds. The 383 came with dual exhaust instead of the low-restriction single exhaust on the four-barrel 273 V-8. Fender plaques announced "383 Four Barrel" to other drivers. Front disc brakes were a mandatory option. The 383 Formula S came with either the four-speed stick or the TorqueFlight auto; bucket seats with console were part of the package. On the downside, you could not order air conditioning or power steering with the 383 Formula S due to under-hood space limitations!

With the successful introduction of the GTX, Plymouth had its big-block musclecar at last. GTX in the ears of a Chevy or Ford driver was not good news. The GTX was not only powerful and fast, it was plush and had the image of an "executive musclecar." Plymouth now had momentum and was looking for other openings in the market.

Of course, 1967 was the second year of the 426 Hemi's production in street Dodges and Plymouths, but that kind of all-out performance came with a steep price tag. Plymouth product planners had been studying the market to see if there was a specific niche to which it could target yet another model. It was a very specific and in-depth market study, and it did indeed reveal there was a place in its product line, and in the consumer market itself, for a more affordable performance car.

You can see the lines reminiscent of the Maserati Mistral and Ferrari Lusso. Interestingly, in describing the Sports Barracuda, Plymouth made use of the name contraction 'Cuda. This would become a distinct model name later.

The addition of two new body styles gave Barracuda buyers freedom of choice. The hardtop offered the more conservative buyer an alternative to the fast-back. Its rear window glass had an unusual upward curl along the top that allowed the roof to extend farther back and still provide ample headroom. The hardtop had a conventional trunk lid.

The convertible was welcomed by open-air driving enthusiasts. The top was power-operated and the rear window was glass so the owner wouldn't have to suffer from a clear plastic window aging to a foggy yellow.

In the interior, buyers were greeted to both the new and familiar. A new sports front bench seat with individual backs and a folding center armrest was standard. Newly designed bucket seats were optional. The for-ward-folding rear seat and security panel conversion fea-

GTX identification was subdued. These badges appeared on the front fender forward of the wheelwell. A GTX badge was also mounted on the trunk lid.

The Plymouth Road Runner, introduced for 1968, established a new automotive genre: a truly affordable big-block musclecar. Eager buyers baffled Plymouth product planners by loading it up with options. The Road Runner was far more popular than the comparably equipped Dodge Super Bee (background).

Enter the Road Runner

In the early winter months of 1967, Chrysler product planner Joe Sturm was in his Highland Park office when he received a call from the Sales Division. The clever minds in the Sales Division had been kicking around an idea and wanted to know what Sturm thought about it. As Sturm recalls, "They asked me, 'Why not offer a car that has the biggest engine we make as standard equipment . . . a car that has no rear seats, no floor mats, and eliminate every piece of trim and ornamentation?' " The car was obviously race-car inspired, and meant to capitalize on Plymouth's successful circle track record.

Sturm discussed the idea with Belvedere product planners Jack Smith and Gordon Cherry and they felt that this kind of stripped-down car would appeal to too small a group of buyers. However, they agreed there was a significant market for a relatively inexpensive car deliberately devoid of interior and exterior frills, with maximum attention to engine, driveline, suspension, and brakes. In order to substantiate the concept and properly target the car, an in-depth look at the high-performance market—both cars and buyers—was conducted. The study revealed five distinct levels of knowledge and interest in cars by enthusiasts, forming a pyramid according to the size of each group.

At the top of the pyramid were the elite professional racers. While this group was small, it exerted the greatest degree of influence of the various groups. Their opinions and actions served to direct and mold the

With the restyling of the Belvedere/Satellite line for 1968, the GTX and Road Runner both benefited. Sheetmetal was carried over for 1969. This 1969 GTX was one of only 625 convertibles built. The blacked-out lower beltline helped to distinguish it from the 1968 model.

desires and attitudes of the balance of the enthusiast market. Next came the hardcore drag racers and road racers, who regard the appearance and reputation of a car of lesser importance than ultimate top speed. The third group consisted of part-time enthusiasts and racers, who owned a dual-purpose machine driven on both the street and the strip. This group put a greater importance on a car's appearance.

The fourth group, Sturm labeled the "executive hot rodders." They liked high performance but placed the most importance on a good-looking machine. These were the principal buyers of the GTX. The last and largest group was, says Sturm, "the Drive-In Set, the street cruisers, spectators, and identifiers who are into performance." The guys in this group, Sturm found, devour the performance-buff magazines for the latest low-buck hop-up tricks because they have the least amount of money of the five groups. However, because of its size, it buys the most cars. This last group was the target group for the car Plymouth was envisioning. Plymouth also studied the high-performance cars on the market for 1967.

"In order to determine what performance level was necessary for this proposed car and what price tag the

car could support," Sturm recalls, "the existing offerings of that time were reviewed in detail. We made a chart giving quarter-mile trap speed vertically on the left and price increasing from left to right. Not surprisingly, we found the more you spent, the faster you went. A cluster of cars over $3,300 was capable of over 100 miles per hour in the quarter mile, but there wasn't one car on the market below $3,300 with the same performance.

With this information, Plymouth's initial goal was to build a car capable of 100 miles per hour in the quarter-mile with a retail price of $3,000. To accomplish this, it would be necessary to eliminate some of

the more costly appointments that characterized the earlier kinds of Supercars. The expense of the extra brightwork and high interior trim level was converted to performance engine and chassis hardware. Rather than use the 440 in this car and compete with its own GTX, Plymouth chose to develop a high-performance version of its venerable 383 cubic-inch V-8. However, the camshaft, valve springs, cylinder heads, intake manifold exhaust manifolds, crankcase windage tray, and related hardware from the high-performance 440 was grafted on to the 383 so the yet-to-be-named Road Runner would have a high-performance engine of its own. The keys to this engine's performance were the high-performance, free-flowing cylinder heads and intake manifold developed for the 440. On the 383, they did wonders.

Beep Beep!

Exactly how did the name for this car come about? "The name Road Runner had shown up on lists off and on for a couple of years," recounts Sturm, "but apparently the product was neither right, nor had the correct 'sell' job been done to get it considered. To make a long story short, Jack Smith and Gordon Cherry sent me

The interior of the GTX was more luxurious than that of the Road Runner and that was the idea. Bucket seats were standard on the GTX and the interior included more brightwork.

BEEP-BEEP! EEEYYOWWWW!

PLYMOUTH TELLS IT LIKE IT IS.

See test results, page 123

To prove a stock Road Runner could break the 100 mph barrier, Plymouth hired Ronnie Sox and under the watchful eyes of the NHRA at Irwindale Raceway, California, proceeded to do just that. With the change to a hotter cam, Holley carb, Edelbrock high-riser intake manifold, Hooker headers, and cheater slicks, the car was in the mid-13s going over 104 mph. It's all in the fine print. The artwork was done by Paul Williams.

home to watch the Saturday Road Runner cartoon show. Incidentally, these cartoons were becoming very popular even in private showings to young people, especially in California where some of the local taverns took time out to watch Road Runner films. It was becoming the thing to do.

"We were amazed to find that we could put a hold on the name Road Runner for a car at the AMA," Sturm continues. "That started the process which eventually led to the Plymouth Division adopting the name Road Runner for the car. Subsequently, agreement was reached with Warner Bros. to use their particular copyrighted cartoon character instead of our own, which we had under development."

In fact, the selection of the name and its association with the cartoon bird was a stroke of brilliance. While the emphasis with other performance cars was on letters, numbers, or an alphanumerical combination, here was a musclecar with a *name*. And it was a name that conveyed exactly the image Plymouth wanted for its new car. The cartoon Road Runner was blindingly, unbeatably fast, yet could stop on a dime. And above all, it could never be caught. And all those young viewers on Saturday morning admired that about the Road Runner. The thing was, countless adults enjoyed watching the Road Runner elude Wile E. Coyote, too. And those adults had the cash to buy the car.

Plymouth didn't stop at the name. Someone, somewhere at Plymouth suggested the car's horn mimic that of the Road Runner's "Beep, Beep!" This gladdened the Sales Division's heart, and the existing Belvedere horn was modified—at considerable development expense— to replicate the cartoon Road Runner's trademark "Beep Beep!" This was achieved by substituting the horn's standard aluminum windings with copper windings. The horn was so accurate that only a trained technician could tell the difference between the car and the cartoon.

Plymouth's product planners realized the car's appearance must be distinct without adding unnecessary cost to the deliberately low-buck Road Runner. All Plymouth B-bodies were getting redesigned for 1968, and a successful redesign it was, too. The GTX was getting a new performance hood for 1968. The new Road Runner would receive the benefit of this hood, but the simulated side vents would display the requisite 383 medallions to announce the Road Runner's displacement. It received a uniquely finished front grille, and the Road Runner nameplate (with all letters in lowercase) appeared on the dash, the doors, and the trunk lid, along with a small caricature of the blindingly fast desert bird.

The proof of the pudding was in the testing. The standard heavy-duty suspension, F 70 Red Streak Wide Boot tires, four-speed manual transmission with standard 3.23 rear end, coupled to the 335-horsepower Road Runner 383 succeeded in getting the Plymouth test drivers through the quarter-mile timing lights at 98 miles per hour. With the suggested retail price of the Road Runner coupe at $2,896, Plymouth did, indeed, succeed in offering an affordable musclecar with the "Most bang for the buck."

Market Dominance–1968-1969

The Road Runner was an ad copywriter's dream. The first Road Runner ad appeared in the September 1967 issue of *Hot Rod*. The double-page color ad done in a whimsical cartoon style showed the Road Runner (car) and the Road Runner (bird) on the Bonneville Salt Flats. The Road Runner (bird) was dangling a racing helmet from the tip of one of its wings, displaying its ever-present and confident smile. It didn't take much to figure out what this car was all about. To remove all doubt, the ad copy was all business: "You say you want to know what our new bird, the Road Runner is all about? Take a look at the standard equipment and you'll

get the idea:" The ad then went on in detail about the car's mechanical specifications, and stating the Road Runner had "A price way below what you would pay for a Supercar." In closing, Plymouth made clear it didn't want this car actually *street* racing. "It's all put together for the guy who really digs cars, knows about tachs and staging lights and how to use 'em. Knows how to use the car in traffic, too, by following the rules and keeping his cool. Our kind of guy."

That meant, of course, trying to keep one's cool behind the wheel of one's Road Runner at the stoplight while the Oldsmobile 4-4-2 next to you just blipped its engine just prior to the light turning green. Adrenaline and testosterone were a powerful combination, especially in a car like the Road Runner. Plymouth knew the car would be street raced, but it wanted to protect itself from any product liability concerns and show itself to be a responsible carmaker.

That note of caution was cast to the winds in an ad that made the connection to stock car racing. This ad appeared in the May 1968 *Car & Driver*. Pictured is

Richard Petty's No. 43 Hemi Road Runner in the background, and a stock Petty Blue Road Runner front and center, with three very prominent words: "The Missing Link." The ad copy was actually the Road Runner's mission statement, and is worth repeating in its entirety: "Until now, there were two distinct types of stock cars. There was the street stock. And, indeed, it was just that. Despite the acquisition of big displacement engines and ferocious nicknames, it was basically a boulevard car. The emphasis was on luxury: expensive interiors, lavish adornments, and lots of brightwork. Then there was the Grand National stocker. You couldn't buy it, and even if you could, your name would have to be Petty or something to get it started on a cold morning. Nevertheless, it was infinitely attractive—the low silhouette; the super wide tires; the stovepipe exhausts; the absence of chrome; the Spartan cockpit—sort of brutally good looking. Obviously, there was a need for a car that combined some of the civilized comforts of the street stock with the integrity of the Grand National type. So we created the Missing Link."

In 1969, the Road Runner was voted the *Motor Trend* Car of the Year. Did Plymouth gloat? Absolutely. This fold-out ad, perfectly in keeping with the character of the car, appeared in the April 1969 issue of *Super Stock Magazine*.

BEEP-
BEEP!

©Warner Bros.—Seven Arts, Inc.

Plymouth was on a performance roll in the 1960s, never letting the competition rest. To unnerve Ford and GM even more, Plymouth released the 1969-1/2 Road Runner 440 6-BBL. The name said it all: Six-barrel induction atop a 440 Magnum, fed by an outrageous and functional hoodscoop.

The Road Runner 440 6-BBL carried the high-performance/minimal adornment theme to the extreme. With nothing more than chrome lug nuts on the wheels, the car displayed a no-nonsense attitude and backed it up with tire-smoking performance.

No wonder the mystique of the Road Runner grew. It would not be a stretch to say the Road Runner became a legend in its own time. This car was already making the executives at Ford and GM sweat. How else can you explain the eventual appearance of the Pontiac GTO Judge, the cult of Dr. Oldsmobile with his side-kick Elephant Engine Ernie, *ad nauseum*?

Despite a very crowded musclecar marketplace, Plymouth managed to carve out a substantial niche for itself by 1968. The GTX and Road Runner were on the lips of street racers and cruisers from Woodward Avenue to Sunset Boulevard. The handsome new Belvedere body was the perfect basis for the GTX and the Road Runner. The Road Runner was offered as a pillarless coupe, or the hardtop with a list of $3,034. The GTX hardtop listed for $3,355, and the new convertible had a base list price of $3,590.

Because of the inherently clean and enduring line of the Belvedere, the 1968 GTX convertible was, and

still is, one of the finest examples of top-down, high-performance driving to come from Plymouth.

Car Life magazine was a popular performance enthusiast magazine during the 1960s. The performance findings at the drag strip for the 1968 Road Runner and GTX were interesting. The Road Runner, with automatic transmission, did 0-60 miles per hour in 7.3 seconds. It covered the quarter-mile in 15.4 seconds, but trap speed was only 91 miles per hour. The four-speed manual transmission offered a dramatic improvement over this. Top speed for the Road Runner was 122 miles per hour.

The GTX with standard 375-horsepower 440 V-8 with TorqueFlight automatic transmission did 0-60 in 6.8 seconds. It crossed the timing lights in 14.6 seconds at 96 miles per hour. Top speed, curiously, was 121 miles per hour. But with the optional 426 Hemi, *Car Life* naturally found the GTX one of the fastest cars it had ever tested in terms of top speed. With Torque-Flight transmission behind all that horsepower, the GTX reached 60 miles per hour in 6.8 seconds. It reached the quarter-mile timing lights in 14.6 seconds—identical to its 440 Wedge counterpart—with a trap speed of 97 miles per hour. Top speed of the 426 Hemi GTX was an astounding 144 miles per hour.

It was precisely this kind of musclecar performance that made these cars popular at drag strips all over America, driven by both amateurs and professionals. Again, the team of Sox & Martin was the most conspicuous in racing Plymouths. For 1968, they chose a street Hemi Road Runner for Super Stock class racing. Against extremely tough competition (Chevys, Fords, and Dodges were neck and neck in the horsepower race), Sox & Martin garnered one NHRA and three AHRA titles that year. When they weren't racing successfully, Ronnie Sox and Buddy Martin conducted the Plymouth Super-car Clinics. These seminars were held at Plymouth dealerships around the country to give Plymouth fans drag racing and car preparation tips. In the larger cities, sometimes over 2,000 people would attend.

Sales Take Off

All this product promotion and undeniable image and performance made the GTX and Road Runner hot

And this was under that hood. The air cleaner spanned the triple two-barrel carbs. The rubber seal ensured only outside air was fed to the engine. It developed 390 horsepower at 4,700 rpm with 490 foot-pounds of torque at 3,200 rpm.

The goal at Chrysler Engineering in designing the six-barrel 440 was to general Hemi-like performance at roughly half the cost to buy and maintain. It also filled the gap between the four-barrel 440 and the eight-barrel 426 Hemi. This factory photo shows an early production unit with air cleaner removed. *Roger Huntington Collection*

sellers. Over 18,000 GTXs rolled out of Plymouth dealerships. But the stunning news was the Road Runner. Sales orders for the Road Runner were pouring from all over America, Canada, and even overseas. A total of 44,598 Road Runners were sold in 1968, surpassing all expectations at Plymouth. The Plymouth product planners and marketing people had done their homework and delivered a car the performance enthusiasts were looking for. Road Runner buyers proceeded to defy the car's premise by loading up the car with options. Seventy-five percent ordered the Decor Package to spruce up the interior and exterior. Sixty percent checked off the Sure-Grip differential—a good choice. Over 30 percent ordered the black performance paint treatment for the hood and a vinyl roof. Forty percent ordered the custom road wheels. In short, the average buyer spent over $500 on options. Only purists and buyers on a shoestring budget left their Road Runner alone.

Not to be overlooked was the Barracuda for 1968. Again, it was aimed at somewhat different buyers, but they still wanted performance. In fact, this car became

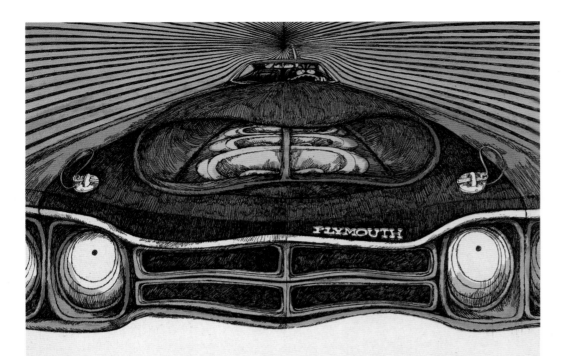

ET'S AND SPECS ON OUR NEWEST ROAD RUNNER:
440 CUBES, GLASS HOOD AND (HEH-HEH!) THREE HOLLEYS!

PLYMOUTH TELLS IT LIKE IT IS.

Special Features:
440 cu. in. V-8, standard.
Edelbrock "6-bbl." Hi-Rise intake manifold, standard.
Three Holley 2-bbl. carbs, standard.
Special low-taper 276°-292°-54° camshaft, standard.
Special hydraulic tappets, standard.
Chromed intake and exhaust valves, standard.
Hemi valve springs, standard.
Fiberglass hood with Super Stock air scoop, standard.
Four pin-type hood latches, standard.
Low-restriction "Air-Grabber"-type air cleaner, standard.
4.10:1 Sure-Grip rear axle, standard.
Dual-breaker distributor, standard.
Heavy-duty 26" radiator, standard.
Viscous-drive fan, standard.
4-speed with Hurst shifter or Torque-Flite automatic, standard.
Extra-heavy-duty "Hemi" suspension, standard.
Heavy-duty 11" drum brakes, standard.
Extra-wide 15 x 6" rims, standard.
Extra-fat G-70 x 15" Polyglas Red Streak tires, standard.

Drag Test:
Date: March 31, 1969
Location: Cecil County Dragoway
Test car: 440 6-bbl. Road Runner (4-speed)
Options on test car: power brakes, power steering, radio, heater, exterior decor package, lighting package.
Weight: 3,765 lbs.
Remarks: Test car in absolutely pure-stock condition—air cleaner and mufflers operating, street tires only; no special tuning.
Witnessed by: Jim McCraw and Roland McGonegal, Super Stock Magazine.

Professional Driver: Ronnie Sox

Run #	ET/Secs	Trap Speed/mph
1	13.21	110.02
2	13.24	110.42
3	13.24	110.29
4	13.22	109.89
5	13.12	110.83
6	13.02	111.52
7	13.14	110.70
8	13.22	111.11
9	13.00	111.52
10	13.00	110.15
Average:	13.14	110.65

Amateur Driver: Roland McGonegal

Run #	ET/Secs	Trap Speed/mph
1	13.95	107.27
2	13.32	109.89
3	13.42	109.22
4	13.48	109.75
5	13.33	110.42
Average:	13.50	109.31

Beep-Beep your *what?!?* To say our new 440 Six-Barrel is the Hot setup is the understatement of the year. Goes to show that nothing shrinks time and distance like cubic inches and a good induction system. Best of all, the whole rig costs a couple of hundred skins less than a Hemi! When you get yours and decide to see what she'll do, just follow our example and do it at a sanctioned strip. Saves wear and tear on the ol' driving record. Dig?

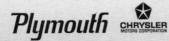

61

This was the ad Plymouth ran detailing the astounding performance of the Road Runner 440 6-BBL. The ad even came out and flatly stated, "Best of all, the whole rig costs a couple of hundred skins less than a Hemi!" Numbers don't lie.

the basis for Plymouth's Super Stock program—a full-race, 426 Hemi Barracuda built in limited numbers for sanctioned drag racing. (The Super Stock program is outlined in Chapter Five.) Plymouth had this to say about the 1968 Barracudas: "Call them unique. They are. The one-of-a-kind sports cars with a zest for the fun life. These are the cars that are coming on strong all over America. The Plymouth win-you-over beat goes on."

While the 1968 Barracuda may have defied the traditional definition of a sports car, it definitely met the criteria in performance and handling, with none of the old drawbacks of "rain burbling under the windscreen, the heater wheezing at your ankle, and the wind screaming through the leaks in your side-curtains," as one Barracuda ad put it.

Plymouth expanded the availability of the Formula S package to include the hardtop and convertible. The 273 V-8s were dropped and in their place were a new 318 V-8 and a 275-horsepower, four-barrel 340 V-8. The high performance 383 received 20 more horsepower via a new four-barrel intake manifold and cylinder heads so as not to be outdone by the high-performance 340. Thus, the Formula S came as either the 340-S or the 383-S. Chrome hood louvers announced the displacement. Handling was improved somewhat with Super Wide Oval Red Streak tires. A wild option on the '68 Barracuda was the red plastic wheelhouse liners for $46.55. These really stood out on black and dark-blue cars.

Plymouth did careful chassis engineering with the Formula S, tailored according to displacement. The Formula 340-S came with 103 inch-pound front torsion bars and 132 inch-pound rear leaf springs. The Formula 383-S came with 115 inch-pound front torsion bars and 150 inch-pound rear leaf springs. In addition, the Formula S with the 340 had a 0.88-inch diameter front stabilizer bar, while the Formula 383-S came with a 0.92-inch diameter front stabilizer bar. Sure-Grip axle ratios available included the 3.23, 3.55, and 3.91:1 with the four-speed manual transmission and the 3.23 and 3.55:1 ratios for the TorqueFlight-equipped cars.

The Plymouth GTX, Road Runner, and Barracuda Formula S balanced nicely the offerings from the Dodge Scat Pack with its Charger R/T, Coronet Super Bee, and Dart GTS. Although sales for the Barracuda dipped somewhat in 1968, that was as much to do with the very competitive offerings from General Motors and Ford, not to mention the available performance cars from Chrysler itself. It was a very tough year to make a decision on a performance car; there were so many to choose from!

The Air Grabber Appears

For 1969, Plymouth chose to improve on the GTX, Road Runner, and the Barracuda, but to do it in subtle ways—and one not-so-subtle way. In the late 1960s, Chrysler rejected the premise of the annual model change, so there was no radical change in sheet metal. That was good news, because the Belvedere body that was the basis for the GTX and Road Runner was an outstanding design and one that would prove to be enduring. Plymouth offered the Road Runner as a convertible, but there would be an even bigger surprise in a Road Runner offering later in the model year.

The performance hood differed slightly on the GTX and Road Runner for 1969, but the big news was the optional Air Grabber hood that made it functional. The Air Grabber was actually introduced late in the 1968 model year and was missed by many GTX and Road Runner buyers. Fresh-air induction was the rage in the late 1960s, and dense, cold air was proven to boost performance—at least on the racetrack.

The Air Grabber was not a hoodscoop in the conventional sense, but drew cool air in from the side openings of the performance hood. The Air Grabber ductwork was made of fiberglass and bolted to the underside of the hood. It was painted a bright red-orange and an Air Grabber decal was affixed to it. The ductwork straddled a large oval air cleaner as the hood was closed. Rubber seals between the ductwork and the air cleaner ensured proper performance. Air control doors within the ductwork could be opened or closed by the driver. The Air Grabber was optional in the Road Runner and GTX, costing only $55.30; it was standard when the 426 Hemi was ordered.

Stylistically, it was difficult to distinguish a 1969 model from the 1968. The lower body of the GTX was painted flat black, and the grille featured a two-bar motif in red with GTX mounted in the center. The grille on the Road Runner was also new, and the taillights of both cars were now recessed. The most welcomed news was the expansion of axle ratios in the Road Runner and GTX, and these had a greater impact on performance than the Air Grabber.

The Performance Axle Package ($102.15) included a 3.55:1 axle ratio with Sure-Grip differential. A viscous-drive fan with fan shroud and extra-wide 26-inch

In 1970, Plymouth unleashed the Rapid Transit System. It comprised the 'Cuda, GTX, Road Runner, Sport Fury GT, and the Duster 340. Plymouth proudly stated in its brochure: "The Rapid Transit System. Anybody can offer a car. Only Plymouth offers a System."

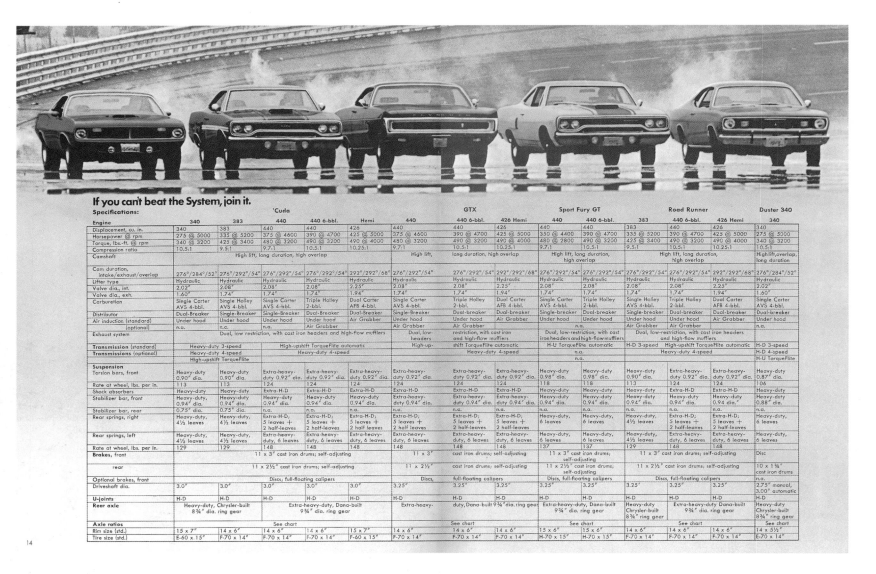

If you can't beat the System, join it.

The Rapid Transit System sits for its portrait at the Chelsea Proving Grounds.

Specifications:

	'Cuda					GTX			Sport Fury GT		Road Runner			Duster 340
Engine	340	383	440	440 6-bbl.	Hemi	440	440 6-bbl.	426 Hemi	440	440 6-bbl.	383	440 6-bbl.	426 Hemi	340
Displacement, cu. in.	340	383	440	440	426	440	440	426	440	440	383	440	426	340
Horsepower @ rpm	275 @ 5000	335 @ 5200	375 @ 4600	390 @ 4700	425 @ 5000	375 @ 4600	390 @ 4700	425 @ 5000	350 @ 4400	390 @ 4700	335 @ 5200	390 @ 4700	425 @ 5000	275 @ 5000
Torque, lbs.-ft. @ rpm	340 @ 3200	425 @ 3400	480 @ 3200	490 @ 3200	490 @ 4000	480 @ 3200	490 @ 3200	490 @ 4000	425 @ 2800	490 @ 3200	425 @ 3400	490 @ 3200	490 @ 4000	340 @ 3200
Compression ratio	10.5:1	9.5:1	9.7:1	10.5:1	10.25:1	9.7:1	10.5:1	10.25:1	9.7:1	10.5:1	9.5:1	10.5:1	10.25:1	10.5:1
Camshaft	High lift, long duration, high overlap					High lift, long duration, high overlap			High lift, long duration, high overlap		High lift, long duration, high overlap			High lift, long duration
Cam duration, intake/exhaust/overlap	276°/284°/52°	276°/292°/54°	276°/292°/54°	276°/292°/54°	292°/292°/68°	276°/292°/54°	276°/292°/54°	292°/292°/68°	276°/292°/54°	276°/292°/54°	276°/292°/54°	276°/292°/54°	292°/292°/68°	276°/284°/52°
Lifter type	Hydraulic	Hydraulic	Hydraulic	Hydraulic	Hydraulic	Hydraulic	Hydraulic	Hydraulic	Hydraulic	Hydraulic	Hydraulic	Hydraulic	Hydraulic	Hydraulic
Valve dia., int.	2.02"	2.08"	2.08"	2.08"	2.25"	2.08"	2.08"	2.25"	2.08"	2.08"	2.08"	2.08"	2.25"	2.02"
Valve dia., exh.	1.60"	1.74"	1.74"	1.74"	1.94"	1.74"	1.74"	1.94"	1.74"	1.74"	1.74"	1.74"	1.94"	1.60"
Carburetion	Single Carter AVS 4-bbl.	Single Holley AVS 4-bbl.	Single Carter AVS 4-bbl.	Triple Holley 2-bbl.	Dual Carter AFB 4-bbl.	Single Carter AVS 4-bbl.	Triple Holley 2-bbl.	Dual Carter AFB 4-bbl.	Single Carter AVS 4-bbl.	Triple Holley 2-bbl.	Single Holley AVS 4-bbl.	Triple Holley 2-bbl.	Dual Carter AFB 4-bbl.	Single Carter AVS 4-bbl.
Distributor	Dual-Breaker	Single-Breaker	Single-Breaker	Dual-Breaker	Dual-Breaker	Single-Breaker	Dual-breaker	Dual-breaker	Single-Breaker	Dual-breaker	Single-Breaker	Dual-breaker	Dual-breaker	Dual-breaker
Air induction (standard)	Under hood	Under hood	Under hood	Under hood	Air Grabber	Under hood	Under hood	Air Grabber	Under hood	Under hood	Under hood	Under hood	Air Grabber	Under hood
(optional)	n.a.	n.a.	n.a.	n.a.	Air Grabber	n.a.	n.a.	n.a.	Air Grabber	Air Grabber	Air Grabber	Air Grabber		n.a.
Exhaust system	Dual, low restriction, with cast iron headers and high-flow mufflers				Dual, low-headers	restriction, with cast iron headers and high-flow mufflers			Dual, low-restriction, with cast iron headers and high-flow mufflers		Dual, low-restriction, with cast iron headers and high-flow mufflers			
Transmission (standard)	Heavy-duty 3-speed	High-upshift TorqueFlite automatic			High-up-	shift TorqueFlite automatic			H-U TorqueFlite automatic		H-D 3-speed	High-upshift TorqueFlite automatic		H-D 3-speed
Transmissions (optional)	Heavy-duty 4-speed	Heavy-duty 4-speed				Heavy-duty 4-speed			n.a.		Heavy-duty 4-speed			H-D 4-speed
	High-upshift TorqueFlite								n.a.					H-U TorqueFlite
Suspension														
Torsion bars, front	Heavy-duty 0.90" dia.	Heavy-duty 0.90" dia.	Extra-heavy-duty 0.92" dia.	Extra-heavy-duty 0.92" dia.	Extra-heavy-duty 0.92" dia.	Extra-heavy-duty 0.92" dia.	Extra-heavy-duty 0.92" dia.	Extra-heavy-duty 0.92" dia.	Heavy-duty 0.98" dia.	Heavy-duty 0.98" dia.	Heavy-duty 0.90" dia.	Extra-heavy-duty 0.92" dia.	Extra-heavy-duty 0.92" dia.	Heavy-duty 0.87" dia.
Rate at wheel, lbs. per in.	113	113	124	124	124	124	124	124	118	118	113	124	124	106
Shock absorbers	Heavy-duty	Heavy-duty	Extra-H-D	Extra-H-D	Extra-H-D	Extra-H-D	Extra-H-D	Extra-H-D	Heavy-duty	Heavy-duty	Heavy-duty	Extra-H-D	Extra-H-D	Heavy-duty
Stabilizer bar, front	Heavy-duty 0.94" dia.	Heavy-duty 0.94" dia.	Heavy-duty 0.94" dia.	Heavy-duty 0.94" dia.	Heavy-duty 0.94" dia.	Extra-heavy-duty 0.94" dia.	Extra-heavy-duty 0.94" dia.	Extra-heavy-duty 0.94" dia.	Heavy-duty 0.94" dia.	Heavy-duty 0.94" dia.	Heavy-duty 0.94" dia.	Heavy-duty 0.94" dia.	Heavy-duty 0.94" dia.	Heavy-duty 0.88" dia.
Stabilizer bar, rear	0.75" dia.	0.75" dia.	n.a.	n.a.	n.a.	n.a.	n.a.	n.a.	n.a.	n.a.	n.a.	n.a.	n.a.	n.a.
Rear springs, right	Heavy-duty, 4½ leaves	Heavy-duty, 4½ leaves	Extra-H-D; 5 leaves + 2 half-leaves	Extra-H-D; 5 leaves + 2 half-leaves	Extra-H-D; 5 leaves + 2 half leaves	Extra-H-D; 5 leaves + 2 half-leaves	Extra-H-D; 5 leaves + 2 half-leaves	Heavy-duty, 6 leaves	Heavy-duty, 6 leaves	Heavy-duty, 4½ leaves	Extra-H-D; 5 leaves + 2 half-leaves	Extra-H-D; 5 leaves + 2 half-leaves	Heavy-duty, 6 leaves	
Rear springs, left	Heavy-duty, 4½ leaves	Heavy-duty, 4½ leaves	Extra-heavy-duty, 6 leaves	Extra-heavy-duty, 6 leaves	Extra-heavy-duty, 6 leaves	Extra-heavy-duty, 6 leaves	Extra-heavy-duty, 6 leaves	Heavy-duty, 6 leaves	Heavy-duty, 6 leaves	Heavy-duty, 4½ leaves	Extra-heavy-duty, 6 leaves	Extra-heavy-duty, 6 leaves	Heavy-duty, 6 leaves	
Rate at wheel, lbs. per in.	129	129	148	148	148	148	148	148	137	137	148	148	148	
Brakes, front	11 x 3" cast iron drums; self-adjusting					11 x 3"	cast iron drums; self-adjusting		11 x 3" cast iron drums; self-adjusting		11 x 3" cast iron drums; self-adjusting			Disc
rear	11 x 2½" cast iron drums; self-adjusting					11 x 2½"	cast iron drums; self-adjusting		11 x 2½" cast iron drums; self-adjusting		11 x 2½" cast iron drums; self-adjusting			10 x 1¾" cast iron drums
Optional brakes, front	Discs; full-floating calipers					Discs,	full-floating calipers		Discs, full-floating calipers		Discs, full-floating calipers			n.a.
Driveshaft dia.	3.0"	3.0"	3.0"	3.0"	3.0"	3.25"	3.25"	3.25"	3.25"	3.25"	3.25"	3.25"	3.25"	2.75" manual, 3.00" automatic
U-joints	H-D	H-D	H-D	H-D	H-D	H-D	H-D	H-D	H-D	H-D	H-D	H-D	H-D	H-D
Rear axle	Heavy-duty, Chrysler-built 8¾" dia. ring gear		Extra-heavy-duty, Dana-built 9¾" dia. ring gear			Extra-heavy-	duty, Dana-built 9¾" dia. ring gear		Extra-heavy-duty, Dana-built 9¾" dia. ring gear		Heavy-duty Chrysler-built 8¾" dia. ring gear	Heavy-duty Chrysler-built 9¾" dia. ring gear		Heavy-duty Chrysler-built 8¾" dia. ring gear
Axle ratios	See chart					See chart			See chart		See chart			See chart
Rim size (std.)	15 x 7"	14 x 6"	14 x 6"	14 x 6"	15 x 7"	14 x 6"	14 x 6"	14 x 6"	15 x 6"	15 x 6"	14 x 6"	14 x 6"	14 x 6"	14 x 5½"
Tire size (std.)	E-60 x 15"	F-70 x 14"	F-70 x 14"	F-70 x 14"	F-60 x 15"	F-70 x 14"	F-70 x 14"	F-70 x 14"	H-70 x 15"	H-70 x 15"	F-70 x 14"	F-70 x 14"	F-70 x 14"	E-70 x 14"

14

The Rapid Transit System sits for its portrait at the Chelsea Proving Grounds. The last two pages of the R.T.S. brochure listed complete specifications.

radiator helped keep the engine cool during racing. A Road Runner Hemi suspension was also included, but this was standard on the GTX due to the 440 Magnum's power. The Trak Pak ($142.85) included a Hurst four-speed shifter, extra-heavy-duty Dana 60 3.54:1 rear axle with Sure-Grip differential, viscous-drive fan, and dual-breaker distributor. The Trak Pak was available only on the GTX and Hemi-powered Plymouths. Finally, there was the Super Trak Pak ($256.45), included the Trak Pak itself, but substituted a 4.10:1 axle ratio and included power front disc brakes.

There were also new performance appearance options to distinguish your mighty Mopar in 1969. To set off the performance hood of your Road Runner or GTX, you could order the new optional performance

hood treatment with two broad bands of flat-black paint that ran from the windshield to the grille. The center of the hood "scoops" were painted red for dramatic effect. Besides the handsome five-spoke steel road wheels, there were also new cast-aluminum five-slot road wheels. There were 19 striking paint colors to choose from. With names like Scorch Red, Seafoam Turquoise Metallic, Sunfire Yellow or Limelight Metallic, how could you go wrong? Many GTX and Road Runner buyers opted for a vinyl roof in a contrasting color.

Without a doubt, however, A12 was the ultimate Road Runner option. This was a new engine and appearance package that removed all doubt about the true function of your Road Runner. Introduced in the spring of 1969, this option gave you a six-barrel 440

V-8 with 390 horsepower and 490 foot-pounds of torque. As on all Road Runners, a four-speed manual transmission and Hurst shifter were standard, as were 11-inch heavy-duty drum brakes. Included was a maximum-capacity cooling system and a 4.10:1 Sure-Grip differential. The car rode on Goodyear G70x15 Red Streak tires mounted on 15x6-inch wheels with no wheel covers—only no-nonsense chrome lug nuts. The *coup de grace* was a fiberglass hood with huge functional hoodscoop. The hood was finished in a special flat-black paint with four chrome locking hood pins to secure it, similar to the way the hood operated on the Super Stock Hemi Barracuda and Dart drag

cars. With the pins removed, the hood could be placed on the roof of the car for engine servicing. A "440-6BBL" decal appeared on the sides of the scoop. The car was offered in four brilliant colors: Performance Red, Bahama Yellow, Rallye Green, and Vitamin C Orange—as well as White, if the other colors did not suit you. The best news of all was the price—$462.80 over the base list price of the Road Runner.

The goal in developing the 440 six-barrel V-8 (for the complete story on this engine, see Chapter Two) was to offer a 440 V-8 with Hemi-like performance without the Hemi's expense. The 440 six-barrel Road Runner was cheaper to buy and maintain than a Hemi Road

For 1970, the Barracuda was completely restyled and reengineered. It was considered then and remains to this day one of the finest musclecar designs to come from Chrysler. The high-performance 'Cuda model came standard with the high-performance 383, but could be options instead with the high-performance 340, 440 6-BBL or even the 426 Hemi.

Runner and—if Plymouth's own ads were to be believed—faster in the quarter-mile! Roland McGonegal, with *Super Stock* magazine, averaged a 13.50-second elapsed time (E.T.) at 109.31 miles per hour. Chrysler's own Dick Maxwell, one of the charter members of the Ramchargers, averaged 13.59 seconds at 105.63 miles per hour in a Hemi Road Runner. With performance like this, it's no wonder the Road Runner was one of the hottest-selling performance cars in 1969. Sales nearly doubled that year to 85,000 units. No doubt the Road Runner lured away some prospective GTX buyers, since sales of the GTX dropped from 18,940 in 1968 to 15,608 in 1969. No doubt Road Runner sales were boosted by *Motor Trend's* Car of the Year award. Plymouth's product planners were feeling pretty good in 1969.

But what of the Barracuda? Plymouth chose to continue the current body style for one more year. The car received a mild facelift with a new grille. Absent were the chrome hood louvers. The 'Cuda Performance Package was new this year, available on the fastback and hardtop only. Essentially, it was an appearance option with Formula S underpinnings. The package consisted

The third generation Barracuda finally focused the car's identity as an honest rival to other ponycars on the market. The 'Cuda displayed perfectly the long-hood short-deck theme that would be seen on streets, boulevards, and drag strips from coast to coast.

of two hoodscoops, two black hood stripes, and black lower-body paint treatment all around. You could order a 'Cuda 340 or a 'Cuda 383. In either case, it came standard with a four-speed manual transmission with Hurst shifter. Although not mentioned in the 1969 brochure, Plymouth released a 440 'Cuda later in the model year. One magazine tested the car. With a curb weight of 3,405 pounds, the 440 'Cuda fastback did 0-60 miles per hour in an astounding 5.6 seconds and the quarter-mile in 14 seconds flat. The Formula S 340 and Formula S 383 were still available. Sales of the Barracuda continued to decline, however, and by the end of the model year, Plymouth had sold just under 27,400 units. Spy photos of the 1970 Barracuda somehow managed to get into some automotive publications, and despite the fuzzy photos, the new 'Cuda looked really sharp. Car buyers would not have long to wait.

The Rapid Transit System

By 1970, virtually every American car manufacturer was offering performance cars in various sizes and performance packages. In an effort to stand out from the others and draw attention to its product line, Plymouth created the Rapid Transit System (R.T.S.). When Plymouth ran ads in the October 1969 issue of *Car & Driver* and other car magazines announcing the R.T.S., it generated a lot of excitement among enthusiasts in general and Mopar enthusiasts in particular.

The System was not just a fleet of cars, but a whole support network between Plymouth and its performance car buyers. While some manufacturers imitated Plymouth's approach, none offered such a comprehensive package. The System included factory-sponsored racing of practically all kinds, Supercar Clinics hosted by the likes of Sox & Martin and Don Grotheer for the benefit of high-performance Plymouth owners, availability of performance parts through Plymouth dealers, and tips on how to make your car go faster. The cars of the R.T.S. were the 'Cuda, GTX, Road Runner, compact Duster, and full-size Fury. The 440 six-barrel Road Runner—the "package car" as Chrysler identified such offerings, was gone, but the 440 six-barrel Wedge V-8 was expanded across the R.T.S. and was available in the 'Cuda, GTX, and Road Runner.

Plymouth published a double-page specifications sheet on the cars of the R.T.S. and the engines available in them. The 'Cuda was available with the 275-horsepower 340; the 335-horsepower 383; the 375-horsepower 440;

the 390-horsepower 440 six-barrel; and the 426 Hemi. The GTX again came standard with the 375 horsepower 440, but the 440 six-barrel and 426 Hemi were optional. Then there was the Sport Fury GT. It came standard with a 350-horsepower 440 with the same level of torque as the 375-horsepower 440, but at a lower 2,800 rpm. According to this spec sheet, the Sport Fury GT could be ordered with—get this—the 440 six-barrel. Wedge V-8! Chrysler historian Galen Govier has confirmed that 61 440 six-barrel Sport Fury GTs were built. Next in the R.T.S. was the Road Runner with standard 335-horsepower 383, with the 440 six-barrel and the 426 Hemi optional. Bringing up the compact contingent was the Duster 340, with the same 275-horsepower, small-block Wedge offered as standard in the 340 'Cuda.

The 'Cuda Redux

Plymouth stylists had been hard at work coming up with a third-generation Barracuda for 1970. The car was completely redesigned both inside and out. The wheelbase remained the same, but overall width was increased more than 5 inches and front and rear tracks increased 3 inches, primarily to accept the massive 426 Hemi and 60-series tires to handle all the extra weight and power.

The shaker hoodscoop that sat atop the 440 six-barrel in this 1970 'Cuda came standard when this engine or the 426 Hemi was ordered. It could also be ordered on the high-performance 340. Availability of the 440 six-barrel was expanded to include the 'Cuda and the GTX in 1970, as well as the Road Runner.

The Plymouth B-body line received some restyling for 1970, which benefited the Road Runner and the GTX aesthetically, but didn't boost sales from the previous record year. The Air Grabber with pop-up hoodscoop was available for the first time. The Road Runner, however, could not outrun rising insurance rates.

The new Barracuda was much more clean, crisp, and taut. The long hood/short deck theme was more obvious and the high trunk, short roof, and smooth, undisturbed sheet metal gave it a more balanced look.

Plymouth stylists paid particular attention to design and manufacturing details to maintain the uncluttered theme of the car. The windshield wipers were now recessed. The front-end sheet metal was carried right to

the leading edge, then sharply turned under. The same was done to the rear of the car. By doing so, Plymouth did away with the molded plastic caps that would have aesthetically broken the lines of the car. The rectangular dual exhaust tips exited through the rear-end sheet metal on the 'Cuda model.

Over the years, the Barracuda had picked up the slang name 'Cuda among Woodward Avenue cruisers as well as others around the country, so Plymouth adopted 'Cuda as a tough-sounding name for a new model appropriate to its image. The name suited the new look of the car. Plymouth was now addressing a specific market it hadn't before: street racers who wanted a high-performance Plymouth in the Ford Mustang Cobra-Jet league.

Distinguishing the 'Cuda from the Barracuda itself was the standard performance hood, which sported two handsome, rakish, nonfunctional scoops. Because the hood was stamped steel, plastic moldings had to be used at the openings to resolve the undercut problem. Hood pins were standard on the 'Cuda, as were two high-intensity driving lights mounted below the front bumper. The performance hood and hood pins were optional on the Barracuda and Gran Coupe. The sole identification on the 'Cuda was the word "Cuda" in silver on the right rear license plate holder, which stood out against the recessed, flat-black rear-end panel.

An interesting appearance option was the elastomeric front and rear bumpers. Molding a smooth skin of urethane over the chrome bumper, it was then painted in one of nine body colors. Two packages were available. One included the elastomeric treatment on the front bumper in any one of nine body colors, plus racing mirrors, and the other included front and rear bumpers and racing mirrors in Rallye Red only.

Another appearance option let everybody know just what you had under the hood. An inverted "hockey stick" flat-black paint stripe started above the door handle, followed the fender line toward the rear of the car, and just after turning down, read "340," "383," "440," or "HEMI." Engine displacement was also shown on a badge affixed to the sides of the functional shaker hoodscoop. This was a corporate scoop, optional also on the Dodge Challenger, and available with all performance engines in the 'Cuda.

The 'Cuda came standard with a high-performance four-barrel 383 rated at 335 horsepower—essentially the same 383 that had been offered in the Road Runner.

Optional engines included the four-barrel 340 with 275 horsepower; the 375-horsepower, four-barrel 440; the 390-horsepower, six-barrel 440; and the 425-horsepower, eight-barrel 426 Hemi. These engines had exhaust systems to match their power potential. The 'Cuda 383 featured 2-1/4-inch exhaust pipes with tuned low-restriction mufflers and 2-1/4-inch tail pipes. The 'Cuda 340 got the same system. 'Cudas powered by the 440s or the 426 Hemi received 2-1/2-inch exhaust pipes, tuned low-restriction mufflers, and 2-1/4 inch tail pipes.

'Cuda buyers did not have to pay extra for heavy-duty suspensions on their cars; they came standard, and were engineered specifically for each engine chosen. Says Larry Shepard, "We offered our cars with a complete package, not just a big motor. The guy at the local drive-in could talk about his Mopar with Super Stock springs, heavy-duty rear axle, TorqueFlight transmission with high-stall converter and so on, and the Chevy guys didn't have any of that. All they could do was point to the SS on the side of the car and talk about the motor."

With such a range of performance available in the 'Cuda, the "fish" was a popular test car in 1970. *Road Test* magazine put a 383-powered 'Cuda through its paces. With a TorqueFlight automatic transmission and a Sure-Grip 3.91:1 rear end, the car did the quarter-mile in 14.4 seconds at 98.87 miles per hour. *Car Craft* tested a Hemi 'Cuda with four-speed manual transmission and 3.54:1 Sure-Grip axle. This car did the quarter in 13.10 seconds at over 107 miles per hour. *Motor Trend* got behind the wheel of a 440 6-barrel 'Cuda with the same axle setup as the *Car Craft* test car, and did the quarter in 14.4 seconds at 99.88 miles per hour, but others recorded better times.

Many magazines suspected that their test cars received factory super tuning to the ignition and/or car-buretor to enhance test results. Chrysler was no exception. Such tuning on Mopars was usually limited to replacing the distributor springs and weights and bumping the spark advance. These modifications greatly improved driveability and performance. In truth, any enthusiasts could perform these same modifications and achieve similar results.

The 1970 'Cuda was one of the high performance bargains that year. With those aggressive good looks and the long list of standard equipment, the suggested list price of $3,164 was a deal. The 'Cuda convertible was $3,433. Few could resist the temptation of adding many options that they wanted. The entire 1970 Barracuda line was a winner with buyers, and more than 50,000 were sold that year, including 2,724 of the exotic AAR 'Cuda (see Chapter Five). Curiously, though, only 550 'Cuda convertibles were sold—just slightly more than one percent of total production.

Perhaps the rarest of all the cars in the Rapid Transit System was the Sport Fury GT. Not many were built in 1970, and few exist today. Plymouth called it a Q-ship because it was relatively quiet and unassuming. Powered by the same engine in the GTX, it was luxurious and fast.

Bread-and-Butter Belvedere

The Plymouth styling studio had also been burning the midnight oil on the new Belvedere. The Belvedere was the bread-and-butter of the Plymouth line and it was important to produce a more contemporary look that would appeal to a broad range of buyers. In a word, they succeeded. The car still rode on a 116-inch wheel-base. The sharp creases that were previously along the fender flanks were shaved off. A nonfunctional scoop was sculpted into the sides between the rear wheels and the door. The hood received a prominent power bulge; the dual hoodscoops were eliminated. The front and rear ends were redesigned as well.

Although the roofline remained unchanged, the reworking of the sheet metal gave the car a completely new look. The result was to produce the best-looking Road Runner and GTX to date. With only 625 GTX convertibles sold in 1969, Plymouth decided to drop this model for 1970, but the convertible Road Runner was again offered. The most rapid car in the R.T.S., the Superbird, was not included in the original lineup ad. When Richard Petty said he was not going to race at an aerodynamic disadvantage and defected to Ford the year before, Plymouth responded with the Superbird. Benefiting extensively from the Dodge Daytona's development, the Superbird succeeded in luring Petty back for 1970. The full development story of the Superbird is covered in Chapter Five.

Other than looks, was there anything new under the skin? In terms of powerplants, no. The one-off 440 6-barrel Road Runner package car of 1969-1/2 did not return for 1970, but that engine was optional in the Road Runner and GTX. There were no new engines offered, but then, none were really needed! The engines entered a period of refinement, or were left alone altogether.

Air Grabber Performance

The biggest performance-related news was the new Air Grabber. Unlike the shaker hoodscoop available on the 'Cuda, the Road Runner and GTX could be ordered with the pop-up Air Grabber scoop. An electric solenoid switch inside the car operated the vacuum-actuated trap door in the center of the hood's power bulge to raise or lower the Air Grabber. This design did away with the restrictive and cumbersome system used before. The 1970 Air Grabber forced cool outside air directly to the air cleaner. It also provided the ultimate form of intimidation at stoplights. If the "440+6" decal on the side of the power bulge wasn't enough to shake up the driver of the GTO or SS454 next to you, a flip of the switch popped up the Air Grabber with its menacing graphics. That was usually enough to rattle the confidence of most street racers. Plymouth stated the new Air Grabber was good for knocking a tenth of a

second off quarter-mile times and added 1.5 miles per hour to trap speeds.

The Air Grabber, in fact, played a very prominent role in an ad for the Road Runner. A Road Runner is pictured on a dry lake bed, and out of the Air Grabber emerged a huge, three-dimensional representation of the ever-smiling Road Runner. This ad appeared in *Life*, no less.

A Quick Duster

Plymouth's compact performance offering in the Rapid Transit System for 1970 was the Duster 340. The Duster was really a new model, with a more sporting flavor than the Valiant. Once again, the Valiant was the stepfather of a new addition to the Plymouth line. The Duster was designed to use the same front-end sheet metal, wind-

shield, running gear, and 108-inch wheelbase as the Valiant. However, Plymouth's stylists succeeded in giving this car a unique look by using a modified fastback configuration with a good degree of curvature to the side glass.

The time available to get the Duster into production was at a premium. Dick Macadam was vice president of styling at the Plymouth studio during the late 1970s, and he had this to say about the new car: "It was a very late program, under extreme pressure, and needed a shot in the arm very quickly. It was sold through product planning, sales division, and finally corporate management in a very short period of time—a few weeks." While most automotive designs are a team effort, the initial Duster sketches were drawn up by one person, Neal Walling, *continued on page 90*

continued on page 90

Those who saw the writing on the wall scraped money together and bought the last of the big-block mighty Mopars, like the 1971 440-6 'Cuda. From the Shaker hoodscoop to the screaming billboard graphics, it was the last of a breed. Chrysler could not justify production of such a car in the face of plummeting sales, tightening emissions, and stratospheric insurance premiums.

It took no effort at all for the 440-6 'Cuda to light 'em up in 1971. For the nearsighted, the 440 graphics on the side dispelled any doubt what was under the hood. This was the end of the line for the high compression, big-block Wedge V-8.

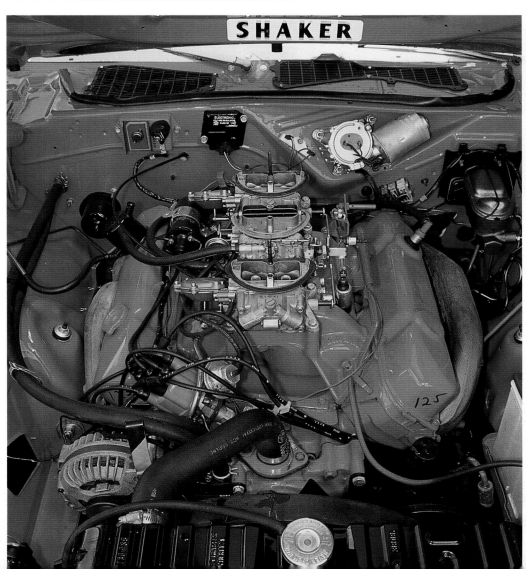

continued from page 87

The Plymouth B-body line was completely restyled for 1971, and this also was an aesthetic success. In an effort to skirt high insurance premiums, Plymouth made the 275-horsepower 340 V-8 available as an option in the Road Runner.

who then carried them out in clay model form. That, perhaps, is why the design was able to go through the approval process so quickly.

The Duster appealed to the economy-minded Plymouth buyer, but the Duster 340 was conceived with the economy-minded *performance* enthusiast. With the 275-horsepower, four-barrel 340, the Duster 340 had

the makings of a sleeper. With a list price of $2,547, it was the least expensive car in the Rapid Transit System. And, with a relatively low weight and high-output small-block Wedge V-8, the Duster 340 had a favorable power-to-weight ratio. Plymouth remarked on this in its R.T.S. brochure:

"We think Supercars should be affordable. Heck, what's the sense of liking anything if you have to wait until you're pushing 30 and your second million to

enjoy it? With that in mind we set about to do an encore to Road Runner and create the industry's lowest-priced high-performance car. Better yet, we decided to make it a sleeper that would blow the doors off hulking, pretentious behemoths twice its size. For a start, we needed a body shell that was strong, simple, and inexpensive to produce. It also had to be lightweight and compact, so that it could achieve a Supercar power-to-weight ratio with a relatively small displacement engine.

We figured that with a good driver and (optional) 3.91 gearing, it should be able to just touch the 13-second bracket. (In fact, it would *have* to; because any car that can't cut a 14-second quarter doesn't qualify for R.T.S. membership.)" In fact, that high-performance 340 V-8 was quite an engine, cranking out 275 horses at 5,000 rpm with 340 foot-pounds of torque at 3,200 rpm. It was ably fed by a Carter AVS four-barrel carb, and ran a 10.5:1 compression ratio. The timing of the camshaft was 276 degrees intake, 284 degrees exhaust, and 52 degrees of overlap; this was only slightly less radical than the camshaft in the four- and six-barrel 440 V-8s.

To keep the price down, the three-speed manual shift was standard; the heavy-duty four-speed was an expensive option—nearly 10 percent of the base list on the car, but many chose to order it. Again, Plymouth did its homework on the heavy-duty suspension, so the car was a pretty good handler. The Duster 340 was the only car in the R.T.S. with front disc brakes standard. The handsome Rallye wheels were also standard.

To really extract the maximum performance from the car, the four-speed was a must, Sure-Grip differential ensured the power got to the pavement and stayed there, and a higher numerical axle ratio than the standard 3.23:1 ratio was a necessity. With a select few other options it didn't take long to push the price of the Duster 340 into the $3,000-plus range.

Sport Fury GT

At the other end of the R.T.S. spectrum was the Sport Fury GT, today the rarest of all the cars in the R.T.S. This seemed like a good idea, because not all performance-minded buyers were under 25. GM and Ford had been selling full-size performance cars for years. The average age for buyers of the Chevrolet Impala SS model, for example, was on the far side of 30. So, it made sense for Plymouth to include the Sport Fury GT in the R.T.S. After all, the Sport Fury was the performance standard-bearer at the top of Plymouth's car line during the early 1960s.

It was a simple matter to drop the high-performance four-barrel 440 from the GTX into the Sport Fury GT, but Plymouth did some numbers juggling. All the internal specifications of the engine in the GTX and Sport Fury GT were identical. Rated output was different. Again, the GTX was rated at 375 horsepower at 4,600 rpm with 480 foot-pounds of torque at 3,200 rpm. In the Sport Fury GT, the engine was rated at 350 horsepower at 4,400 rpm with 480 foot-pounds of torque at a leisurely 2,800 rpm.

When the data sheet for the R.T.S. was drawn up, the Sport Fury had only one optional engine—the six-barrel 440. There it was in black and white! However, very few buyers selected the 440 six-barrel option. Consequently, the 1970 Sport Fury GT with this option is among the rarest of the Supercars of 1970. This was the only year the Sport Fury GT made its appearance in the R.T.S.

The Class of 1971

In some respects, 1971 marked both an apogee and a perigee for the R.T.S. The entire Belvedere Satellite line, now know simply as Satellite, was completely redesigned, and it was an absolute winner. The Plymouth styling studio had done it again and produced a striking design that would also prove timeless. At the

same time, sales of high-performance cars were plummeting due to the prohibitive cost of insuring the cars. Musclecars were involved in more than their share of accidents, and the insurance companies responded with rates that made car buyers reconsider their decision. This was the last year Mopar buyers would have the wealth of choices in terms of powertrains and models to choose from.

Plymouth again issued a R.T.S. brochure for 1971. The Barracuda featured only minor changes, to its front grille and virtually no change to the rear end. The car now had four headlights instead of two. The grille had six large cutouts in a silvertone finish. There were four small louvers set into the sides of the front fenders, which helped to distinguish the 1971 'Cuda from the 1970 model.

The standard 383 four-barrel V-8 in the 'Cuda suffered a one-point drop in compression ratio to 8.5:1, to

Several options made this 1971 Road Runner visually unique. The color-keyed left- and right-hand racing mirrors (G36), the matching painted bumpers (M73), and the backlight louvers (J68) make this Tor-Red monochrome Mopar a show winner.

allow it to run on regular gas. Its gross horsepower was down from 335 to 300. Net horsepower ratings were also being adopted industry-wide to give a more realistic rating of rear wheel horsepower; this put the 383 in the 'Cuda at 250 net horsepower. Output of the high-performance 340 remained unchanged, despite a minor 0.2 point drop in compression. The four-barrel 440 was dropped from the 'Cuda line. The six-barrel 440 was still offered, but it too dropped slightly in compression, from 10.5 to 10.3:1, with a loss of five horsepower. The 426 Hemi was still rated at 425 horsepower. Interestingly, the unsilenced air cleaners on the 440 six-barrel V-8 and 426 Hemi engines were not available in California because of that state's new drive-by noise standards. A quieter air cleaner was used to muffle induction roar on those engines bound for California.

There were many "lasts" this year in the Plymouth line. This was the last year for the 426 Hemi and 440 six-barrel V-8s. It was also the last year for the 'Cuda convertible, and the last year for the GTX. If we had known then what we know now. . . .

The Road Runner and GTX were now wrapped in a completely new body shell. The contours were softer and more rounded—what Plymouth referred to in its brochure as "fuselage" styling. The Satellite had pronounced wheelwell bulges, which gave the Road Runner and GTX a particularly muscular look. A new performance hood had outward-facing simulated vents that showed off the displacement, either 383, 440, 440+6, or HEMI depending on the standard or optional engine. The Air Grabber hood scoop was again available. In fact, all the high-performance goodies that had made both these cars among the fastest and best musclecars of the era could still be ordered.

The Duster 340 did not undergo any dramatic changes for 1971, merely improvement on a winning design. Only the front grille and taillight designs were new. There was a new body-side tape stripe with the number 340 featured prominently on the rear quarter panels. The Duster could really be made to stand out with such colors as Tor-Red, Curious Yellow, In-Violet, Sassy Grass Green, or Bahama Yellow. There was a new, and striking, blackout hood treatment available with stock car-sized "340" in large white outline letters, with the word "Wedge" in orange, painted vertically within the 4. For 1971, Plymouth switched from a Carter AVS four-barrel carb to a Carter Thermo-Quad on the high-performance 340 offered among the Duster 340, 'Cuda

340, and the Road Runner. It was again rated at 275 horsepower, with a net rating of 235 horsepower.

By all appearances, the 1971 Rapid Transit System was alive and well. These cars were as fast as they had always been. They were better looking than ever. Despite all this, sales continued to plunge. Sales of the 'Cuda dropped from more than 50,000 units in 1970, to just over 16,000 for 1971. Over 39,000 Road Runners were sold in 1970, but only 13,000 in 1971. Only 2,626 GTXs were sold that year. Among Road Runners and GTXs ordered with the 426 Hemi, the numbers descended into the collector status range. Only 55 Road Runners came with the 426 Hemi; 27 with the TorqueFlight auto tranny, and the rest with the four-speed manual. A mere 30 GTXs were ordered with the Hemi, 19 with TorqueFlight, and only 11 with the four-speed manual!

Decline and Fall

The prohibitive cost of insuring big-block muscle-cars was having a stunting effect on the sales of the cars. Consequently, Plymouth made a number of decisions that made sense from a corporate sales point of view,

Small-block Road Runners were not ashamed of their displacement. The large, recessed hood louvers announced the number of cubic inches under the hood. A total of 1,681 340 Road Runners were sold in 1971.

The 340 ci high-performance Wedge V-8 in the Road Runner had a rating of 275 gross horsepower. The net rating adopted that year put the number of ponies at 235. The engine still ran a 10.3:1 compression ratio, requiring premium fuel. There was still some Beep-Beep! left in the Road Runner.

center divider. Those who had hoped to buy a 'Cuda convertible in 1972 were disappointed to learn there was none. The standard engine in the 'Cuda was now a two-barrel 318 with single exhaust with only 150 horsepower. The high-performance four-barrel 340, with 240 horsepower, now cost a whopping $221 and the performance hood was an extra-cost option, too. This was the hottest engine that could be ordered; there was no 400 cubic-inch V-8 and certainly no 440.

Sales of the V-8 'Cuda slid even further in 1972, to just over 6,300 units. The Duster 340 soldiered on as the economy Plymouth street machine. The big news here was the price—it went down! List price was $2,742. Plymouth was trying to lure buyers as best it could. Instead of trumpeting performance only, the combination of performance with an even lower price was the sales hook. Of course, the Duster 340 had to be significantly lower, because the Road Runner listed for just over $3,200.

The automotive magazines were reciting the last rites over the musclecar. It didn't take a rocket scientist to figure that out. But then, why should Plymouth market something when the demand just wasn't there? And everyone knew why the demand was driven into the basement. Not only insurance, but ever-tightening emissions were having a dramatic impact on power, and it was due to get much worse. There was talk in the press that in a few years, catalytic converters would be required to clean up exhaust emissions. Already Chrysler was dedicating increasing amounts of development money toward this technology. Performance in the traditional sense was vanishing from the engineer's vocabulary. Chrysler engineering became preoccupied almost totally with safety issues and emissions.

Against this backdrop, Plymouth introduced its new line of cars for 1973. The Road Runner returned, but the big shocker came from the engine compartment. The standard engine was now a two-barrel 318 producing 170 horsepower. The car was definitely underpowered with the small-block Wedge V-8, but this was selected to keep the price of the car right around $3,000. The Satellite line received all-new front-end sheet metal and it was a handsome change. Underneath, all the suspension pieces were there to make the "bird" handle. The news regarding power wasn't all bad. Optional engines included the 240 horsepower, 340 cubic-inch V-8; the 260 horsepower, 400 cubic-inch V-8; and a 280 horsepower, 440 cubic-

but it still shocked many Mopar enthusiasts who thought the performance era would go on indefinitely. Not surprisingly, the GTX was dropped for 1972. Also gone were the 426 Hemi and the six-barrel 440. The R.T.S. was losing its rapidity, as it was now made up of the Road Runner, the 'Cuda, and the Duster 340.

The Road Runner came standard with the four-barrel 400 cubic-inch V-8 (the 383 with a larger bore), three-speed manual transmission, heavy-duty suspension and brakes, front and rear stabilizer bars, and F70x14 tires. Tightening emissions resulted in the compression ratio being lowered to 8.2:1, with net horsepower now 255. There was a GTX option package with a 280 horsepower, four-barrel 440 V-8. When this engine was ordered, special GTX designations appeared on the sides of the car and the trunk lid. And, the Air Grabber was still available, except in California.

The 'Cuda underwent subtle restyling, front and rear. The four-headlight design of 1971 reverted back to a two-headlight configuration for 1972, with a grille very similar to the 1970 model, except for slots in the inch V-8. With the optional four-speed manual or TorqueFlight automatic transmission behind one of those big-block Wedge V-8s, and a Sure-Grip differential, the Road Runner was still a respectable performer. Buyers welcomed the changes in the Road Runner, and sales shot up to over 17,000 units!

Over in the 'Cuda and Duster camps, virtually all specifications were carried over from the year before. The clean lines of the 'Cuda remained handsome, marred only when the optional gaudy tape strip was slapped on the side. The Duster had become Plymouth's best-selling model, so little was done to change it.

If there was any change, it was to de-emphasize performance. Plymouth chose to put the R.T.S. to sleep at the end of 1972. For 1973, Plymouth stressed "Extra care in engineering." However, Plymouth continued to advertise the Duster 340 in the enthusiast magazines. This ad copy proved Plymouth was still in there swinging: "Try to find a performance car that comes with heavy-duty torsion bars, heavy-duty rear springs, a front sway bar, high-control shocks, a dual exhaust system, 3.21:1 ratio rear axle, unibody construction and an engine equal to our 340-cubic-inch Wedge. Try to find a car like that for around $2800. Just try."

Plymouth was right. An equivalent car from Ford, Chevy, or Pontiac cost hundreds of dollars more than the Duster 340. It was a lot of car—and fun—for the money. That 340 still pumped out 240 net horsepower.

In 1974, the last year for the catalyst-free era, Chrysler increased the displacement of the 340 to 360 cubic inches, and with four-barrel carb, was rated at 245 horsepower. It was available in the 'Cuda, Duster, and Road Runner. Plymouth chose to curtail production of the Barracuda line in 1974. The official production total was 11,734. Of that, 4,989 were 'Cudas. These often-overlooked 'Cudas from 1973 and '74 are affordable collectibles, when they can be found.

And the Road Runner? Well, it was tough competing against the likes of Super Duty 455 Pontiac Trans Ams, and the like. Still, the Road Runner was a survivor, and it could still boast a big-block Wedge under the hood if so optioned. Nevertheless, the uncatchable Road Runner was on its last legs. To paraphrase General MacArthur, the cars of the Rapid Transit System didn't die, they simply faded away. The musclecar era was much richer and more interesting for their having been there. Today they make some of the most exciting and interesting cars to own and drive.

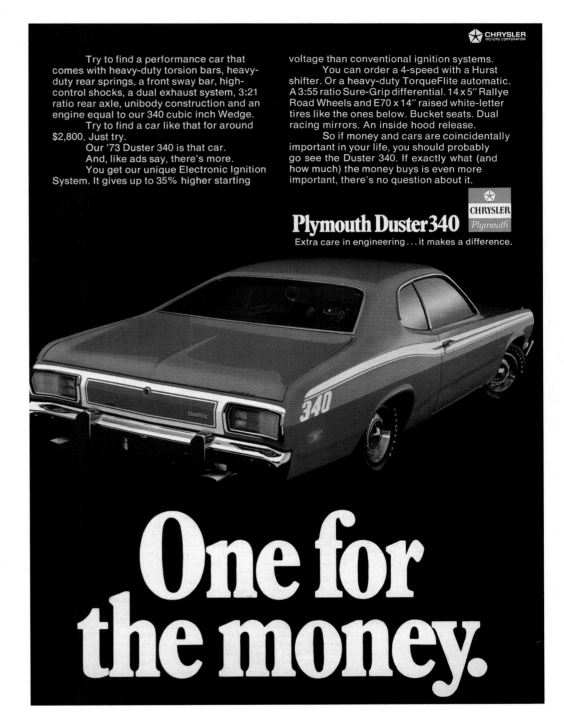

The Rapid Transit System was gone by 1973, but surprisingly, performance in a small package could still be found, and at an affordable price. The high-performance 340 V-8 was a good performer in the Duster 340, and Plymouth advertised that fact in 1973. A new generation of Mopar enthusiasts are discovering the Duster 340 as a car worth restoring and driving.

CHAPTER FOUR

A New Hemi Era

In the brutal and high-stakes arena of Grand National stock car auto racing, corporate prestige has always been the real prize. That prestige could only be secured by making it to the winner's circle. For Chrysler in the early 1960s, that prestige meant a great deal to the corporation's management. Unfortunately, Chrysler's prestige in NASCAR was suffering at the time in the early 1960s, and something needed to be done about it.

The problem Chrysler was facing in Grand National stock car racing stretched back to the late 1950s. Chrysler had won the Grand National title with its Chrysler 300 in both 1955 and 1956. Chrysler, however, began a reengineering program that would eventually replace the Hemi with V-8s using a Wedge head design in all its cars. This had a direct bearing on the corporation's success in NASCAR. By 1958, Chevrolet—yes, Chevrolet!—topped the list of wins in NASCAR by getting the checkered flag 23 times; Ford won 16 races and Oldsmobile won 7. In 1959, Ford was on the top of the heap with 14 wins, followed by Chevrolet with 13, Plymouth with 9, Oldsmobile with 5, and Pontiac with only 1. Interestingly, Lee Petty won 5 races driving the Oldsmobile, then switched to Plymouth, winning 9 races.

During the 1960 NASCAR season, Fords won 15 races, Chevrolet won 13, Plymouth 8, Pontiac 7, and

Dodge only 1. The following year, Pontiac was once again back on top, winning an amazing 30 of 52 races, Chevrolet won 11 Grand National races, and Ford won 7 races. Richard Petty managed to garner 3 wins for Plymouth in 1961. Clearly, Chrysler Corporation did not have the V-8 firepower it needed to win on the high, banked ovals. The new 413 Wedge did not alter the equation much in 1962, although the engine was a beast on the quarter-mile strip. The problem was the Wedge head's breathing ability in the sustained, high-rpm environment of stock car racing. The mood at Highland Park was one of frustration.

"The 413 Wedge was less successful as a Grand National stock car engine," Hoover admits. "If the Wedges had been more successful in Grand National racing, the need for the 426 Hemi wouldn't have existed, because the Wedges were doing a good job in drag racing, and that success was related to modifying the TorqueFlight automatic transmission for drag racing purposes. Pontiac was the job to beat at the time, if I recall correctly. It became evident that in order to really make a big splash . . . in the Grand National cars, we needed a better level of power."

Certainly, those in Chrysler's engine group were aware of the problem. Willem L. Weertman was manager of Chrysler engine design at the time. He could see the 413 and later the 426 Wedges were superb on the

The 1970 Coronet R/T with optional 426 Hemi was not, perhaps, the best-looking Mopar on the street, but it was certainly among the fastest. The Ramcharger fresh air hoodscoops came standard as part of the Hemi option that year.

This Plymouth idles at 30 mph.

The '64 "Melrose Missile" and its driver went hauling to Top Stock Eliminator at NHRA's 1964 Winternationals. And the new 1965 "Missile" (shown above) is presently making mincemeat of last year's records.

The 426 Hemi is at the heart of the matter, of course.

If last year's Plymouth Super Commando 426 Hemi was a full house, then this year's is a straight flush. The '65 Hemi has been improved. It has a magnesium intake manifold. Aluminum cylinder heads. More chrome on the valve stems. A longer duration camshaft. Aluminum oil pump. Valve relief in the pistons. And a roller type timing chain for increased durability.

Our engineering staff's bulletin reads: "The Plymouth Super Commando 426 is designed to be run in supervised, sanctioned competitive events."

With twin four-barrel carbs, ram-tuned intake manifold, non-silenced air cleaner and equal-length streamlined tubing exhaust headers—this is the engine to beat.

If you can't beat us, join us. It's an ancient tactic, but it wins trophies.

THE ROARING '65s
FURY
BELVEDERE
VALIANT
BARRACUDA
Plymouth

PLYMOUTH DIVISION ✦ **CHRYSLER** MOTORS CORPORATION

The street Hemi legend was built up around the many victories of the racing 426 Hemi which supplanted the 426 Max Wedge in 1964. The Melrose Missile was among the most successful cars racing the Hemi. This rare ad details the new features of the 1965 Hemi, including the magnesium intake manifold and aluminum cylinder heads.

quarter-mile, and more than adequate for the street, but plainly lacking in NASCAR.

Weertman had joined Chrysler in 1947 and entered the Chrysler Institute of Engineering. After graduating from C.I.E., he began work at the Plymouth Road assembly plant. When the Mound Road engine plant was built for the production of the V-8 engines, he was selected at the first resident engineer of the plant. In 1955, Bob Rarey, as the new assistant chief engineer of engine design, selected Weertman to be manager of engine design.

"We had a fairly strong factory effort with the Wedge V-8 in 1962 and '63," Weertman says, "but it was obvious to those managing the program we were not competitive with it. About that time, in late '62 and early '63, it was a collective decision by our race policy people, which included Bob Rodger, who said in effect, 'Either we do something big or we should get out. What we are doing is not meaningful to the company, to our dealers, or to car sales.' So, Rodger, Tom Hoover, and Bob Rarey had to think about what might be possible and immediately the thought came to their minds, 'Can we have a Hemi version of our B and Raised B engines?' "

Designing a New Hemi

The discussions centered on using the existing 426 Wedge engine block, and designing a new hemispherical combustion chamber cylinder head to bolt to it. There were a number of sound engineering and economic reasons for doing this. The Hemi was, again, a proven performer, and there were definite advantages to using an existing block; they would not have to incur the expense of engineering and tooling up a new block or its related components. Also, the more parts Chrysler could employ from existing production, the less likely it would receive scrutiny from the NASCAR tech inspectors.

"I remember exactly where I was on the second floor of the main building in Highland Park," Hoover says in describing one of those life-changing events in one's life. "Don Moore was there. I was there and a couple of other people. It was the winter of '62-'63 and the big Wedges had not done well in NASCAR. A couple of us offered up the argument, I suppose it was Don Moore and myself, 'If we're going to make a new head for the engine, let's go with what we know is right. We know the Hemi will do the job, and we have all the

A311 and Cunningham background upon which we can rely to proceed forward.' Jack Shirapar picked up the ball and he's the one who carried it right up to the executive committee. I got to carry the drawings up there for Jack. He made the pitch and Townsend didn't hesitate a bit. [He said] 'Do it.'"

However, there was a very big caveat—the engine had to be ready in time for the February 1964 Daytona 500 race. Hearts almost stopped for many of those seated in that meeting. The Hemi design engineering team was suddenly faced with an almost impossible deadline. Thus, the decision was made to use the same basic machining dimensions as the 426 Wedge in order to use existing tooling. In March 1963, the project was given to Chrysler's advanced engine group, under Bob Dent. Frank Bialk was the lead designer in that group.

"We had the displacement set up," says Weertman, "now we had the challenge of trying to put the Hemi head on that engine. A critical decision was made by that group to stay with the included valve angle from the old Hemi engine, because we had a background that describes the chamber, valve sizes, and the performance of the engine. One thing that we had on the new engine that was better than the old engine was the headbolt pattern. Our B and raised-B engines had a five-bolt headbolt pattern as compared to four on the prior engines. The ability to clamp the head is crucial to how much you are ever going to get out of the engine."

The problem the engineers faced in doing the Hemi became the solution that made a real engine out of it: how to handle the fifth headbolt. The fifth head-bolt was literally in the way of the pushrods and intake port. That area would be so restricted it would not have produced much more power than the Wedge-head engine. In a stroke of brilliance, Bialk decided to bring the bolt up from underneath.

The juxtaposition of the intake and exhaust valve within the hemispherical combustion chamber was also crucial. If the two valves were equidistant from the bore centerline, the resulting engine would be so wide it wouldn't fit into the cars for which it was designed. The solution was to rotate the included valved angle across the hemisphere toward the intake manifold. However, the rocker arms for such a valve arrangement were also a headache.

"We looked at that rocker arm and that thing kept looking like a huge pump handle," Weertman laughs. "We reduced its length until we thought 'That's going

The Dodge Ramchargers didn't steal all the racing thunder with the 426 Hemi. Plymouth's counterpart to the Ramchargers was the Golden Commandos. Here, engineer Forest Pitcock performs work on a Hemi Plymouth in January 1965. *Roger Huntington Collection*

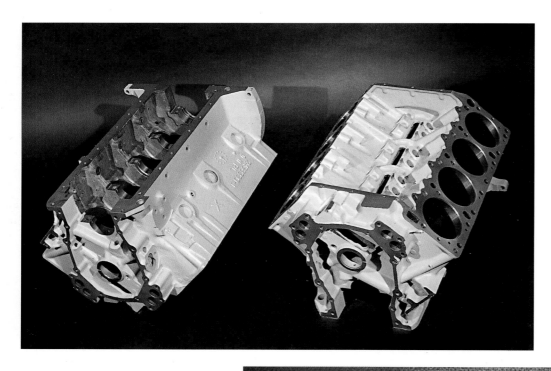

to work.' That set where the valve was going to be. We had daily meetings on the board to see what Frank had, then we'd let him work for several days to come up with his best thinking. He was really an amazing guy. He would say, whenever he would get into a corner, 'Sometimes I just go home and I'll have a vision. I'll come back to work and [it will be] just fine.' "

The Hemi's bottom end was also vitally important. With a maximum vertical separating load of 18,800 pounds at 7,200 rpm along the crankshaft centerline, durability of the bottom end was crucial. To ensure durability and rigidity, the main bearing cap design of the 426 Wedge was abandoned. Bialk designed a new set of number two, three, and four main-bearing caps that took advantage of the current deep-skirt walls of the raised-block by adding cross-bolts that went through the block walls into the bearing caps. The forged steel connecting rods went through two redesigns before being finalized. The forged steel crankshaft was also unique to the 426 Hemi.

The key to the 426 Hemi's amazing strength was in the engine block. Although based on the 426 Wedge block, the Hemi block was extensively modified and improved. Note the cross-bolt hole access in the bottom view of the block on the left, and the fifth cylinder headbolt location above the cylinder bore in the top view of the block on the right.
Roger Huntington Collection

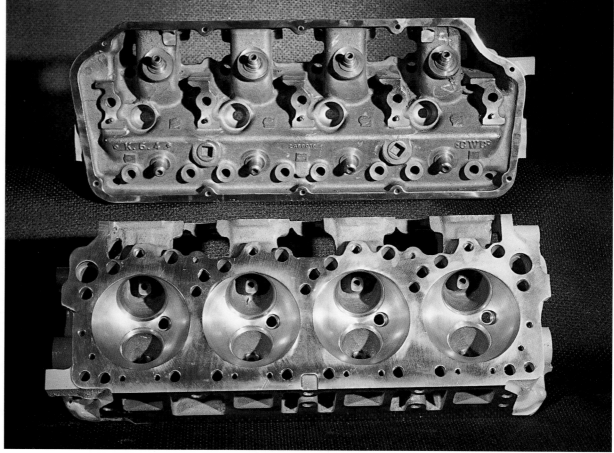

In the 426 Hemi, this was the center of the universe. The aluminum cylinder heads were released in the racing 426 Hemi in 1965, but were never made available on the street Hemi. Note the C.W.C. foundry mark on the cylinder head in the top view.

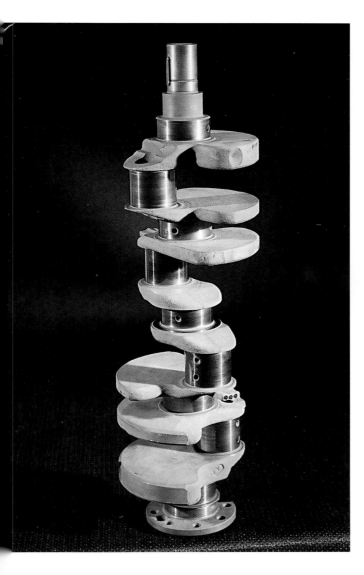

The 426 Hemi crankshaft was stout, to say the least. Basically, the same crank also went into the street Hemi. Chrysler knew Hemi owners would take their cars to the strip, and they didn't want to have to worry about warranty disputes.

In fact, there were few parts common with the 426 Max Wedge. The NASCAR 426 Hemi and the drag racing 426 Hemi were engineered concurrently, but some of the reciprocating and rotating parts differed in material. The intake manifolds, designed by Forbes Bunting, were unique to each engine, with the drag Hemi using a dual four-barrel design almost identical to that used on the Max Wedge, while the circle-track engine used a single four-barrel Holley on a high-riser dual-plane manifold.

From Casting to Testing

Once the design for the cylinder block and heads was finalized, these two long-lead items were procured for manufacturer. Chrysler's American Foundry Division in Indianapolis, Indiana, was chosen for casting the cylinder block. Campbell, Wyant and Cannon Foundry in Muskegon, Michigan, was selected to cast the cylinder heads. The raw cylinder blocks and heads were shipped from their respective foundries to Chrysler's Trenton, Michigan, engine plant for machining. Changes were made to the 426 Wedge-block line to allow for the Hemi's requirements.

Although the eventual production of the 426 race and street Hemis were to be assembled at Chrysler's Marysville, Michigan, engine plant, the test and early racing engines were assembled at the engine labs in Highland Park, Michigan. The Hemi parts shipped there from the Trenton plant underwent minute inspection and checking before being approved for final assembly. The first 426 race Hemi build-up started the last week in November 1963 and was ready for lab testing the first week in December. The Daytona race was only two months away.

The pistons in the 426 Hemi were drop-forged, domed for 12.5:1 compression, and notched for intake and exhaust valve clearance. The pistons for the street Hemi were 10.25:1 compression, still requiring premium gasoline. *Roger Huntington Collection*

The intake manifold designed for NASCAR competition was a high-riser configuration fed by a Holley double pumper. It featured huge passages for developing high-rpm horsepower needed on the high-banked ovals. *Roger Huntington Collection*

Several different intake manifolds were designed for the 426 Hemi, depending on the application. The "bathtub" manifold (upper left) was a later development for NASCAR events. The manifold designed for drag racing (upper right) was nearly identical to that used on the Max Wedge 413s and 426s. The street Hemi used two in-line four-barrel carburetors (lower left). The original stock car intake manifold (lower right) was used for several years.

Roger Huntington Collection

On the dyno, the first 426 Hemi was slowly brought up to speed primarily because the dyno engineers didn't know precisely how much power the engine would produce, and they were afraid of breaking the 400 horsepower dyno! At 4,800 rpm the Hemi was developing 400 horsepower. On this first short run, the engine developed over 425 horsepower, and there were smiles all around.

Then began the rigorous race-profile testing. The engines ran headers with an exhaust system that dumped into stacks that went up to the roof of the three-story building. Engineers coming to work in the morning could hear the glorious sound of the Hemi at redline echoing all over Chrysler's Highland Park facility. Problems arose quickly, however.

"We were bringing the engine up to as much power as we could get out of it with this deadline of the Daytona race in February in front of us," Weertman says. "It was in fairly quick succession that they found cracked cylinder bores in the lab engines. In was in my office when Larry Adams, who was in charge of race engine development, came into my office, just sat down in the chair, and said, 'Bill, that engine isn't going to last. We aren't going to finish the race.' I told him, 'Well, Larry, what's it going to take?' He said, 'We have to thicken up the bores. There's really no other way.' I said, 'OK, we'll see what we can do.'"

It was January 28, 1964. Weertman immediately scheduled an emergency meeting of the advance engine

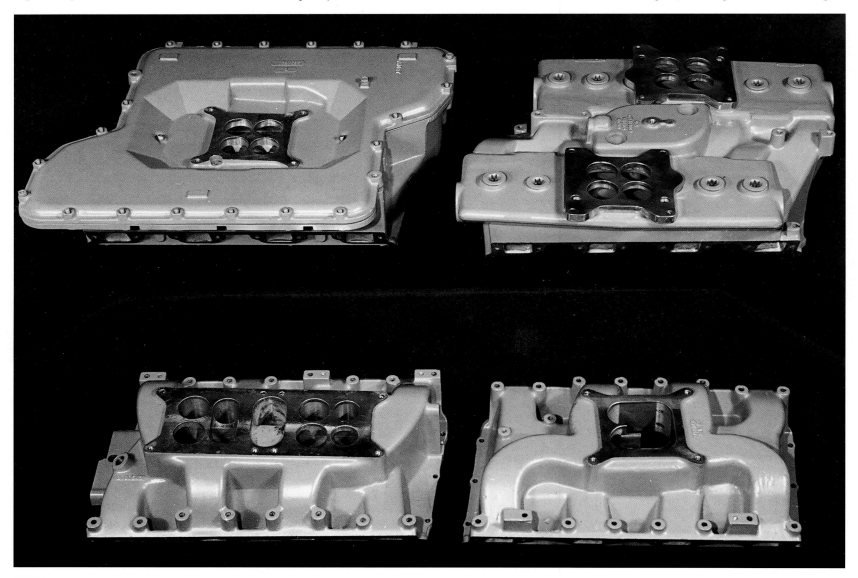

Chrysler engineers developed the D-5 cylinder head to use two spark plugs per cylinder. This ensured more complete and uniform combustion. The D-5 was developed and used for sanctioned drag racing. *Roger Huntington Collection*

Race Hemi development for drag racing took several different configurations to take advantage of the twin-plug cylinder heads. The D5 cylinder head program began in 1970 and included intake manifold development as well.

group to come up with a solution. A template was designed to reduce the diameter of the sand core for the existing water jacket; this effectively thickened the cylinder bore walls. These templates were given to the foundry liaison engineer, Louis Taylor, who flew to Indianapolis with them. When the sand cores were scraped with the templates, the cores cracked. Weertman was advised of this and flew to Indianapolis himself. It was discovered that the sand cores had not been dried properly and when the molten iron hit the cores, the result was an unusable block. With properly dried cores and a slow cooling-down after casting, the block castings were good.

The blocks, and the cylinder heads, were both carefully stress-relieved. Newly assembled engines with these improved blocks showed no problems.

Track testing of the 426 Hemi began even before dyno testing was completed. Testing took place at the Goodyear track in San Angelo, Texas. Race driver Paul Goldsmith was behind the wheel. The first time out, Goldsmith hit 180 miles per hour. Subsequent testing convinced the Hemi could deliver reliable—and winning—power at Daytona.

The 426 Drag Hemi sits for its portrait. The beauty of the Chrysler Hemi was the package car. In 1964, you could order an entire vehicle set-up to go drag racing, as was done before with the Max Wedge. Chrysler backed up the amateur and professional drag racer with technical bulletins, parts, and service. *DaimlerChrysler Corporation*

The "bathtub" intake manifold was introduced on the Hemi for circle-track competition in 1966. It had improved high-rpm capabilities and remained in use for NASCAR through 1970. Rule changes spelled the doom of the 426 Hemi in stock car racing. *DaimlerChrysler Corporation*

The Daytona 500—A Sweep

On the morning of February 24, 1964, race fans began filling the stands of Daytona International Speedway. The racing program talked about the new "Chrysler Corporation's Hemispherical Combustion Chamber Maximum Performance Engine" and countless bets were placed on the outcome of the race.

Pre-race qualifying to determine the starting lineup gave a good indication. Paul Goldsmith held pole position in his Plymouth Belvedere. Next to Goldsmith was Richard Petty in his No. 43 Plymouth. Junior Johnson was in third position, driving a Dodge Coronet. Bobby Isaac was in fourth, also in a Coronet. Buck Baker was behind the wheel of a Belvedere, as was Jim Pardue. David Pearson was in seventh in a Coronet. Jim Paschal was in tenth position in a Coronet. And 426 Hemis were under the hoods of each one.

That day, racing history was made and a legendary engine was born. Three hours and fifteen minutes later, Richard Petty was first across the finish line, followed by Jim Pardue and Paul Goldsmith—a one-two-three sweep by Plymouth. Jim Paschal was fifth, seconds behind the leaders. Junior Johnson was ninth. Hemi cars set a new average speed record of 154.334 miles per hour. Chrysler president Lynn Townsend was jubilant.

The 1964 NASCAR season was a good one for Chrysler, but the 426 drag Hemi also set records from coast to coast. The 426 Wedge was supplanted by the 426 Hemi, and the Hemi proved it could respond to supercharging and other exotic induction setups. All this left street enthusiasts fantasizing about what life would be like with a 426 street Hemi. In fact, Chrysler's engine group had held out the possibility of doing so, but they were preoccupied with getting the race Hemi ready.

The 426 Hemi Drag Cars

Chrysler's racing group wanted to continue the program of offering assembly line–built factory drag racing cars, as it had with its Max Wedge 413s and 426s. In an SAE paper Weertman co-authored with Bob Lechner, they explain the production level anticipated:

"Immediately following the initial introduction of the engine," they wrote, "a production run of several hundred drag racing engines and cars were planned to be built. The production of the several hundred drag engines was completed by the end of the 1964 model year. Another production run of several hundred drag

engines was made for the 1965 model year automobiles, with a considerable weight decrease for the engines obtained by the use of aluminum and magnesium components."

Like the Max Wedge drag cars that came before, the Dodge and Plymouth factory drag cars truly were set up for the strip. The 12.5:1 compression ratio 426 Hemi was factory rated at 425 horsepower at 6,000 rpm but to racers who knew better, this rating was obviously conservative. The standard rear-axle ratio was a Sure-Grip 4.56; optional ratios available ranged from 2.93 to 5.38. Dual Carter AFB four-barrel carburetors sat atop the short-ram aluminum intake manifold, which was practically identical to that used previously on the Max Wedge. The cars came standard with the TorqueFlight three-speed automatic transmission specifically engineered for the drag Hemi.

Dodge called its Hemi the Dodge 426 Hemi-Charger. In its booklet, Dodge added this disclaimer in

The street Hemi was introduced in 1966. It featured two in-line Carter Thermo-Quad carburetors bolted to an aluminum dual-plane intake manifold. Chrysler had set a precedent of using dual four-barrels on its high-performance street engines, and chose not to break with tradition with the 426 Hemi. While a single four-barrel would have been sufficient on the street, image and the possibility of drag racing dictated dual quads. *DaimlerChrysler Corporation*

bold type to discourage any would-be racers from taking the car to the streets:

"The Hemi-Charger 426 engine is designed for use in supervised acceleration trials and other racing and performance competition. It is not recommended for general every day driving because of the compromise of all around characteristics which must be made for this type of vehicle. In view of its intended use this vehicle is sold 'As Is' and the provisions of Chrysler Corporation's manufacturers passenger car warranty or any other warranty expressed or implied does not apply."

The booklet went on to describe the lightweight aluminum front-end package and components available as optional equipment. This included aluminum fenders, hood, dust shields, front bumper, bumper-support brackets, and doors. Door glass and front quarter window winders were eliminated. The rear window was replaced with 0.08-inch thick tempered glass. The hood was fitted with a large air scoop to feed colder, denser air to the angled, oval air cleaner spanning both carburetors.

"The Super Stock drag race cars (Dodge Coronets and Plymouth Belvederes) were intended only for drag strip use," Troy Simonsen states, "but were production-built cars and we built a lot of them, both manual and automatic. They had a minimum amount of equipment in them. You could take one out the door, put a set of M&H tires on it, uncork the headers, and go turn 11.50."

In its second year of production, the 426 street Hemi found its way into such cruisers as this 1967 Plymouth Satellite convertible. Shaker hoodscoops and billboard graphics were not yet in the engineer's or designer's vocabulary—just a low-key displacement badge behind the front wheelwells.

A word of warning to those who would attempt to take this Road Runner in the stoplight matches that inevitably arose. The top-feeding hood vents were functional with the optional Air Grabber fresh air system.

The Road Runner was a runaway best-seller by 1969. Over 82,000 were sold that year. Fewer than 800 were equipped with the 426 Hemi. This one was originally ordered by a Plymouth dealer in Montreal, Canada. Of the 422 Hemi Road Runner hardtops built in 1969, 188 were ordered with the TorqueFlight automatic transmission, like this one.

After the beating Ford and GM took at Daytona in 1964, the corporations did not sit around pondering what to do. They responded with more aggressive engine development programs of their own. Chrysler, of course, assumed GM and Ford would do just that, and pushed the Hemi's development in other directions.

"After the first several races in 1964," Simonsen recalls, "Ford made a major drive and improved their performance of both the engines and the cars, and from then on out, the races were pretty much competitive."

One of the derivations of the Hemi was a dual over-head cam design having four valves per cylinder, with the designation A925. A prototype was built, and although it never ran in Chrysler's dyno labs, this proto-type did have a deterrent factor, as it turned out.

"Ford went down to Daytona for 1965 with their racing engine," Bob Rarey remembers, "which wasn't a Hemi exactly, but was darned near, I guess. They said they wanted to race *that* against us. Ronnie Householder (Chrysler's director of stock car racing) went to Bill France and said, 'Hey, look fellows. If you run that Ford engine, we're running this engine.' He takes the cover off it and shows the four-valve Hemi. This engine had a six-teen-branch intake manifold! It was unbelievable. France just said, 'As of now, the Ford engine isn't running and

Popping the hood was a frequent occurrence with the Hemi Road Runner. When the option code N96 Air Grabber was ordered on the 426 Hemi, an additional decal was placed on the air cleaner that brought smiles.

neither is *that*.' We eliminated the competition with that one engine."

Unfortunately, the NASCAR ban on the Ford single-overhead-cam 427 and Chrysler double-overhead-cam 426 Hemi also extended to the 426 Hemi they were currently racing. Ford and Chrysler filed formal protests, but to no avail. Chrysler withdrew its factory support for the 1965 NASCAR season, but then, it had no other choice. However, the Hemi excelled in NHRA, AHRA, and USAC events in 1965.

One of the other Hemi engine development programs was the A990, which began in August 1964. The goal was to reduce the Hemi's weight as much as possible using aluminum and magnesium components. The new parts included aluminum cylinder heads, oil-pump

body, oil-pump cover, water pump housing, water-outlet elbow, and alternator bracket. The intake manifold was cast in magnesium. The aluminum heads were first cast by Alcoa and later by various small foundries around the country. This engine actually went into production, with an anticipated production of 210 engines. These engines went into the factory drag cars, replacing the iron head Hemis.

Race Hemi in Street Clothing

During the latter months of 1964, product planning meetings were held by Chrysler management to discuss the feasibility of offering the 426 Hemi in Dodge and Plymouth passenger cars. On January 6, 1965, Bob Rodger issued a Product Planning Letter,

which stated in part, "Because of continued requirements for an ultimate performance drag strip and street type engine with expanded usage, the following change in the engine lineup has been agreed upon after discussion with the affected areas. Please release a hemispherical combustion chamber engine for 'B' Series with the following general characteristics:

1. Intake manifold to have two four-barrel carburetors.
2. Cylinder block to maintain cross tie bolt main bearing caps.
3. Cast iron exhaust manifold.
4. Solid lifters are acceptable but not preferred.
5. Pistons—Forged acceptable and thermally controlled preferred.
6. Manifolding and camshaft to be designed to give best

The Dodge Coronet line was restyled for 1970, and this would be the last year for the Coronet R/T. The functional hoodscoops now came standard when the 426 Hemi was ordered. The nonfunctional rear quarter panel side scoops were part of the R/T package. The vivid Green Go paint (option code FJ6) was a mid-year offering.

hood of the B-bodies that would receive it. The right front shock absorber tower was redesigned for easier access. The power brake-cylinder booster had to be moved to clear the left valve cover. However, the booster would still need to be removed when the number-seven spark plug needed replacement, or the valves needed adjustment. Due to the air cleaner's size, the hood hinge torsion bar position and support bracket had to be modified. The dash panel in the area of the heater motor depression required a change for proper valve cover clearance, and the heater hose routing and fittings had to be changed, also for valve cover clearance. These and other changes were already evident when the Hemi was installed in B-bodies in the 1964 and 1965 factory-built drag cars.

The only anticipated changes to the cylinder block were mounting lugs on the side of the block for engine mounts in C-bodies, and some machining of the mounting areas. The only changes to the cylinder heads were those necessary to accept the new, streamlined cast-iron exhaust manifolds. The valves, rocker arms, mechanical lifters, and pushrods were from A864 race Hemi, but the valve spring rates were lowered to avoid premature wear and limit engine redline to keep rated output to the desired 425 horsepower.

high speed power possible while still maintaining a reasonably driveable vehicle for summer/winter.

7. Automatic and four-speed [manual] transmissions required (4-speed to have development priority).

8. No air conditioning required for 'B' Series."

The street Hemi was to be available beginning with the 1966 model year. Due to the overall width of the 426 Hemi, some modifications needed to be done under the

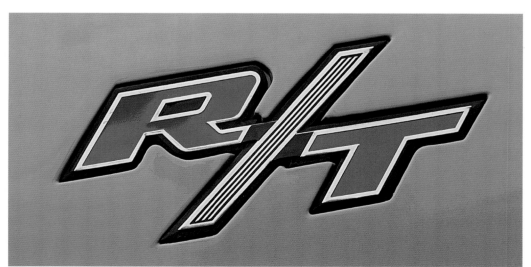

The crankshaft was essentially the racing crank, as were the connecting rods. The pistons, of necessity, featured a 10.25:1 compression ratio so the engine could run on available extra-premium fuel. The camshaft timing was also redesigned to make the engine drivable on the street. The cast-aluminum intake manifold was a dual-plane design to use two Carter AFB four-barrel carburetors mounted inline. While the second carburetor really wasn't needed on the street, Chrysler knew these cars would be drag raced, and felt a dual four-barrel setup would also offer the ultimate in image and performance on the street. In short, only those changes that were necessary to make the racing Hemi streetable were performed.

The fresh air system used on Dodges was appropriately called Ramcharger. In appearance and function, it was identical to the system used on Plymouths. The Hemi Orange Ramcharger and air cleaner against the Green Go engine compartment and hood offer up a riotous color contrast.

It was the era of flower power, and 1970 was the year of 'Cuda Power. Specifically, the Hemi 'Cuda. This was spelled out in lowercase on the shaker hoodscoop. HEMI also appeared on the "hockey stick" tape treatment on the rear fenders.

The 426 street Hemi was assembled at Chrysler's Marine and Industrial Division in Marysville, Michigan. The street Hemi went through its own pre-production testing program almost as tortuous as the race Hemi. Dyno testing of the 426 Hemi offered for the street proved the horsepower would be as advertised.

"The factory rating for the street Hemi of 425 horsepower was right on," says Ted Flack, one of the Hemi dynamometer test engineers. "When we did a scuff test, we'd fire up a green engine—no hours on it—and run it at maximum horsepower for two hours. Those things made 425 horsepower like clockwork."

To enthusiasts familiar with the race Hemi, the beauty of the street Hemi was knowing the engine underwent the identical manufacturing and assembly procedures as the circle track and drag racing engines. This had to be done because the 426 Hemi Dodges, Coronets, and Plymouth Belvederes available in Chrysler showrooms truly were street/strip machines. Chrysler could not afford to suffer reliability problems with this engine that had achieved such notoriety in NASCAR, NHRA, AHRA, and USAC competition. It had to uphold the 426 Hemi's racing heritage. This explained why the 426 Hemi option cost nearly $600 when offered for 1966; this included heavy-duty driveline components to handle the awesome torque and horsepower the Hemi produced.

In the fall of 1965, the Chrysler Corporation Engineering Office issued a publication titled *Chrysler Corporation's Hemi-426 for 1966*. It was meant to give a complete description of the street Hemi in response to countless requests from magazine editors, newspapers, and interested individuals. In part, the publication read, "Because of the increased demand and popularity, the Hemi-head engine is now available as a regular production option for 1966 Plymouth Belvedere and Dodge Coronet. Belvederes powered by this high performance option are identified by the 'HP2' emblem on the fenders. Coronets by the '426 HEMI' medallion."

Initially, the "HP2" emblem on the 1966 Hemi-powered Belvederes raised the obvious question: What does it mean? It meant High Performance Plymouth. While the Dodge medallion was to the point and self-explanatory, the Plymouth badge was curiously vague. After several months of production, the "HP2" medallion was replaced by the "426 Hemi" emblem.

The Rapid Transit Authority.

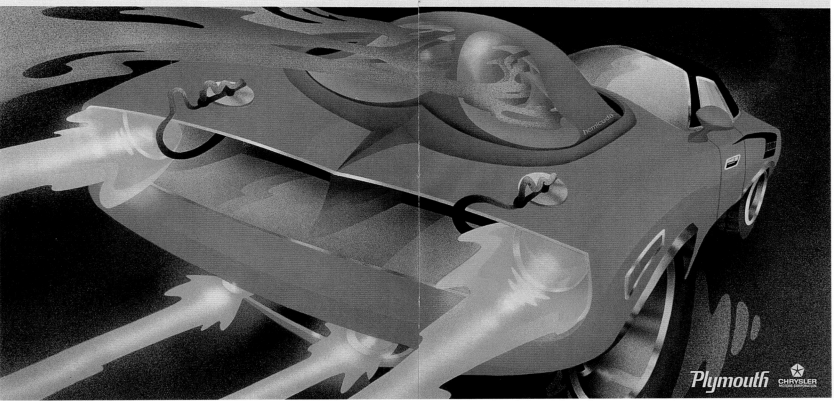

It's Hemi-'Cuda. Our angriest, slipperiest-looking body shell, wrapped around ol' King Kong hisself.

Ah yes, and we've perched the entire setup atop the ruggedest ponycar suspension in the industry. The front suspension is the same extra-heavy-duty combination used on Hemi Road Runners and GTXs—the same torsion bars, shock absorbers, anti-sway bar, spindles, ball joints, etc. Ditto the rear suspension, which carries two extra half-leaves in the right rear spring, to prevent torque steer off the line.

As for the brakes, they're giant 11-inch diameter drum-type units.

The standard transmission is (1.) a heavy-duty 4-speed with Hurst linkage and our new "Pistol Grip" shift handle, or (2.) Chrysler's famed TorqueFlite 'auto' with our new "Slap-Stik" shifter.

Tires? Fiberglass-belted F60 X 15s.

Air induction? That's courtesy of Air Grabber, which sticks right up through the hood. Aside from the fact that it looks tough and the girls dig it, it's good for .15 to .20 of a second in the quarter. And the Hemi it connects to now has hydraulic lifters, so it stays in tune longer.

Availability? Why, at your Plymouth dealer's Rapid Transit Center, of course. There you'll find 'Cudas of all denominations—340s, 383s, 440s, and 440 Six-Barrels.

Giving people what they want is easy. When you have a System.

Plymouth CHRYSLER MOTORS CORPORATION

Selling the 426 Street Hemi

With all the excitement surrounding the introduction of the 426 street Hemi, the automotive magazines couldn't wait to get their hands on a 426 Hemi Charger, Coronet, Belvedere, or Satellite. *Car Life* tested a Hemi-powered 1966 Plymouth Satellite with TorqueFlight automatic transmission. The performance figures were 0-60 miles per hour in 7.1 seconds and the quarter-mile was covered in 14.5 seconds, hitting 95 miles per hour through the lights. Very poor results, indeed, in light of the engine's capabilities. In fact, a 1966 Plymouth Satellite with a 325-horsepower 383 with TorqueFlight was just as quick to 60. It was only at the end of the quarter-mile that the Hemi showed its abilities. In elapsed time, the Hemi-powered Plymouth was the fastest car that the magazine tested in 1966, but clearly, the Hemi

was hamstrung with narrow, bias-ply Blue Streak tires and its closed exhaust system.

Advertising for performance cars in the 1960s was a genre that rarely has been duplicated. Some of the most clever ad lines, ad copy, and graphics made up the advertising of the era to draw the youthful buyer and the young at heart. An ad promoting the 1966 Charger featured a Hemi-powered Dodge Charger at speed, with "Boss Hoss" and then a picture of the 426 Hemi below. The ad read in part, "Dodge Charger with a big, tough 426 Hemi up front makes other steeds look staid. Both for show and go, Charger looks beautifully quick just standing still. And the optional Hemi V-8 supplies a kick to match, with 425 muscular horses. Not a pony or a kitten in the bunch. The hot setup? You bet."

continued on page 120

Plymouth called on famed illustrator Bob Grossman to do this illustration of the 1970 Hemi 'Cuda in the Rapid Transit Authority advertisement. The ad copy was brief and to the point.

The last year of the street Hemi's production was 1971. Coincidentally, only 71 Dodge Challenger R/Ts were ordered with the 426 Hemi that year. This one is appropriately painted in Hemi Orange. Hoodscoops became functional with installation of the Ramcharger that came as part of the 426 Hemi option.

New tape stripes were offered on the Challenger R/T in 1971. Option code V9X put black stripes on this Hemi Challenger R/T. The rear quarter panel scoops came on the R/T and were for appearances only. The optional rear deck spoiler would increase downward aerodynamic pressure if placed at the correct angle.

The 1971 Hemi 'Cuda was the last of a mighty breed. The 426 Hemi output remained an honest 425 horsepower right to the end of production. Devoid of any graphics, this Hemi 'Cuda painted in Sno White is contrasted by the flat-black shaker hoodscoop. Factory records show 108 hardtop 'Cudas got the Hemi in 1971.

The interior of the Hemi 'Cuda showed the full instrumentation needed to keep an eye on what was going on under the hood. The pistol grip shifter used with the optional four-speed manual transmission was ergonomically designed and remains one of the best shifter designs to see production.

The 426 Hemi spawned many drag racing vehicles, but in the early days of the "elephant motor" perhaps none became more famous than the Little Red Wagon and the Hurst Hemi Under Glass.

With the introduction of the 426 Hemi in drag racing mode, creative drag racers considered the possibilities of this engine in all manner of cars and trucks. With the help of those fine folks at the Woodward Avenue Garage, a.k.a. the Ramchargers, a most unique Hemi-powered machine literally rose from the garage floor. Like most great drag racing vehicles, this one was the product of several experienced race car builders and drivers, but the focus of their attention was offbeat: a Dodge A-100 compact pickup. In standard trim the 90-inch wheelbase A-100 came standard with the 101-horsepower straight-six engine. The concept was to replace that engine with a 425-horspower drag Hemi. Well . . .

Initially, four men were involved in the design and construction of what would become the Little Red Wagon. They were Jim Schaeffer and John Collier, who built the special, heavy-duty 75-inch by 36-inch wide rectangular steel tube frame to support the Hemi and TorqueFlight transmission, shortened drive shaft, and heavy-duty differential. This frame was mated to the A-100's unibody using thick gusset plates from the frame up to the truck's unibody, with two 9/16-inch bolts up front and the leaf-spring rear suspension in the rear. Thus, it was a simple matter to drop the A-100 over engine and frame—except for one thing. Portions of the truck bed and passenger compartment wall had to be cut away to clear the big Hemi and the velocity stacks of the Hilborn fuel-injection system chosen in place of the factory dual four-barrel induction system. Stuffed into the rear wheel wells were 10-inch wide drag slicks. To properly slow the Little Red Wagon without melting the factory brakes, a bright yellow drag chute was mounted to the open tailgate.

The Wheelstand Kings

To ensure the Hemi delivered the desired show and go, Roger Lindamood and Dick Branstner, also of Detroit, selected and tuned the Hilborn fuel injection system for what is believed to be the first application of F.I. on the 426 Hemi for drag racing. The final horsepower output of this engine was a closely guarded secret but rumors of 450 to 500 horsepower were circulating. The truck, appropriately, was painted a bright red and huge bold text on the side announced the "LITTLE RED WAGON." When Lindamood and Branstner trucked the LRW to Detroit Dragway to test the vehicle, little did they realize the wheelstanding capability of the mighty Hemi-powered A-100. Whoa—talk about weight transfer!

After they learned to control the LRW in wheelstanding mode, they were able to hustle through the quarter-mile at nearly 130 miles per hour running in the 11-second range, with an eye on the high 10s. The Little Red Wagon made its debut at Cecil County Drag-O-Way in Maryland on September 19, 1964. To say it was a crowd-pleaser is an understatement. Bill "Maverick" Golden took over driving duties, and so enjoyed taking the Little Red Wagon around the country—and setting records—that he bought it and built a second one as a backup show vehicle. During one mishap, the LRW got away from Maverick and it was severly wrecked—the built-in rollcage did its job. Maverick towed the tattered LRW home and put it in mothballs, and pressed Little Red Wagon No. 2 into service. At the 1998 Chryslers At Carlisle event, Golden put on display the original, unrestored Little Red Wagon. And yes, Virginia, there was more than one Lassie, too.

The other wheelstand king that vied for attention during the sixties was the Hurst Hemi Under Glass. George Hurst, who had become a household name among enthusiasts, primarily due to his rugged shifters and other performance products, decided to unleash Hurst Research on a vehicle powered by the new 426 Hemi. Discussions centered around using a 1965 Plymouth Barracuda and locating the Hemi just behind the driver and passenger seats. Hurst put Jack Watson in charge of the project. Watson's team engineered a unique manual transaxle to bolt up to the Hemi, and it was engineered to withstand anything the engine could dish out. This drivetrain was bolted to a new frame designed to mate to the existing Plymouth frame and bodywork. The driver's seat had to be moved forward considerably to clear the intrusive Hemi. An aluminum plate shield separated the new engine compartment from the "passenger" compartment.

Interestingly, the radiator was moved to the very rear of the car and was assisted by two electric fans. To ensure coolant flow, an electric water pump rated at 30 gallons per minute would keep the Hemi from overheating. A new fuel tank was located underneath the hood and was pressurized. An airduct ran from the grille area to a sealed air cleaner spanning the staggered carburetors. This first Hemi 'Cuda was fitted with the necessary wheels and tires—and something more.

Watson and his team knew the new center of gravity for the Hemi Under Glass would make the car do some very interesting things. Wheelie bars were a must, but just to be sure, they were designed to take the entire weight of the car as it reared up on its haunches.

Their suspicions were correct. After the first initial burnout and timid wheelies at Detroit Raceway, Bill Schrewsberry unleashed the Hemi Under Glass, pulling a wheelstand so high the car nearly went over onto its roof. This would take some getting used to!

As Schrewsberry and the Hurst engineers sorted the car out, the Hemi Under Glass was able to put down some very impressive numbers. More important, the car would be a rolling testbed of ideas for Hurst and get the corporate name before hundreds of thousands of drag racing enthusiasts. Talk about product promotion, this was it!

In 1966 Bob Riggle became the driver of the Hemi Under Glass. He campaigned the car for Hurst until 1975. It was not until 1991 that the idea of getting this classic, crowd-pleasing car back on the quarter-mile strip started to haunt Riggle. With the encouragement of the ever-lonely Linda Vaughn and support of Hurst, Riggle embarked on building an exact replica of the famed Hemi Under Glass. In August 1992, the car made its appearance at the NHRA U.S. Nationals at Indianapolis, with Riggle behind the wheel. The huge crowd was on its feet, cheering, as the Hemi Under Glass once again lifted first its front wheels, then its rear wheels, before coming back down to earth and roaring off down the strip.

The rarest of the rare: a mere seven Hemi 'Cuda convertibles were built in 1971. Don't ask what this one is worth.

The Hemi 'Cuda convertible was the twilight of maximum performance top-down driving. These cars have become one of the greatest automotive investments of the musclecar era, but few had the vision to consider that possibility in 1971.

continued from page 115

Over the next two years, *Car Life* tested two other Hemi-powered Mopars. In 1967, they tested a Hemi Charger, again equipped with a TorqueFlight automatic transmission. The car reached 60 miles per hour in 6.4 seconds and did 96 miles per hour through the timing lights. Top speed was 134 miles per hour. The 1967 Hemi charger had the lowest elapsed time and the highest top speed of all the cars the magazine tested that year. In 1968, the magazine tested a 426 Hemi GTX. Performance was nearly identical to the Charger tested the year before. With TorqueFlight automatic transmission, the GTX took 6.3 seconds to reach 60, and did the quarter in 14.0 seconds doing 97 miles per hour through the lights. Top speed was 144 miles per hour.

In 1969, *Popular Hot Rodding* tested a pair of Chargers—one with a TorqueFlight and the other with a manual four-speed. The automatic car covered the quarter-mile in 14.01 seconds at 100 miles per hour. By advancing the ignition and removing the air cleaner, the car reached the end of the quarter-mile in 13.75 seconds at 104 miles per hour. The Hemi Charger equipped with the four-speed manual did much better. The E.T. was 13.60 seconds at 107.44 miles per hour. And this was with a 3.23 Sure-Grip rear end and vehicle weight of more than 4,100 pounds!

The Coronet Super Bee and Coronet R/T were dropped after 1970. The Super Bee and R/T options were offered only on the Charger in 1971. This R/T was optioned strictly for performance: 426 Hemi with Ramcharger hoodscoop, hood pins, front and rear spoilers, four-speed manual transmission, and Super Trak Pak with 4.10 Sure-Grip differential.

In 1970, Chrysler rebodied the Plymouth Barracuda and introduced the new Dodge Challenger to the pony-car wars. Both of these handsome E-bodies were designed from the outset to accept the 426 Hemi. *Road Test* magazine tested a 1970 Challenger R/T with the Hemi, four-speed manual transmission, and 4.10 Sure-Grip differential for the June 1970 issue.

"It takes courage to specify the Hemi option in a Challenger," the editors wrote. "You must face a drivetrain warranty foreshortened to six months, a whopping $1,227.50 increase in the $2,953 list for a basic Challenger V-8 to cover the Hemi and its mandatory related accessories, insurance and operating costs matched by no other U.S. nameplate except maybe a Hemi Plymouth and the certainty that no fuzz will let you pass unnoticed.

"In return, you get power that can rattle dishes in the kitchen when you start it up in the driveway, extra attention in any service station, respect from owners of 428 Fords and SS427 Chevys, a measurable bonus in pride of ownership and immediate status as *the* car expert on your block."

Road Test recorded a quarter-mile E.T. of 14.0 seconds at 104 miles per hour. In summary, the editors wrote, "If brute power over all other considerations is your forte, the Hemi is still boss on the street and if you'll note what most people put under a supercharger in Top Fuel Eliminator, it's boss on the strip as well."

Of all the Hemi-powered Dodges and Plymouths built for the street, perhaps the most distinctive was the 1970 Hemi 'Cuda. It wasn't a distinct model in the

The purposeful look of this Hemi Charger R/T is enhanced by the color-keyed elastomeric front and rear bumpers, black tape striping, and bone-stock hubcaps sans wheel trim rings.

The decal on the sides of the Ramcharger hoodscoop featured the familiar bumble bee. On the sides of the hood bulge was the alpha-numeric badge that gave pause to all those who challenged this car's supremacy on the street.

'Cuda, the ads for the Hemi 'Cuda gave the impression of being a distinct model.

The Hemi 'Cuda received a respectable share of advertising dollars. One ad showed a 1970 Hemi 'Cuda in a field of psychedelic-colored flowers, with the tag line "'Cuda Power." It described the new performance Barracuda, the 'Cuda, and what the 426 Hemi could do for the 'Cuda. At the bottom of the ad it stated, "See the 1970 Hemi 'Cuda at your Plymouth Dealer's September 23."

Then there was the famous Bob Grossman airbrush illustration of the Hemi 'Cuda that appeared as a two-page spread. This ad was the product of Plymouth's advertising agency, Young & Rubicam. Jim Ramsey and Joe Schulte were the account executives. The ad shows a wildly distorted Hemi 'Cuda, rendered in Grossman's unique style, shown in Hemi Orange paint and black vinyl roof with headlights and driving lights blazing. Almost erupting through the hood was the shaker scoop of mammoth proportions, glowing ominously from within, with a curious purple vapor being drawn into the "nostrils" of the scoop—sniffing out the poor, unfortunate competition, perhaps? The tag line above this outrageous, eye-catching illustration read, "The Rapid Transit Authority." The first paragraph of ad copy read, "It's Hemi 'Cuda. Our angriest, slipperiest-looking body shell, wrapped around ol' King Kong hisself." This indeed was the golden age of musclecar advertising!

The Twilight of Hemi Power

Few Mopar enthusiasts realized that 1971 would be the last year for the Chrysler 426 street Hemi. After all, the market had seen Hemi Coronets, Hemi Super Bees, Hemi Chargers, Hemi Challengers, Hemi Belvederes, Hemi Road Runners, Hemi GTXs, Hemi 'Cudas—even Hemi Daytonas and Hemi Superbirds. The fact was, the numbers just weren't there. Sales of Hemis were plummeting in the face of staggering insurance premiums. Sales in 1971 were even worse. For example, only 71 Challenger R/Ts were ordered with the 426 Hemi in 1971. The Hemi 'Cuda was only slightly better, with 108 hardtops and only 7 convertibles built! Only 22 Dodge Charger Super Bees and 63 Charger R/Ts were optioned with the Hemi. The Hemi Road Runner was put on the endangered species list; a total of 55 were built in 1971. There were only 30 GTXs with the 426 Hemi. The buyers of these cars were among the prudent few who saw the handwriting the wall and knew this would be their last chance to buy a street Hemi.

With the 1971 Ramcharger using a single scoop centered in the hood, there was less ductwork taking up underhood real estate. Where tenths of a second made a difference on the quarter-mile, this could reduce elapsed times by a few tenths.

new 'Cuda line that year, but when you ordered the 426 Hemi in your 'Cuda it was identified as such on the standard shaker hoodscoop with "hemicuda" on the sides of the scoop. The rear quarter panels received subdued graphics with the word "Hemi" as additional identification. It was the only Mopar during the 426 Hemi's 1966-'71 production in which "Hemi" was used in the name of the car. Despite being an option in the

In hindsight, many Mopar enthusiasts wish they had had the wisdom and the money to walk into a Dodge or Plymouth dealer and place an order for a Hemi Mopar of their choice. Better yet, to have ordered two—one to drive and the other to keep in storage with zero mileage, for true investment appreciation. However, car collecting has always been this way. Certain cars are never thought of as collectible during their day, only years or decades later. Those who did buy Hemis may have lost interest, found a new "love," had a change in financial priorities, wore the cars out and sold them, or perhaps even wrecked them. Few original owners actually held onto them.

In addition to all this, the Hemi faced the specter of performance-robbing emission controls. Chrysler had run emissions tests on the 426 Hemi and was having difficulty meeting the projected emissions levels.

"It was a matter of qualifying it for emissions," Tom Hoover says, "and the fact the insurance companies had come down hard on the people who were buying the cars at the time. It was prohibitive to own one, and the market dried up."

While production of the 440 Wedge V-8 continued into the 1970s with the engine suffering annual drops in power, the 426 Hemi today is remembered as an uncompromised high-performance V-8. Whether it was a 1966 Dodge Charger or a 1971 Plymouth Hemi 'Cuda, all churned out 425 horsepower. The 426 Hemi's nickname as the "elephant motor" is apropos, the elephant being the largest and most powerful beast to walk on the face of the earth today. Ceasing production of the 426 street Hemi in 1971 kept it that way.

The clean interior of this Charger R/T featured bucket seats but no console. The pistol grip Hurst shifter really let the driver keep a handle on things when the action got hot, which it often did with this car. That's what Hemis were for.

CHAPTER FIVE

Race on Sunday, Sell on Monday

Almost from the time the automobile was invented and "speed" was discovered, competition was not far behind. Manufacturers saw automotive racing as a way to convey to prospective customers the ruggedness and durability of their cars. The excitement of racing and, more important, the thrill of winning, were the means of lending panache to the cars on the showroom floor.

Stock car racing and drag racing were two of the ways Chrysler brought glory to Highland Park. The privateers did the stock car racing in the mid- and late-1950s, as recorded in Chapter One. Aggressive factory support would not start until the early 1960s. Drag racing was approached somewhat differently at first, with a small internal band of engineers who were visionary, loved the Dodges and Plymouths they worked on, and strove to make them go faster.

Birth of the Ramchargers

For many years, Chrysler had operated the Chrysler Institute of Engineering as the "finishing school" for degreed, graduate engineers who joined Chrysler Corporation. In the late 1950s, a small group of young, talented Chrysler Institute engineers with an unabashed love of performance slowly and informally started forming by word of mouth. Tom Hoover was one of the men in that group. He had received a master's degree in

physics in 1955, joined Chrysler, and graduated from the Chrysler Institute in 1957. While having lunch in the Chrysler Engineering cafeteria in the summer of 1958, Hoover and fellow engineer Wayne Erikson kicked around the idea of forming a group to go to drag races and help one another with their own cars.

"Initially, it was a confederation," Hoover says. "Each of us had cars we were working on. I had a 1957 Plymouth convertible and I had the good fortune to buy from salvage one of the engines from the 392 program, which was the Raised Block version. Wayne Erikson had a 1953 Dodge two-door sedan; he had the low-block Chrysler 365 Hemi in his car. We did everything we thought we could learn using the A311 program data reports, which were a gold mine of information. Barnes Daniels had a '57 Plymouth that had an 'A' engine in it. Pete McNichol had a 354 Chrysler Hemi in a '57 T-bird. Herman Moser ran a small-block Dodge Red Ram 241 Hemi in a '53 Dodge. Troy Simonsen drove the L-head six-cylinder car, and Pete McNichol became the slant six guy."

They became a chartered club with the NHRA, calling themselves the Ramchargers. This engineering brain trust was the cutting edge of Chrysler Corporation drag racing, only Chrysler didn't know it yet. In one of their bench-racing sessions, the Ramchargers conceived a plan to build their own club car for C/Altered class to

The 1969 Dodge Charger Daytona followed quickly on the heels of the Charger 500, bringing the Charger to the apex of aerodynamic development for use in Grand National stock car competition. It became the fastest stock car ever raced up to that time. Due to its amazing stability, it proved very popular with all the drivers who raced it. The street Daytona, built for only one year, turned heads and stopped traffic.

The only chance you'll get to pass Richard Petty's Hemi!

Small wonder, what with its high-performance 426-cubic-inch hemispherical-head V-8. Plymouth Belvedere . . . a beautiful piece of hairy machinery! Everything about the Hemi package is designed to move you out, fast. Like four-barrel carbs. Dual-breaker distributor. High-lift, high-overlap cam. Special plugs, pistons and double valve springs. Low-back-pressure, dual-exhaust system. Special Blue Streak tires. Wide-base, Safety-Rim wheels. Oversize front torsion bars. Sway bar.

Added-leaf, high-rate rear springs. And heavy-duty shocks. For performance stops, optional front-wheel disc brakes. Now that we've told you what goes into making a Hemi-powered Plymouth such a great winner, we'll tell you what it takes to beat one. Another Hemi-powered Plymouth.

PLYMOUTH DIVISION — CHRYSLER MOTORS CORPORATION

Plymouth . . . a great car by Chrysler Corporation.

A prime example of "race on Sunday, sell on Monday" advertising. Plymouth never passed up the opportunity to capitalize on Richard Petty's wins with his 426 Hemi Plymouths. This ad appeared in the July 1966 *Road & Track*.

The first thing they did was pull the Plymouth's engine, to make way for something much more potent.

"Dan Mancini and I built the engine," Hoover says. "Gale Porter over at Dodge got for us a 354 Hemi truck engine that had dropped an exhaust valve. It became the engine for the *High and Mighty*. It was a joke with us at the time because we had roughly $200 invested in it. We bought a new set of Jahns pistons. Jim Hider had a place over near Detroit Airport. We came up with a camshaft profile and ol' Jim would do it for a reasonable price. Jeff Baker at Chrysler designed the plenum-ram manifold, and we used reinforced radiator hose for the trumpets. The primary performance people in the engine lab before I got there were John Platner, Don Morre, and Jeff Baker. Jeff did the mapping of the inlet manifold to get the ram effect. We used Jeff's recommended plenum dimensions. The information from the A311 Indianapolis program, along with Jeff's work, gave us, essentially, 21 inches from the plenum to the valve seat. The *High and Mighty* was the granddaddy of the tunnel-ram manifold."

The resulting engine was never dynoed, but slide rule calculations indicated some very serious horsepower. Getting all this newfound horsepower to the ground with the limitations of tires and suspensions of the day was a challenge. How would the Ramchargers harness that power and get the desired traction?

"With the *High and Mighty* we sat down and thought about the vehicle dynamics of drag racing," Simonsen recalls. "The problem was getting all the traction you can. We wanted the car high, to get weight shift. We had a unique suspension that was intended to transfer the weight equally to both the rear wheels so that the torque of the driveshaft and the tendency to lift the right wheel were offset. That car was tall enough that you could crawl under it on your hands and knees, almost."

The *High and Mighty* made its debut at the 1959 NHRA Nationals, which were held in Detroit that year. The car proceeded to set the C/Altered record and won the class at the Nationals. It was a rolling testbed of ideas, and was refined—and repaired—while it was raced in 1959 and 1960. Dick Maxwell was hired by Chrysler in February 1959 and graduated from the Chrysler Institute in 1961. While attending the Institute he joined the Ramchargers.

"That's where the whole thing got started," says Maxwell. "We ran the car in '59 and '60 and finally destroyed the engine and didn't have any parts to repair

compete in sanctioned drag racing. The Ramchargers didn't have a budget per se; any funds would come out of their own pockets and material donations were welcome. They latched onto a 1949 Plymouth Business Coupe, took it to the home of Ramcharger Jack McPhearson, and sequestered in his garage to be extensively modified.

it. At that time, Jim Thornton was head of the group, and he went to Frank Wylie (in Dodge Public Relations) and sold him on the fact that we should go Super Stock racing. So, the company got involved in drag racing in 1961, legitimately in 1962, to build an image. We were virtually invisible on the street—the drive-in scene or the stoplights—-wherever you wanted to go. There weren't any of our cars. The only thing we had on the street in those early days [1959 and 1960] was the 383, which wasn't bad, but it wasn't recognized because in order to go fast, you had to have a Chevy or a Ford."

That fact was anathema to Lynn Townsend, who became Chrysler president in mid-1961. The timing, and the man, were fortuitous for Chrysler. Townsend did not become president by being aloof to market trends or failing to respond to them. He came up through the ranks at Chrysler seeing what the Hemi engine had done for Chrysler's market share and image, but the original Hemi was gone by the time he became president; he had inherited the Wedge era.

Chrysler began releasing some impressive multiple carbureted V-8s by the 1961 model year in both 383 and 413 "Maximum Special Police Packages." The hottest of these was the 375-horsepower, dual four-barrel carburetors mounted on a "Runner" manifold with a 10.0:1 compression ratio. As impressive as this engine was, it was designed for the street. If Chrysler was going to go drag racing, it needed a drag racing engine.

The *High and Mighty* built by the Ramchargers made its debut at the NHRA Nationals held in Detroit in 1959. It set the C/Altered record and won its class. It also redefined the possibilities of tunnel-ram intake manifolds and megaphone exhausts. *DaimlerChrysler Corporation*

Coupled with this fact were the tales of woe Townsend would hear from his two teenage sons at the dinner table. This particular vignette has taken on the mantle of legend at Chrysler, and the exact words spoken between father and sons were never recorded, but the gist of it is this: Townsend's sons frequented Woodward Avenue and their reports back to their father were not good. Dodges and Plymouths were not represented in the stoplight duels that took place, and the Chrysler 300 was an old man's car. Chrysler did, in fact, have some pretty hot engines by 1961, but that fact wasn't filtering down to the street level. Lynn Townsend set about to change Chrysler's image on both the street and strip.

The Max Wedge 413

Townsend was not alone in his belief that the performance image of Dodge and Plymouth in all quarters had to change. Bob Rarey was another. He had joined Chrysler in 1942 and became assistant chief engineer of engine design in 1955 when Mel Carpentier died. By the early 1960s, Rarey had become chief engineer in

The Ramchargers raced the *High and Mighty* for two years. In 1961, the group received Dodge division support through Frank Wylie in Public Relations. They were given a Dart Phoenix with a 413 equipped with the dual four-barrel tuned-runner Daytona package. Then the Ramchargers went to work on the engine. Compression was bumped to 13.5:1, Tom Hoover made and installed the tube headers, and other modifications were done. This car won the match race against Don Nicholson's 409 at the 1961 NHRA Nationals with Al Eckstrand behind the wheel. *Roger Huntington Collection*

Chrysler released its maximum performance 413 for sanctioned drag racing in 1962. Dodge called its 413 the 413 Ramcharger, and Plymouth, the Super Stock 413. Racing enthusiasts called it the Max Wedge 413. It was available with standard 11.0:1 compression, or optional 13.5:1 compression. *Roger Huntington Collection*

These were the heavy-duty components that went into the 413 Ramcharger and Super Stock 413. The cylinder heads featured 25 percent larger parts compared to stock. With 11.0:1 pistons, the engine was factory rated at 410 horsepower.
Roger Huntington Collection

charge of engine, transmission, and engine electrical. When asked by Bob Anderson to take on the added responsibilities of racing-engine development at Chrysler, Rarey balked. However, he agreed to set up a separate group, apart from production-engine design, to handle this activity. That responsibility would fall on Tom Hoover's shoulders.

Hoover was in constant contact with others at Chrysler who were in agreement that a strong high-performance program had to be implemented if Chrysler wanted to shake off its dowdy image, offer exciting cars, and increase its market share.

"There were," says Hoover, "encouragements from Bob McCurry over at Dodge, certainly Gale Porter, Frank Wylie from Dodge public relations, and Jack Shirapar. Jack was our champion. He was the guy who could carry the message from the trenches—from North Woodward and Detroit Dragway—right upstairs. Jack knew what had to happen out on North Woodward. When Mr. Townsend, by whatever mechanism, let it be known that it was time to change the image of our product, it was just like having the clouds separating and the sun shining through.

"Engineering Division was given the directive to get some cars out there that would do the job," Hoover recalls. "I was made engineering coordinator for the whole Engineering Division for the race program. A program began in October 1961 to release in the standard-size cars performance packages based on the RB engine, which at the time was 413 cubic inches. I'll never forget that because Mr. Townsend himself had signed the project request to initiate it, that was like walking into engine design with a blank check."

Chrysler's Central Engineering department was immediately tasked with designing an engine to withstand the rigors of drag racing. The Ramchargers had already learned a great deal from their racing in 1960 and 1961 and were already thrashing a 413 with numerous performance enhancements when the racing 413 engine program was launched. During the summer of 1961, the Ramchargers raced a '61 Dodge with a 413 that had received the Ramcharger treatment. The car competed at the NHRA Nationals in Indianapolis in SS/S class and made a very impressive showing.

The longhorn, cross-ram intake manifolds used on the dual four-barrel carburetor Wedges provided superb torque, but high-rpm horsepower was needed for drag

The Max Wedge 413 was short-lived, replaced in 1963 by the 426 Ramcharger and Super Stock 426. Displacement was increased to coincide with changes in allowable displacement by the sanctioning bodies. Appearance was identical; the difference could be discerned by the labels on the valve covers.

strip competition. Testing and racing resulted in a short-ram one-piece aluminum intake manifold with 15-inch runners, running from the carburetor mounting plate to the intake valves. The two Carter carburetors were staggered atop this manifold to achieve the required internal runner length for maximum horsepower above 4,000 rpm.

The cylinder heads were also new, with 25 percent larger ports, no heat crossover passage, and a strengthened deck structure for more positive head gasket sealing needed for the much higher compression ratios. As added insurance, stainless-steel cylinder head gaskets were used. In addition, the heads were lightened by removing cast iron from areas of the head where it wasn't needed. The intake valves were enlarged to 2.08 inches. The exhaust

valves were also bumped up in size, to 1.88 inches, and the cylinder bores of the engine block were notched to provide the necessary clearance. In place of the standard stamped steel rocker arms, malleable cast-iron rockers designed for marine applications were used; these rockers had a screw adjustment for setting valve lash. Dual valve springs were incorporated with heavy-duty machined steel retainers.

Little was left untouched within the short-block assembly of this 413. This engine used, of course, mechanical rather than hydraulic lifters. The new 300-degree duration camshaft incorporated a hefty .510 valve lift. The stock pushrods were discarded, and beefed-up steel pushrods were designed. The stock

Nothing was under the hood but full-race, high-compression horsepower. These factory cars were the terror of the quarter-mile strip in the early 1960s. They were too unruly for the street, but that didn't keep some owners from venturing out onto Woodward Avenue or Hollywood Boulevard at night.

This was the view from the driver seat. A Hurst-Campbell three-speed manual shifter was ordered for this, but the heavy-built TorqueFlight automatic transmission could be ordered instead. The engine worked beautifully with either transmission.

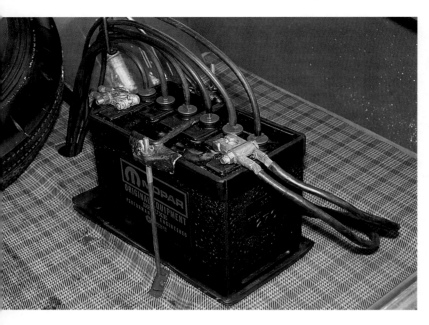

The battery in these factory drag cars was relocated to the trunk to put just a bit more weight on the rear wheels.

1963 was a very good year for the Ramchargers. In fact, they were so good they often squared off against each other in national events. Dodge ran this ad in *Hot Rod* showing Jim Thornton and Herman Mozer (upper photo) battling for S/SA honors at the NHRA Nationals at Indianapolis. Thornton won. In the bottom photo, Al "Lawman" Eckstrand squared-off against Mozer for Top Stock Eliminator. Mozer won with an E.T. of 12.22 seconds.

forged-steel connecting rods were retained, but were magnafluxed to check for microscopic cracks. Forgedtrue supplied the pistons; the standard compression ratio was 11.0:1 for Special Police Pursuit duties, or 13.5:1 for strictly sanctioned drag racing use. The forged-steel crank was flame hardened and the journals shot-peened. Harder F-77 tri-metal main bearings were part of the package. The Ramchargers even designed a new oil pan with deeper sump that incorporated anti-slosh baffles. Perhaps the wildest pieces to be bolted to this engine, visually speaking, were the new cast-iron headers. Indeed, they were headers and not exhaust manifolds. The individual runners swept up, over, and then down with a generous 3-inch exhaust. Even the under-car exhaust system was carefully designed with crossover pipe and removable blockoff plates. When these blockoff plates were removed at the strip, the 3-inch diameter header pipes were totally unrestricted, and close to 70 horsepower was unleashed in the process.

In testing the engine on Chrysler's dynamometers, the high-performance 413 generated 410 horsepower at 5,400 rpm running the 11.0 pistons, and 420 horsepower at 5,400 rpm running the 13.5 pistons. However, the engine was designed to operate up to 6,500 rpm! Chrysler truly had an awesome engine on its hands. Lynn Townsend had been waiting patiently to have a look at the first mule once the car had been sorted out.

"The first of the cross-ram, eight-barrel 413 Wedge cars we got running," says Hoover, "was a white Plymouth two-door. Mr. Townsend himself, the chairman of the board, came out to the Chelsea proving grounds one day and I took the car out there. He stood out there at the east-west

straightaway and had me make a pass with the car so he could listen to the car and watch it. He had the ability to understand what it meant, and I'll go to my grave believing it was his two teenage boys who put that sparkle there."

Townsend was all smiles. Here was the engine and the car that were going to take the wind out of the sails of General Motors and Ford. When installed in 1962 Plymouths, it was referred to as the Super Stock 413; in Dodges it was called the Ramcharger 413. The Max Wedge moniker was never officially attached to the engine, but was an informal label the engine acquired over the years, and the name stuck.

Knowing that publicity was everything, Chrysler made sure it made cars available to the automotive press. *Motor Trend* was one of the first magazines to wring out a pre-production car, a 1961 Dodge Dart equipped with the Ramcharger 413. The lucky editor to

Jim Thornton and Herman Mozer (979) coming off the line in S/SA class.

Some days you win

Mozer and Al Eckstrand in final run for Top Stock Eliminator title.

Some days you lose

check the car was none other than Roger Huntington. The Ramchargers agreed to meet Huntington at Central Michigan Dragway in Stanton, Michigan. There were actually four cars there when he arrived, and he was greeted by Jim Thornton, Al Ekstrand, Tom Hoover, and Mike Buckel. All the cars came with the 410-horsepower 413. The *Motor Trend* test car was equipped with 3.91 rear gears and TorqueFlight automatic transmission. For comparison, there was a second car with three-speed manual transmission with 4.30 rear end, a third car with the three-speed manual and 4.56 rear end, and finally a car with TorqueFlight automatic and 4.30 rear end.

The *Motor Trend* test car, driven by Warren Tanzola and Wally Chandler, got a best E.T. of 13.44 seconds doing 109.76 miles per hour. The second car with three-speed stick and 4.30 rear end driven by Jim Thornton did 113.92 miles per hour, tripping the lights in 12.97 seconds. The third car with 4.56 rear end driven by Tom Hoover and Mike Buckel got a best E.T. of 13.30 seconds doing 112.51 miles per hour. Al Eckstrand, driving his car with 4.30 rear end and TorqueFlight did a best of 13.12 seconds at 111.11 miles per hour.

Writing in the August 1962 issue of *Motor Trend*, Huntington waxed eloquent: "Dodge's new 'Ramcharger 413' package gives more performance per dollar than any other factory-assembled car in America. And, if present trends continue, by the end of the summer it will be right at the top of the stock car heap—*regardless of price.*"

And just what was the price of admission to become a hero at your local drag strip? The package was a mere $374.40 on top of the base list price of a Dodge Dart equipped with the standard V-8 with TorqueFlight transmission. The bright red booklet that accompanied the car, "Your New RAMCHARGER Dodge," had this to say to the new owner:

"You have just purchased one of the finest automobiles ever produced on an American assembly line for maximum performance, the 413 Cu. In. Ramcharger powered Dodge. This car has been designed and developed to satisfy the specific desires of the performance enthusiast who demands peak acceleration ability." The *Plymouth Service Bulletin*, dated July 25, 1962, stated, "The 413 cu. in. engine with the 11 to 1 standard compression ratio and 13.5 to 1 (optional at extra cost) compression ratio, is designed for maximum acceleration from standing start. This makes it ideally suited for Special Police Pursuit work and competition driving." Of course, what went unmentioned, specifically, was street racing; but then, one could consider that competition driving—yes? Fact was, the Ramcharger 413 and Super Stock 413 cars hit the strip *and* street. Boy—did they!

"Those cars hit the drag race scene like an H-bomb," Hoover remembers. "They just blew everything else away by 8 to 10 miles an hour. I think that there's no question that the experience that all the Ramchargers had gained the preceding three or four years at the drag strip and North Woodward was fundamental to making those cars successful." Dick Maxwell remembers the tremendous impact of these cars and the excitement they generated for Chrysler.

With each factory drag car, Dodge and Plymouth included owners manuals specifically written with the racing engine in mind. The manuals issued by Dodge for its 413 and 426 Ramcharger V-8s gave information, advice, and specifications to ensure the cars maintained peak performance.

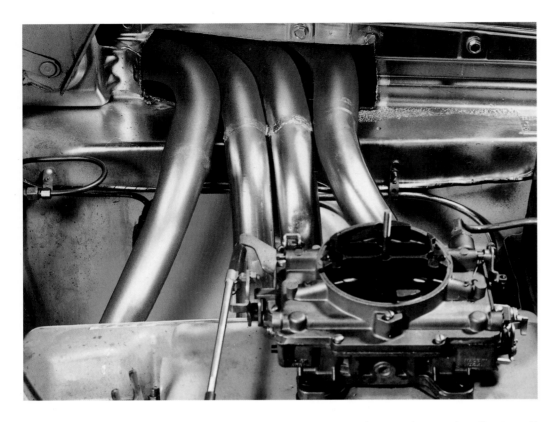

To extract as much horsepower as possible from the 426 Ramcharger, Dodge released these exotic tuned headers. They required cutting a 3.5x11.5 opening in the inner fenders. Tube diameter was a whopping 2.0 inches. *Roger Huntington Collection*

"We went out there with our 413s," Maxwell remembers, "and used them as our image cars on the drag strips and did *very* well with them. That was our first real racing venture—those 413s we built in 1962. And the guys took them out on the street and did even *better*. This stirred up interest in the 383. As a result, we sold a lot of 383s, but not too many 413s because the

413s were really more than most guys could handle. The thing was pretty close to a race car in those days, and it was a real handful on the street. Those things—in '62, '63, and '64 until we brought the 426 Hemi out—were absolutely unstoppable on the street."

The Ramchargers made impressive showings around the country with the Ramcharger 413, and many independent racers who took delivery of Chrysler's first factory drag cars were setting records with them as well. According to NHRA official records established with the Ramcharger 413 included a 12.71 E.T. set by Dick Ladeen in SS/S, a 12.50 E.T. set by "Maverick" in SS/SA, the Golden Lancer setting an A/FX record of 12.26, and a breathtaking 8.59 E.T. set by Jim Nelson in AA/D. At Fresno, California, the "Flying Dutchman" set a strip E.T. record of 12.42 seconds in SS/A doing 114.40 miles per hour. Ramcharger Al Eckstrand put down Pontiacs from Hagerstown, Maryland, to Central Michigan Dragway, running 112.5 miles per hour/12.4 E.T. at Hagerstown and 112.50 miles per hour/12.80 E.T. at CMD. The story was very much the same around the country.

At the Fremont, California, Drag Strip on July 15, 1962, Tom Grove, driving the *Melrose Missile*, became the first racer to crack the twelve-second barrier in a production stock passenger car with factory option engine. Behind the wheel of the Plymouth with the 413 Super Stock engine, Grove clocked an 11.93-second elapsed time at 118.57 miles per hour. Grove had this to say about the 413 Super Stock engine:

In July 1963, Dodge and Plymouth released a Stage II version of the Max Wedge 426. Improvements included an improved cylinder head combustion chamber to relieve the intake valve and new intake ports, and enlarged primary bores to match the secondary bores in the intake manifold with new Carter AFB-3705S carburetors.

"I feel the Plymouth has the strongest potential in the Super Stock field—more horsepower and less car weight per cubic inch than any of the competition. The engine is a beauty—none better. And Plymouth is just starting to really tap its power. I have pulled numerous 430 rear-wheel horsepower readings on Melrose's 500-horse dyno. These are steady readings that have been held—not flash readings. The best that the 1962 *Missile* has pulled is a steady 450 rear-wheel horsepower. Can any of your slide rule mathematicians compute the actual shaft horsepower? Wow!"

The Ramchargers were having the desired effect and the performance image of both Dodge and Plymouth started to skyrocket. The production of the Max Wedge 413 was short-lived, however. It was replaced in 1963 with something bigger and better.

The 426-III, or Stage III of the racing 426, featured new cast-iron exhaust manifolds with improved flow and tuned length incorporating a Tri-Y header design and numerous other improvements. A new four-speed manual transmission was available, in addition to the three-speed manual and the automatic. The engine became available in August 1963. *Roger Huntington Collection*

In 1964, the Max Wedge 426 was replaced by the 426 Hemi. Dodges and Plymouths could be ordered with lightweight aluminum front end sheet metal and other aluminum components. This 1965 Dodge Coronet is one of those Hemi-powered factory lightweights.

The Max Wedge 426

Chrysler chose to take advantage of rule changes regarding maximum displacement by the sanctioning bodies for both drag and stock car racing. This was achieved by enlarging the bore in the 413 to 4.25 inches, resulting in 426 cubic inches. The Carter 3447 carburetors used on the 413 were initially carried over on the 426, according to a Chrysler Plymouth Service Bulletin issued in December 1962. In fact, virtually all other specifications and parts, other than pistons and rings, were carried over also. The rated output of the Dodge Ramcharger 426 and Plymouth Super Stock 426 also remained at 415 and 425 horsepower according to compression ratios.

The Ramchargers, however, were spending many hours in the Highland Park dyno labs and various drag strips developing the 426 further. By the middle of 1963, the Stage II, or 426-II in official corporate identification, made its appearance. The entire top end was new and improved. The previous carburetors were replaced with Carter AFB-3705-S carburetors with larger 1-11/16 inch primary bores, matching the size of

The interior of the 1965 racing package cars was Spartan, and that was the idea. Even the existing seat track assemblies were replaced with lightweight, fixed mounts. This Coronet was fitted with the TorqueFlight automatic transmission, a good match for the Hemi.

The 426 Hemi made the factory drag cars formidable competitors in the hands of amateur and professional racers alike. The Hemi would go on to become the premiere drag racing engine by thousands of racers with a longevity marked in decades, not just years. In short, the Hemi became a legend.

the secondaries. The primary throttle bores of the short ram intake manifold were enlarged to match. New air cleaners with larger mounting plates were installed. The Ramchargers had also been working to improve the air-flow of the cylinder heads. The combustion chamber adjacent to the intake valve was relieved, and a portion of the intake port above the valve seat was relieved an additional 15 degrees to improve flow. Horsepower ratings remained unchanged at 415 and 425 respectively—but performance was dramatically improved!

The big payoff for the 426-II Max Wedge occurred at the 1963 NHRA Winternationals. The previous year "Dyno" Don Nicholson had won the Winternationals running his 426 to a winning 12.84 E.T. at 109.22. At the '63 Winternationals, Ramcharger Al Eckstrand proved the 426-II Max Wedge's worth by driving through the timing lights at 115.08 miles per hour, tripping the Chrondecks in 12.44 seconds and seizing the Stock Eliminator title. Before the enthusiastic crowd, a jubilant Eckstrand was congratulated by NHRA president Wally Parks himself. When Lynn Townsend got word of the National title win, he was grinning from ear to ear. It was the best form of advertising; Chrysler built winning race cars, and you could buy one and win too.

The Ramchargers had not just confined themselves to engine development. During 1963, an aluminum front-end package became available. This included the front fenders, hood with hoodscoop, and other parts that reduced the weight of the cars equipped with the 426 Max Wedge by nearly 150 pounds. This was a substantial weight reduction that would be reflected in the elapsed times at the strip.

Development continued on the Max Wedge 426 to extract the maximum amount of power from this potent engine. Chrysler engineers found they could lower the lofty 13.5:1 compression ratio to 12.5:1 with no loss of performance. This had the added benefit of extending engine life. The 426-III still had the same factory rating of 415 and 425 horsepower. The cylinder heads were refined by eliminating the aluminum pedestals for the rocker arm shafts with pedestals cast into the heads.

Ramcharger Herman Mozer displayed the 426-III's winning potential at the 1963 Nationals by surpassing Haydin Proffitt's 1962 winning time of 12.83 at 113.92 miles per hour by racking up a 12.22 second E.T. at a blistering 116.73 miles per hour. In fact, 1963 was one big massive win for Chrysler on the drag strip,

whether the drivers were Ramchargers or privateers behind the wheel of their own Dodge Ramcharger or Plymouth Super Stock.

During the 1960s, Dodge had a news bureau in New York City. *Cars* magazine also had its editorial offices there. It was a heady decade for the magazine and its editor Martyn "Marty" L. Schorr. The magazine would often gets calls for the editorial staff to check out the latest wheels from Dodge. One day, in the spring of 1964, Schorr got a call from Dodge public relations in Manhattan informing him there was a rather special car they would like the magazine staff to check out for a week or so. All Schorr had to do was go over to the Chrysler West Side service center to pick the car up. No specifics on the car were given over the phone, so it was a couple of days before Schorr made it across town to the Chrysler dealer.

When Schorr walked into the service center, there was a 1964 Dodge Ramcharger Candy Matic with 426

At the start of the 1964 Daytona 500, Paul Goldsmith (left) held the pole position with Richard Petty to his immediate right. By the end of the race, Petty took the checkered flag and fellow-Plymouth driver Goldsmith was third. The 426 Hemi had proved its worth the first time out.

Paul Goldsmith, in his No. 99 Hemi-powered Plymouth, is shown on his way to a third-place win at the 1964 Daytona 500. The engines that went into the winning cars had been assembled just weeks before using strengthened and recast blocks. Until the Daytona race, the blocks were unproven in stockcar competition. *Roger Huntington Collection*

The 426 Hemi also successfully competed in USAC (United States Auto Club) competition. Norm Nelson drove his No. 1 Plymouth GTX to numerous wins and top-place finishes during the mid-1960s. *Roger Huntington Collection*

Stage III that had been displayed at the New York Auto Show Coliseum. With its wild striped paint job and *"Ramchargers"* emblazoned across both sides of the car, it was the ultimate in high-profile high performance. Schorr realized the Dodge News Bureau was having some fun with the editors at *Cars*.

This was a factory-built drag car, not a street vehicle. As page one of booklet "1964 Dodge 426 Ramcharger" stated in bold text: "THE 1964 RAMCHARGER 426 ENGINE IS DESIGNED FOR USE IN SUPERVISED ACCELERATION TRIALS. IT IS NOT RECOMMENDED FOR GENERAL EVERY DAY DRIVING BECAUSE OF THE COMPROMISE OF ALL-AROUND CHARACTERISTICS WHICH MUST BE MADE FOR THIS TYPE OF VEHICLE."

The editors were a bit perplexed about what to do with this embarrassment of high-performance riches. The car was due to be displayed at the New York World's Fair so the car could not be trucked out to the drag strip, even though that was the car's element. Schorr decided to have the timing adjusted as much as possible, drain the tank of its low-octane fuel, and put the highest octane gas he could get in the tank. Still, driving the car around the streets of Manhattan produced more than its fair share of stalls and flameouts. The car had been shipped from Detroit to New York for the show without even being tuned for competition. It took several days to get the car sorted out before Schorr ventured over to Woodhaven Boulevard, New York City's answer to Woodward Avenue. They pulled into the local pasta joint and the restaurant and nearby vehicles emptied out immediately. Up went the hood, and down went the lower jaws. Talk about public relations—Dodge knew what it was doing!

The Chrysler "Skunk Works"

Chrysler engineering had scored a stunning coup with its development of the 426 Hemi for stock car racing and the engine was also designed to take over the duties of the Max Wedge 426 for drag racing. However, Chrysler's fledgling race group was faced with a corporate structure that was not experienced in building the race cars needed to get the job done. The development of the 426 Hemi for NASCAR and sanctioned drag racing made that clear. There was no convenient place to do prototype development cars at Highland Park. In order to do the job professionally and avoid corporate

DODGE DIVISION — CHRYSLER MOTORS CORPORATION

Dodge cools off Winter Nationals competition . . . again

Cool gas means hot runs. So drag racers pack intake manifolds with ice, as the famed Dodge Ramchargers are doing above. This gives the densest possible mixture per cylinder.

But gas was the only cool thing about Dodge at the '65 American Hot Rod Association Winter Nationals at Bee Line Dragway, Arizona. New '65 Dodge Coronets, specially equipped for drag race competition, took Top Stock Eliminator—a class Dodge also topped in '64. They walked away with Mr. Stock Eliminator and turned low elapsed time and top speed among stock cars.

Mike Buckel won Top Stock Eliminator title in the Ramchargers' Dodge, blasting to a 10.73-second elapsed time and 132.15-mph top speed during eliminations. Bud Faubel and his "Hemi-Honker" roared through one of the fastest 16-car fields in stock car dragging history to become Mr. Stock Eliminator. Other competition-equipped Dodges took three of the four major stock class wins.

How's that for openers in a new season? Can't hardly beat it with a club. Like you can't hardly beat Dodge's great way of going . . . and going . . . and winning. Try it.

Hot '65 Dodge

JUNE, 1965

The Ramchargers made excellent use of the 426 Hemi and continued their winning streak. In this ad, Ramcharger Jim Thornton is shown cooling down the intake manifold of his Hemi Coronet to improve the density of the incoming air charge. At the 1965 NHRA Winternationals, Ramcharger Mike Buckel took Top Stock Eliminator with a 10.73-second E.T. at a blistering 132.12 mph. Independent Bud Faubel in his "Hemi Honker" seized Mr. Stock Eliminator.

red tape that would slow progress, a separate facility had to be found.

"There was really no place inside engineering where we could do the sort of things we wanted to do," Maxwell says. "We needed a specialized facility where we could do prototype race cars, or whatever."

After some searching, Hoover felt he had found the ideal building: a former Pontiac dealership on Woodward Avenue. Its location was appropriate, too. Woodward Avenue had become the street to cruise—and race. It had developed a mystique and was known to enthusiasts all over the country. Still, what went on behind the garage doors had to remain secret—until the appropriate time.

Dan Mancini was put in charge of running Chrysler's new race shop. He had joined Chrysler in 1953 as a driver and mechanic and quickly moved on to the dynamometer lab. Later, he was responsible for engine buildup for the engines that were tested in the lab. This was followed by work in the carburetor lab. While working there he learned of the Ramchargers and became involved.

The Ramchargers didn't get all the glory during the 1960s. A friendly corporate rivalry evolved with the Plymouth Golden Commandos. In 1965, Dodge and Plymouth built a small number of Altered/Factory Experimental cars to compete in A/FX class. These cars had an altered wheelbase and used exotic Hemi engines. Here, Golden Commando Al Eckstrand pilots his A/FX Plymouth down the quarter-mile.

While the 1968 Dodge Charger was indeed sleek, the deeply recessed grill and tunnel backlight created severe lift, drag, and turbulence on NASCAR super speedways. Wind tunnel testing resulted in installing a flush grill and rear window, boosting the car's top speed. Homologation rules required a minimum production of 500 units, and the Charger 500 was born. Bobby Allison is shown behind the wheel of his 1969 Charger 500.

The race garage was to become the automotive equivalent of the Lockheed "Skunk Works" in California where the aerospace company built its prototype jets and other classified projects for the U.S. military.

Mancini gathered a crew of five mechanics from within Chrysler with a keen interest in racing and skill in engine building and car fabrication. These were Roger Lindamood, Larry Knowlton, Fred Schrandt, Dan Knapp, and Ted Macadaul. "This was where we built the racing mules for testing," Mancini says, "whether they were for drag racing or NASCAR. Tom Hoover and Jim Thornton supervised the drag cars and Larry Rathgeb handled the stock cars."

The men at the Woodward Avenue garage were given the task of drag car development for the 1965 racing season, coupled with transitioning from the 426 Max Wedge to the 426 Hemi. For 1965, this took the form of two vehicles, one mild and the other wild. Mild consisted of the factory Super Stock offering, but with changes from what was offered in 1964. The NHRA changed the rules again for the upcoming 1965 season, and cars raced in Super Stock now had to have steel body panels and the cars had to weigh a minimum of 3,400 pounds. The Ramchargers on Woodward shortened the wheelbase of the Coronet from 117 to 115 inches to improve weight transfer. This could be done without

No sooner had the Charger 500 been released than development work began on boosting the Charger's top speed even further. By installing an aerodynamic nose and a rear spoiler—actually a combination of horizontal and vertical stabilizers—drag coefficient was reduced, top speed significantly increased, and high-speed stability improved. Dodge raced the car into production for competition in 1969. This 1969 Charger Daytona was one of just over 500 built.

The vertical stabilizers on the 1969 Daytona were cast aluminum, while the horizontal airfoil was an aluminum extrusion. These same pieces were used on the Daytona for NASCAR competition. The height of the spoiler was necessary so the trunk lid would open!

Standard engine on the 1969 Charger Daytona was the four-barrel 440 Magnum rated at 375 horsepower. Bench racers liked to kick around theoretical top end for the street Daytona. For the highest top speed possible, a low numerical axle ratio was required.

altering the sheet metal; all that was required was equipping the car with correspondingly shorter driveshaft and modifying rear spring attachment to the frame. The 426 Hemi for the drag cars (street production would not commence until the 1966 model year) featured a cast-magnesium short-ram manifold, cast-aluminum cylinder heads, and other weight-saving pieces. The race mule that emerged sported a 50/50 weight balance, which was better than the 1964 offering even with aluminum front end. Production orders were issued to Chrysler's Lynch Road assembly plant where the super stock factory drag cars were to be built as in previous years.

On the wild side of the drag car equation was the very limited production of the A/FX, or factory experimental cars. This was a radical push by the Ramchargers to produce a weight-saving and weight-transfer vehicle. This was a Coronet two-door hardtop with the rear wheels moved 15 inches forward and the front wheels moved 10 inches forward, with a final wheelbase of 110 inches. The front fenders, front bumper, hood, doors,

dashboard, and rear trunk lid were fiberglass, manufactured by Plaza Fiberglass Manufacturing Co. in Dearborn, Michigan. The car also featured a redesigned front K-member that saved 25 pounds over the stock unit. The pieces were also available separately for those who wanted to modify their own vehicles. All this effort was expended to keep the car at 3,200 pounds, the minimum allowable weight mandated by the NHRA for A/FX class cars.

One of the most successful of the privateers in drag racing on the East Coast during the early 1960s was Bud Faubel of Chambersburg, Pennsylvania. He was the owner of a Dodge dealership there. He spread the banner of Shivley Motors up and down the eastern seaboard with his winning Dodges. Running under the nickname "The Honker," he won more than 180 class trophies and earned another nickname: Mr. Stock Eliminator, after the class he virtually dominated for 10 years.

With that kind of winning record, he had no difficulty securing one of the six factory A/FX Hemi Dodges built. These cars, delivered "in the white," were custom painted by the racers themselves. Faubel painted his car, #708, the familiar two-tone color scheme with his "The Honker" and duck logo on the doors. At the 1965 AHRA Winter Championships held in Phoenix, Arizona, Faubel took Mr. Stock Eliminator honors, while Mike Buckel in the Ramchargers' 1965 Coronet won the Top Stock Eliminator class. In fact, Chrysler's factory drag cars were doing well all over the United States during the 1965 season. However, the Ramchargers and other privateers were getting considerable grief from the single overhead cam (SOHC) 427 Mustangs also competing in A/FX. In fact, it was the SOHC 427 Mustang that took the A/FX title at the NHRA Nationals at International Raceway Park in September of 1965. However, Mopars were king in the Super Stock and Super Stock Automatic classes.

With the bruising Chrysler took with its foray into the exotic A/FX class in 1965, not to mention the expense in developing such a car and the limited financial return, Chrysler chose to stick to its efforts where it could be most successful, Super Stock. The 426 Hemi was proving its worth in drag racing, and after NASCAR got over its fit of jealous rage over the 426 Hemi in 1965, the Hemi Dodges and Plymouths returned to circle track racing in 1966. The Hurst Hemi Under Glass was a car Chrysler engineers felt was better left to the privateers, but it did get the creative Ramchargers thinking. When the newly designed Barracuda was introduced for 1967, it was a fortuitous event for the Ramchargers in particular and Chrysler in general.

The 1968 Super Stock Program

When the second-generation Barracuda was designed, it was established that the car would accept both small-block and big-block Wedge V-8s. Since a 440 was no bigger in overall dimensions than a 383, fitting the biggest-block Wedge Chrysler made into the car for drag racing purposes could be accomplished. But the 440 Wedge was not Chrysler's drag engine, the 426 Hemi was. It got Ramcharger and engineer Dick Maxwell putting pencil to paper, and the more he thought about it, the better he liked the idea of stuffing the Hemi into an A-body for Super Stock drags. After putting together a thorough presentation, Maxwell proceeded to pitch the idea to the race group.

The 1968 Super Stock program was the most ambitious Chrysler had ever undertaken, but the procedure for getting corporate approval and funding was the same as previous race car programs.

"We usually had to get sales division approval to do something like this," Maxwell says. "The race group at that time was in product planning. The first thing we would do was go to the product planners and sign them up in supporting the program. Then, we'd go to our leader, Bob Rodger, and get him behind it, and then the sales division and sell them on it, which wasn't hard because there was so much enthusiasm for racing in those days and drag racing in particular because of the musclecar boom. We were doing so well in that market. Once we had that done, it was a matter of scraping up money—which was sales division money—to pay for the program."

Since the A-body Dodge Dart and Plymouth Barracuda had similar chassis and body dimensions and clearances, it was felt only one prototype had to be built. A Barracuda was selected as the mule and shipped to the

Bobby Allison's Charger Daytona undergoes technical inspection prior to a race. Racing Daytonas did not have functioning headlights; they didn't need them. The appearance of pop-up headlights was molded into the racing Daytona's fiberglass nose cone. Production Daytonas featured vacuum-operated headlights.

Woodward Avenue garage. Bob Tarrozi was the mechanic and engineer who first worked out all the calculations on paper, then went about extensively modifying the car. He was looking to drastically reduce weight while strengthening the car to handle horsepower and torque levels for which the A-body was never designed.

"That car," says Maxwell, "was the mule—the test car. Everything was worked out in that car, and the purchase order contract was let to Hurst Performance, which opened up a facility in Hazel Park and built the cars for us."

Stock Barracudas and Darts were shipped to the Hurst facility where the cars were modified and the 426 drag Hemi installed according to Tarrozi's manual that had been compiled from the prototype. The cars were left in the gray primer so the racers could add their own color scheme. Dodge and Plymouth cranked up the public relations mill, getting the word out about Chrysler's new Super Stock drag cars.

"We had no trouble selling those cars," Maxwell remembers. "We originally scheduled 50 cars each, and we had so many orders we went back and built 25 more. We built 75 of each. I don't remember what the prices were but they were pretty reasonable, and they could be ordered through the dealers."

"I can remember," Hoover says, "at the time I argued that we should keep the Hemi in the B-body because that's where we sold to people, but I'm glad that Dick prevailed because by many standards, they are the world's nastiest, meanest production cars that people could go out and buy."

The biggest names in drag racing lined up to buy the Super Stock Barracuda or Dodge Dart. Sox & Martin ordered up a Barracuda, while Dick Landy naturally plunked down his money for a Dart. There were also lesser-known privateers who also ordered up their cars, and they never regretted it.

Back to the Ovals

With the stunning success of the Super Stock drag car program, efforts at the Woodward Avenue garage shifted back to stock car racing development. The first-generation Charger proved adequate on the high-banked super speedways, along with the Dodge Coronets and Plymouth Belvederes, using brute Hemi power. It was thought the even sleeker 1968 Dodge Charger would be a real asset during the 1968 NASCAR season, but in fact the car had to be sorted out aerodynamically.

Chrysler engineers were coming to the conclusion that they had taken horsepower as far as could be realistically developed from the 426 Hemi; if they wanted to boost top speed, the key lay in improved aerodynamics.

The Charger 500

Testing of the race Hemi Dodge Chargers and Road Runners at Chrysler's Chelsea, Michigan, proving grounds initially looked promising. John Pointer was test engineer at the proving grounds and recalled their findings.

"Our preliminary tests indicated the Charger and Road Runner were winners," Pointer says. "We got to the Beach and the cars were indeed running just about the way we expected to—183, 184 miles per hour, which was 3 miles per hour over the old lap record. The problem was the Fords were running 187 and the Mercurys were running 189. It was a very embarrassing situation."

As supervisor of the Special Vehicles Group, Larry Rathgeb put his finger on the problem: "When we took the '68 Charger to Daytona, we found we couldn't run

the thing very fast because we had a tremendous amount of front-end lift."

Not only did the Charger encounter severe front-end lift due to the deeply recessed grille area (the front end on the first generation Charger being virtually flush), they would also find dramatic turbulence in the backlight area between the rear roof pillars. That translated into drag. In its existing form, the Charger would prove to be uncompetitive. More power was not likely to be the answer. By Pointer's estimate, it would have cost roughly five million dollars to design and tool a new

Richard Petty had always raced Plymouths but the division did not offer an aerodynamic equivalent for him to race in 1969. Rather than drive at an aerodynamic disadvantage, he drove for Ford that year. Smarting from this loss, Plymouth started its own aero program using the Belvedere Road Runner, and the Superbird was the result. Petty got behind the wheel of the Superbird for 1970.

There were aspects of the Charger Daytona that could only be revealed on the test car at Chelsea. One of them was the nose cone opening for engine cooling; another was the chrome wind deflectors at the windshield A-pillars. When tunnel test revealed the high incidence of turbulence coming off the windshield, Reeker suggested the deflectors to smooth the flow and the results were verified at Chelsea. The front fender scoops evolved from testing at the proving ground to provide more tire clearance when the car was at speed and aerodynamic pressures were at their greatest.

During all track testing, Pointer had been limited to 120 miles per hour due to corporate rules in the interest of safety. In July 1969, the time had come to test the car at full race speeds. The track was closed one Sunday to permit the test. Together with Charlie Glotzbach and Buddy Baker, Pointer says, "We had a crew there that rode in cars over to the back side of the oval, which is almost five miles around. We split into two groups and we each walked every inch of the track to make sure there weren't any pebbles, stray parts—nothing on the track."

"At the time," Rathgeb says, "we were involved with Nichol's Engineering in Griffith, Indiana, and they brought up a Charger 500. We ran a Charger 500 against the Daytona to see what the differences would be." People were stationed every quarter-mile around the track, and an ambulance and firefighting equipment stood by. With Glotzbach at the wheel, the Daytona went significantly faster than the 500, hitting 194 miles per hour. It did not break the 200-mile-per-hour barrier because of engine problems. Nevertheless, it was a milestone day for Chrysler, and the nation. It was Sunday, July 20, 1969—the day the astronauts Neil Armstrong and "Buzz" Aldrin landed on the moon. The following Sunday, Chrysler was back to finish what it had set out to do. Glotzbach climbed into the Daytona and lapped the Chelsea track at over 204 miles per hour.

Pointer fondly remembers the experience of driving a race Daytona at Chelsea some weeks later: "It was the eeriest feeling. In about half a mile, shifting at 4,000 rpm, I was doing 135 miles an hour going into the north turn of our track and I thought, 'Wow, this thing is really unbelievable,' because it was so smooth. It was like driving an ordinary car and accelerating up to 60. I got on the back straightaway and there was not a soul in sight. I had on the helmet and had a full NASCAR rollcage, so I said, 'Okay, let's see what it's really like. You've never driven a car like this before and you may never get a chance to drive one again.' And that's when I heard the secondary on the four-barrel click in. In a very brief period, instead of being six lanes wide, our oval track seemed a quarter of an inch wide, and the south turn was coming at me like nothing I'd ever seen before in my life. I glanced down and I was doing between 180 and 185 and climbing. I looked back up again and my brain told me that the car would easily take that curve at 200, but my right foot said 'Not with me on board you don't.' The car was so effortless and smooth, it was more like flying."

Racing driver Buddy Baker had glowing praise for the Daytona: "That wing makes driving a whole new world," he said in an article for the 1970 Darlington Raceway Rebel 400 program. "The car is so stable you can't believe it at first. Normally, when you try to go under someone in a corner, the draft starts to pull the back end of your car around. Most people think that drafting is just the slingshot action when the rear car zips past the first. They ought to ride in a race car and find out. When you're drafting, you get quite a ride in a regular car. But the Daytona is just as stable in a draft as it is when it's all by itself on the track. With the Daytona, you just aim low and motor on by."

After the winning 1970 NASCAR season with Bobby Isaac behind the wheel of the red K & K Insurance-sponsored Daytona, Nord Krauskopf decided to break some longanding speed records with the same car. On the morning of September 12, 1971, the familiar No. 71 Daytona backed out of a transporter onto the Bonneville Salt Flats. Chief mechanic Harry Hyde and his crew prepared the car and the next day Isaac began breaking records. Over the space of five days, Isaac established 28 new marks in the USAC record book, including four wold records, and breaking Ab Jenkins' long-standing record. Today, the car is ensconced at the Talladega museum.

The Daytona at Speed Testing and Record-Setting

race engine, with no guarantee it would be any faster than the 426 Hemi.

"Basically, we decided that the key to it had to be in the aerodynamics of the cars," Pointer says. "We didn't see any way clear to find enough horsepower to make up the difference. We couldn't race what we made, we had to make what we wanted to race. This led to the development of the Charger 500."

Dale Reeker, then product planner, said there was an ulterior motive. "At that time, one of the things that triggered us was the fact that Bill France had allowed Ford a two four-barrel carburetor to compensate for the fact that their engine was a pushrod engine. The two four-barrel 427 Wedge high-rise Ford was a better engine when it was all said and done than the single four-barrel 426 Hemi. I think the original idea came out of the frustration of the way they were Mickey Mousing the rules, so we tried to improve the drag coefficient. I had enough knowledge about the vehicles to see a way to get high track performance, especially at Daytona, by aerodynamics, because we had gone as far as we could within the rule structure of improving the chassis and horsepower output of the engine."

To really define the extent of the high-speed aerodynamic problem with the 1968 Charger, wind tunnel tests had to be conducted. This was typically done with aircraft but rarely with cars. Chrysler had no facility, so after some searching, Wichita State University was contracted to test a 3/8-scale model of the car in the university's wind tunnel. The tests graphically confirmed what the Chrysler engineers had suspected.

"The tunnel backlight in the Charger was a source for a fair amount of concern," Reeker said, "because it caused the airflow over the roof and down over the deck lid to be turbulent. We could see there was a good chance to convert that surface into, essentially, a fastback in terms of how air would flow over it."

On the basis of discussions with the Special Vehicles Group and Product Planning, Pointer did a sketch in the Champion building at Daytona in December 1967 showing the car with a flush grille and backlight. It was calculated that such modifications would boost top speed by a considerable 5 miles per hour. At the speeds the Charger would race, the Hemi would have had to pump out 17 additional horsepower for every 1 mile per hour boost in speed.

The vice president and general manager of Dodge, Bob McCurry, did not like seeing his cars lose on the track and gave the green light to proceed with the required modifications. A clay mockup revealed the

Road Runner Superbird decals were placed on the vertical stabilizers and on the nose cone. The Road Runner holding a racing helmet was a clever touch.

The standard mill in the Superbird was the 375-horsepower 440. The 390-horsepower 440 six-barrel and 425-horsepower 426 Hemi were optional. This Superbird was ordered with the 440 six-barrel. The Air Grabber could not be ordered.

One of the most formidable drag racing partnerships during the 1960s and 1970s was the team of Sox & Martin. They were partial to Plymouths and especially liked the 426 Hemi. They campaigned the 1968 factory Super Stock Barracuda with great success. Here, Ronnie Sox is checking the throttle return spring on his SS/B Barracuda.

work involved. The Special Vehicles Group called in the specialists at Chrysler's Woodward Avenue garage to build a running prototype. While the flush grille could be borrowed from the Coronet and fitted with little problem, the flush backlight would now be carried back to the middle of the trunk lid. The trunk lid would have to be shortened, a custom rear window tooled up, and a plug to go below the window. When the car was ready, Bill McNulty, the high-performance supervisor at the Chelsea, Michigan, Proving Grounds scheduled the car for testing, which confirmed the modifications improved the Charger's aerodynamics and boosted its top speed several miles per hour.

NASCAR regulations required a minimum of 500 production units of a given body type in order to race that vehicle. Said Rathgeb, "NASCAR really didn't have rules that wouldn't allow us to run them. As long as we stayed within the limits of those rules, we felt we were doing the right thing."

It was here Reeker's background proved invaluable in getting the car into production. "I had recently come from the race group," he said. "I knew the people, I knew in detail how the sanctioning bodies operated and how the teams operated because I had done a fair amount of that kind of work. My new job in Product Planning allowed me to get the thing done."

Such a limited production car precluded the modifications being done at Dodge. Reeker contacted Vern Kopin, Charlie Shell, and Lou Wiser at Creative Industries in Detroit to handle the work. The NASCAR minimum requirement gave the car its name. Ronnie Householder, in charge of Chrysler's circle track racing, welcomed the Charger 500 with open arms. Dodge News Bureau cranked up the promotion mill and produced a slim brochure announcing to the unsuspecting *continued on page 156*

continued on page 156

The Cars that Never Were

In the war to race on Sunday and sell on Monday, there were some casualties—cars that never made it into production. To be precise, there were two cars that did not continue production into their second year. These cars were the Dodge Charger Daytona and the Dodge Challenger T/A.

While the Dodge Charger Daytona was racking up Grand National points during the later half of 1969, Dodge marketing believed it should also build a 1970 Daytona. To prepare the 1970 Dodge Scat Pack brochure, it brought together the racing greats of the day, each one to drive a specific model in the Scat Pack and give their impressions for use in the brochure. A great marketing idea. "Big Daddy" Don Garlits would drive the Challenger R/T. Dick Landy would evaluate the Super Bee Six Pack. Funny Car drag racer Charlie Allen is called on to give his impressions of the Swinger 340. USAC champion Don White got behind the wheel of the Charger R/T. And—Bobby Isaac is called on to give his impressions of the Charger Daytona.

When Dodge laid out the 1970 Scat Pack brochure, right there on the front page was a bright red Daytona. Anyone picking up the brochure would assume Dodge would offer the Charger Daytona for 1970 also, and that was initially the plan. Sadly, it never came to pass. NASCAR issued a new production quotient for cars to compete in Grand National competition. If manufacturers wanted to race it, they had to build not 500 units, but 2,000 units. Dodge division didn't think it could sell that many. In additon, Plymouth was selling its Superbird for 1970, and one winged warrior by Chrysler for 1970 was deemed enough. The 1970 Dodge Charger Daytona was never built.

The other car that was promised that never saw the light of day was the 1971 Challenger T/A. Flipping through the 1971 Scat Pack brochure, prospective buyers came across the Challenger T/A. Dodge said it was the "End of the road for the Do-It-Yourself Kit." Interestingly, the standard equipment listed the engine as a 340 four-BBL V-8. Apparently, the 340 Six Pack was replaced on the proposed 1971 model. The color photo of the bright yellow and black Challenger T/A was shown with a 1971 grille. Some say it was an artfully retouched shot of the 1970 T/A with the 340 Six Pack decal airbrushed out and the 1971 grille airbrushed in. Those holding this view point out the 1970 T/A shown in the two-page black and white ad and the 1971 T/A in the Scat Pack brochure are pictured in the rain. The clincher, they say, is that the tire inflation stems are in the identically same place in both shots, although the 1971 car is shown at a slightly different angle.

Those in the opposing camp say a prototype 1971 T/A was built and point out the 1971 car is shown in the color shot with a matching yellow elastomeric front bumper, while the 1970 T/A clearly has a chrome front bumper. It is indeed quite possible that Dodge did build a 1971 T/A and had the car photographed in the same location as the previous year. But the rain . . . the tire stem . . .

If ever a Chrysler X-Files is opened, these two cars will be among the first to be investigated.

CHALLENGER T/A
End of the road for the Do-It-Yourself Kit.

This is one car where the list of standard equipment is longer than the list of options. Hey, man, this isn't the beginning of something great, it's the driving end.

Big bias-belted skins in front, bigger ones in back. The good shift, Hurst style. Power discs up front; drums, heavy-duty, in the rear. Dual exhausts with low restriction mufflers, chrome side exit megaphones.

Challenger T/A. Just the way you'd do it yourself. If you had the time. And the money. Yeah, the money. Frankly, it would probably cost you more to do it yourself. So why bother with do-it-yourself dreams? Check out this bargain for the man who'd rather be moving than building.

Check out the Standard Equipment List carefully. You'll find that everything is in order. From engine to drive train, Dodge puts it all together for you.

STANDARD EQUIPMENT

340 4-bbl. V8 □ TorqueFlite automatic transmission or 4-on-the-floor fully synchronized manual transmission □ Fiber-glass hood with Fresh Air Pack □ Hood pins □ Special Rallye Suspension (includes rear sway bar, larger front sway bar, heavy-duty shock absorbers, increased camber of rear springs) □ Rear duck tail □ Low-restriction dual side exit exhaust with megaphones □ Tires: E60x15, front; G60x15, rear; raised white letters □ 15x7.0JJ wheels □ Power front disc brakes with special semimetallic pads; 10" rear drums □ 3.55 axle ratio—8¾ ring gear □ Vinyl front bucket seats □ Deep-pile carpeting □ Simulated wood-grained door trim inserts □ Locking flip-top gas cap □ Flush outside door handles □ T/A body side tape stripes □ Grille and deck panel blackout.

DODGE ANNOUNCES SCAT CITY
The '70 Dodge Scat Pack is road ready.

Scat City is anywhere competition is hot, keen, and sanctioned.

With the release of the new E-body in 1970, Sox & Martin built a new car powered by the drag racing Hemi, nicknamed "The BOSS." While successfully competing across America, the two also conducted performance clinics at Plymouth dealers for owners who wanted firsthand performance tips from the winning racers themselves. The clinics were always well attended.

The purpose-built 426 Hemi that went into Sox & Martin's 1970 'Cuda was an awesome machine and built to win. The massive Holleys on top of a tunnel-ram manifold worked to generate staggering horsepower without going the route of supercharging.

In 1970, Chrysler attempted to duplicate its success in NASCAR, USAC, and NHRA by competing in the SCCA Trans Am series. Plymouth contracted with Dan Gurney's All American Racers to turn its Barracuda into a Trans Am machine. The AAR 'Cuda was the result. Plymouth ran this ad to let everyone know there was a new member to the Rapid Transit System.

continued from page 151
world the sleek Charger was now even sleeker—and faster. Introduced as a 1969 model, the Charger 500 brochure read, in part:

> ". . . the Charger 500 is offered specifically for the high-performance race track. It is available only to qualified performance participants and is being built to special order on a limited production basis."

With this teaser, coupled with the car's rarity (knowing you would have the only one, in all likelihood,

in your county), enthusiasts flocked to Dodge showrooms to check out the new Charger to admire and, perhaps, to buy. At $3,843, it was less than $300 over the price of the Charger R/T. *Popular Hot Rodding* tested both a TorqueFlight-equipped and four-speed manual transmission Charger 500 in 1969, both with 3.23 rear cogs and the 426 Hemi under the hood. The automatic transmission–equipped car did the quarter-mile in 14.01 at 100 miles per hour. The four-speed car did much better, with the quarter-mile covered in 13.60

In outward appearance, the street AAR 'Cuda differed from the Trans Am car only by the lack of the front spoiler and the need for street wheels and tires. The large NACA hoodscoop was functional on both machines. Production of the car began in March 1970 and finished by April 17, 1970, to comply with SCCA qualification rules. Note the side-exhaust pipes.

seconds at 107.44 miles per hour, and this using street tires! Not bad for a car weighing over 4,100 pounds. Of course, drag testing the Charger 500 missed the whole point of the car. Still, more than a few Charger 500 owners in the midwestern states relished the car's high-speed capability.

No sooner had the Charger 500 debuted at Riverside Raceway in January 1969 with Al Unser behind the wheel than Ford got to work to make its cars even more aerodynamic as well. Within months, Ford and its Mercury division announced the Torino Talladega and Mercury Cyclone Spoiler in answer to the gauntlet thrown down by Dodge. Chrysler engineers had anticipated this, and had been working to improve their car's aerodynamics even further. While the Charger 500s battled the Talladegas and Spoilers at the start of the NASCAR season, Chrysler engineers were in the wind tunnel and on the Chelsea high-banked track.

The Charger Daytona

Valuable data had been gathered when the Charger 500 had been tested in the new Lockheed-Georgia wind tunnel and scale model tested at Wichita State. The Lockheed-Georgia wind tunnel had been constructed as the NASA Apollo program wound down. When Chrysler's space division approached the automobile division with the idea of testing cars, the race vehicles were the first to benefit. John Vaughn, an aerodynamicist at Chrysler's Huntsville, Alabama, facility, was tapped to run the studies.

"Chrysler was the first contract group to go into that new Lockheed tunnel," Vaughn said. "They had not even finished calibrating it. Lockheed had run some stuff with jet models on the centerlines, but you can't do that with a car, you've got to mount it on the floor somehow. We were running not only the first test in the tunnel, but a unique test."

The AAR 'Cuda was shod with E60x15 tires in front and G60x15 tires in the rear, the first time a Plymouth built for the street featured different front and rear tire sizes. The car featured a 340 six-barrel V-8, 3.55 or 3.91 Sure-Grip rear axle, close-ratio four-speed manual transmission, and special Rallye suspension. Manufacturer's Suggested Retail Price (MSRP) for the AAR 'Cuda was $3966.00.

The AAR 'Cuda was powered by a special 340 ci V-8 engineered specifically for this car. It used the same modified block used in Gurney's race cars, but the racing AARs used short-stroke cranks to stay with the 305 ci limit set by the SCCA. The engine also featured special cylinder heads and valvetrain, and unique triple two-barrel induction system. The engine was factory rated at 290 horsepower.

Rathgeb had asked Pointer and another aerodynamicist, Bob Marcel, to sketch up a design based on specific lift and drag figures. Said Pointer, "Shortly before the Christmas of '68, it turned out we more or less sketched the same thing, basically taking the 1970 Charger front end which had a loop bumper, and replacing the bumper with a streamlined fairing. This made it a fairly simple process to put the fairing on because we would use the same mounts."

At this point in the car's conceptual design, there was no rear spoiler. With the sketches in hand, Rathgeb took Reeker to meet with Bob Rodger, chief engineer of Chrysler Product Planning. Rodger had been the prime mover of the famed Chrysler 300, and had been instrumental in promoting other performance models. At the meeting, Rathgeb related, "Rodger said, 'Fine, if you can sell it to either one of the divisions, go ahead and do it, because it looks like somebody is working on a way to make us go faster.' So that's what we did. The Plymouth people didn't want to buy it. That was before Petty had left for Ford. The Dodge people did."

Added Reeker: "It was done purely and simply for one reason and that was to generate a vehicle with optimum aerodynamics to try to get back on top of the Ford guys in NASCAR. We treated it as a public relations project."

The Wichita State University 7x10-foot tunnel and Lockheed-Georgia 16x23-foot tunnel were again employed to develop what would become known as the Daytona. The goal was a 15 percent drag reduction over the Charger 500. In order to get precise baseline readings, a new, highly detailed 3/8th scale model of the 500 not only took into account the under-body features but actually duplicated the engine compartment flow through a scale radiator with a miniature fan driven by a small motor. Tests on this new model were begun at Wichita State. Working closely with the aerodynamicists, Bob Marcell at Wichita and Vaughn at Lockheed-Georgia, Pointer began full-size mockup work at the Chelsea proving grounds.

He used a Charger that had been raced by Bobby Isaac in the 1968 Firecracker 400, one of three Chargers that had been channeled 2 inches to lower the Charger's overall height. Predictably, NASCAR frowned on such bodywork and the car never raced again. The car was, in one sense, useless on the Grand National circuit, but it was a perfectly usable testbed, so Pointer chose this car as the development mule. Work on the nose began in January 1969. By the time of the Daytona 500 that year, Pointer had the first crude prototype completed, and he gave a Polaroid snapshot of the car to Reeker before he took off to the Daytona race.

"I sold it to Bob McCurry on the way back from Daytona where we got tromped by the Ford guys," Reeker said. "It was a pretty crude-looking device, but if you got back far enough it was a pretty mean-looking automobile. McCurry seized the thing as something he wanted to do."

Early testing of the mule at Chelsea proved they had completely upset the balance of the car as far as lift was concerned. If they tried to balance it with a rear deck spoiler, the spoiler would be much too large and would induce additional drag. The general consensus was that an inverted airfoil on struts would be more efficient and have the added advantage of being adjustable. Gary Romberg joined Marcel in wind tunnel testing and they later wrote an SAE paper on their findings.

"We worked in the tunnel with a wide range of shapes for the nose cone and the attitude of the car," says Romberg, "something we could do easier in the tunnel than John Pointer could do on the track. Then John would run on the track the most promising configurations and confirm what we found in the tunnel. The car's drag coefficient depended on the rear wing angle. As we pitched the wing, it changed the induced drag and the rear lift, and that changed the drag on the car."

Two nose cones, 9 and 18 inches long, and three front spoiler locations were evaluated specifically. The 18-inch nose with a front spoiler having a 5-inch chord mounted 13 inches back from the tip gave the best results. The rear deck horizontal stabilizer was a Clark Y inverted airfoil having a 7.5-inch chord and was adjustable from plus to minus 10 degrees. It was mounted 23.50 inches above the rear deck on vertical stabilizers having an NACA 0012 symmetrical airfoil section. The horizontal wing could have been lower but, as was pointed out by Reeker to the chagrin of all concerned, the trunk lid would have to open on the production car.

Much work went into the design and development of the opening for proper engine cooling while still maintaining clean aerodynamics. The size and shape of the opening were critical to ensure the engine did not overheat at race speeds. A 2-square-inch smaller opening than what was required was sufficient to cook the engine. The figure arrived at was 40 square inches.

Another detail was the chrome wind deflectors at the A-pillars. When tunnel tests revealed the high incidence of turbulence coming off the windshield, Reeker suggested the deflector to smooth the flow, and the results were verified on the Chelsea track.

The reverse-facing scoops on the front fenders have been the subject of heated debate for years. Many assumed they were placed there to relieve pressure in the wheelwells or perhaps cool the brakes. In truth, tunnel testing recommended pitching the car slightly forward. This was achieved by dropping the front over its suspension. In track testing, the tires rubbed against the top of the fenders. "We couldn't afford a new fender for the car," Pointer explained, "so we just cut a hole in the top, put this bulge on it, and away we went. In fact, we were very careful to make sure they didn't do anything aerodynamically."

Originally, the Daytona was conceived as a 1970 model but in mid-March 1969, word came down that it would debut at the inaugural race at Talladega, Alabama, on September 14th. Production was to commence June 10th and all 500 cars had to be delivered by September to qualify as 1969 vehicles. Suddenly, there was very little time.

The burden of the Daytona's production now fell on Reeker's shoulders. He had to coordinate the design, engineering, and manufacture of all the parts. Besides the nose cone itself, there were the retractable

Chrysler Plymouth issued special price and ordering information for the AAR 'Cuda, because the base car, engine, transmission, tires, T/A package, six-barrel carburetion, collapsible spare, Sure-Grip differential, and fiberglass hood had to be specifically listed using the correct order codes; the car was not a distinct model per se. This bulletin was issued to Canadian Plymouth dealers. The AAR 'Cuda pictured on the front showed large diameter, straight exhaust pipes that were not adopted for production.

Dodge also campaigned its Challenger in SCCA Trans Am competition in 1970. The production car was the Challenger T/A. Mechanically, it was identical to the AAR 'Cuda, but the fiberglass hood was unique to the Challenger T/A. The hoodscoop was designed to get above the boundary layer and into the flow of air.

headlights. The rear vertical stabilizers had to be cast and the horizontal airfoil had to be extruded in aluminum. There were details such as side marker lights and the need for a scissors jack because the nose couldn't support the car's weight. At the same time, Reeker had to make sure these parts were compatible with the race vehicles and kits to be patched through Bob McDaniel, responsible for giving Mopar racers the needed parts. Once again, Creative Industries handled the chores under a seemingly impossible deadline.

The 1969 Dodge Charger Daytona was introduced with a manufacturer's suggested list price of $3,993. Production Charger R/Ts were shipped to Creative Industries for conversion at the rate of seven per day. Production began in early June 1969. The first Daytona was shipped to a Kingston, Ontario, Canada, dealer on June 27, 1969. The 500th Daytona was shipped to Lafayette Dodge in Lafayette, Indiana, on September 8, 1969. It is reported three additional Daytonas were built by Creative Industries.

Even though the Daytona made a debut late in the 1969 NASCAR season, the cars, with their extended bullet nose and high rear wing, were real crowd-pleasers. With only a few races left in the season, Daytona drivers were still sorting the car out and learning its capabilities by the time the last checkered flag went down. The Talladegas and Cyclone Spoilers continued to be formidable contenders in these races, but 1970 would prove to be a far different story, with the addition of yet another winged warrior from Chelsea.

The Plymouth Superbird

When Richard Petty defected to Ford in 1969 to race the aerodynamic Torino Talladega instead of his usual Plymouth Belvedere, Plymouth realized it had made a mistake in not seizing the opportunity to build an aerodynamic stocker. Petty was not going to race at an aerodynamic disadvantage with a stock Belvedere and battle the likes of Daytonas, Talladegas, and Spoilers. Plymouth was now without its premier driver and the division knew the only way to lure him back was to have an aerodynamic car of its own. Without Petty, Plymouth won only two Grand National races in 1969.

Plymouth immediately got to work on the car. Thanks to the groundbreaking work on the Daytona, Plymouth's car took shape exclusively in the wind tunnel. The car had its own host of development problems. The front fenders of the Belvedere-based Road Runners

The Challenger T/A featured a noticeable rake due to the mixed aspect ratio tires and suspension setup. Dodge ran a double-page black-and-white ad in several magazines briefly listing the car's equipment and stated: "Challenger T/A. The car has never raced, yet it has more firsts than any other car in its class." The car did compete after the ad appeared, but did not do well in Trans Am competition.

were not suited to a nose cone fairing, so Plymouth chose to use Coronet fenders. However, when the nose cone was designed, there was a mismatch with the hood, so a plug had to be tooled to provide a reasonably smooth transition. The rear backlight also required special glass and a plug below it. Unlike the Daytona, Plymouth's car, to be called the Superbird because of its Road Runner roots, came with a mandatory vinyl roof in order to save on the cost of hand-finishing the bodywork.

Wind tunnel work produced two distinct differences from the Daytona. The air inlet on the Superbird was lower and larger, and the rear vertical stabilizers had greater area and were more swept back. Once again, Creative Industries performed the work, but during Chrysler's delay on the decision to build the car,

NASCAR once again shifted gears, requiring 2,000 units to be manufactured to qualify for racing. Also, the cars had to be built before January 1, 1970, to avoid having to conform to stringent new lighting laws with regard to retractable headlights. Creative Industries had to work feverishly to meet the deadline, but the last car was built and Richard Petty would be racing a Superbird for 1970, sporting the familiar blue paint scheme with 43 on the doors.

The Daytonas and Superbird really brought the gold home to Highland Park for Chrysler, justifying all the expense and work to develop these cars. On March 24, 1970, Buddy Baker became the first driver to average over 200 miles per hour in a Grand National race, and he did it in a Daytona at Talladega. The K & K Insurance

Daytona campaigned by Nord Krauskopf and driven by Bobby Isaac entered 47 of the 48 scheduled NASCAR Grand National and short-track races, winning eleven of them, and the Championship. On November 24th, Isaac bettered Baker's speed at Talladega, establishing the world's closed-course speed record of 201.104 miles per hour. Plymouth took the checkered flag 21 times with its Superbirds, but Petty won less than Isaac. However, of the eight super-speedway wins by Superbirds, Petty won five races. Dodge Daytonas won 17 of the Grand National races, capped by a stunning one-two-three sweep at the Darlington Southern 500, with Buddy Baker first in a Daytona, Bobby Isaac second in his Daytona, and Pete Hamilton third in a Superbird. Ford limped home with a mere six wins and Mercury with four. Combined, Dodge and Plymouth won 38 NASCAR events in 1970, the most successful season in Chrysler's history.

The Plymouth AAR 'Cuda and Dodge Challenger T/A

In the late 1960s, SCCA-sanctioned Trans-Am racing drew a great deal of attention from both car manufacturers and enthusiasts. Mark Donohue had raced Camaros and switched to, of all things, AMC Javelins. Parnelli Jones drove a Mustang, and Jerry Titus drove a Firebird to name but a few in the field. Both Chrysler divisions wanted to gain high visibility with their respective pony cars and the Trans-Am series was one of the best ways to do it.

To enter the series, Plymouth had to build 2,500 street versions of its racing 'Cuda. Plymouth contracted with Dan Gurney and his company, All American Racers, to build and race the Trans-Am 'Cuda. Plymouth then got in touch with Creative Industries to design and manufacture the fiberglass hood and rear spoiler that were to go on both the racing and street versions. The AAR 'Cuda was conceived to resemble the racing car as

Detail of the Challenger T/A shows the handsome, clean lines of the car. The rear spoiler showed T/A identification, and T/A appeared in the side tape stripe.

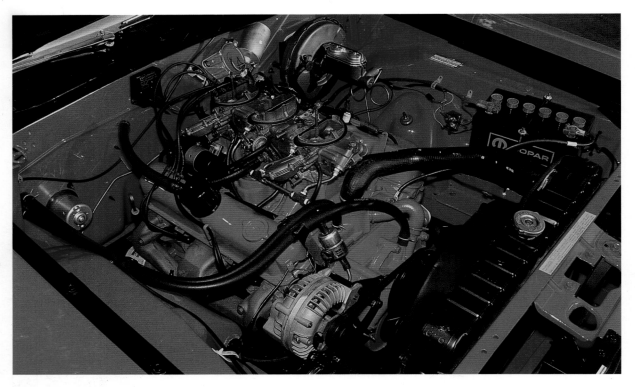

The 340 Six Pack installed in the Challenger T/A was one of the finest small-block high-performance V-8s engineered by Chrysler and made the car one of the most exciting cars to drive on the street. Some magazine editors felt the rated 290 horsepower was really closer to 1 horsepower per cubic inch.

closely as practicality, legality, and cost would allow. In February 1970, Plymouth announced the availability of the AAR 'Cuda by late March.

The sales code for the AAR 'Cuda was A53. The engine was unique to the car: a 340 cubic-inch block with reinforced main webs and filled pail rails, six-barrel carburetion using three two-barrel Holley carburetors on an Edelbrock aluminum intake manifold, with special cylinder heads and valvetrain. This engine was not available in any other Plymouth. The choice of either the TorqueFlight or four-speed manual transmission was standard. The car was equipped with a 3.55:1 rear axle ratio with Sure-Grip differential. A 3.91:1 axle ratio was optional. Front disc brakes were standard. The AAR 'Cuda suspension included special front and rear stabilizer bars and heavy-duty shock absorbers. Special heavy-duty springs raised the rear end to make room for a Trans-Am-type exhaust system with side outlets and to provide room for extra-large G60x15 rear tires. Front tires were E50x25. Plymouth's sharp Road Wheels were standard. Price for this superb car was $3,966.

The AAR 'Cuda's appearance on the street made heads turn. The grille, hood, cowl, and fender tops were flat black. Ornamentation included a black strobe stripe which ran the length of the car on both sides, ending at

the rear in an "AAR 'Cuda" decal with the "AAR" in the form of the Dan Gurney All American Racers crest in red, white, and blue.

These road rockets were a blast to drive on the street. The AAR 'Cuda was much better balanced than the big-block 'Cudas and, with its quick-ratio manual steering, was an exciting machine on twisty roads. The engine, conservatively rated at 290 horsepower, was more than adequate to propel the car.

The key driver behind the AAR 'Cuda on the Trans Am circuit was Swede Savage. Driving against the likes of Mark Donohue, one of the best racing drivers of that era, Parnelli Jones, truly a legend in his own time, and other experienced professionals, Savage was up against formidable competition. Although competent and driving an excellently engineered car out of Gurney's shops, Savage was outgunned, finishing the season behind Chevrolet, Ford, AMC, and Dodge.

The Dodge Challenger T/A was the product of Chrysler's road racing team manager Pete Hutchinson, and the race car was built by Ray Caldwell's Autodynamics.

Like the AAR 'Cuda, the Challenger T/A needed a distinctive hood that would also feed cool outside air to the six-barrel 340 V-8. Cold air induction was a proven performance booster, which is why hoodscoops were standard or at least available options on musclecars during the 1960s and early 1970s. Ramcharger Dale Reeker, inspired by a special scoop he saw on a jet aircraft, sketched up a design that was conceived to get above the hood's boundary layer and into the strong flowing layer of air. The design was a functional and aesthetic achievement. Creative Industries manufactured the hood and rear spoiler. The prototype Challenger T/A was evaluated at the Dodge design studios and approved for production.

For the racing T/A, Ray Caldwell turned to Keith Black to build the racing engine. The Chrysler 340 was de-stroked to the SCCA-dictated 305 cubic-inch limit, and Black performed his modification magic to extract 450 horsepower from the small-block Wedge. The production street engine was identical to the rugged V-8 that powered the AAR 'Cuda. Mechanically, the two street cars were virtually identical under the skin. The

Challenger T/A was an option pack on the Challenger V-8 models, costing $865.70. It could not be ordered on the convertible, but it is a tantalizing thought. A total of 2,399 Challenger T/As were built. The key driver for the Challenger T/A was Sam Posey. By season's end he had placed fourth behind the Javelins, Mustangs, and Camaros. Chrysler's Trans-Am efforts were disappointing to the company, but nevertheless was an excellent way to promote its cars and bring them to the attention of prospective buyers. Said Chrysler's Larry Shepard, "We felt we had better cars and wanted to show it. You have to compete, even if you don't win, to get attention."

By any standard, 1970 marked the apex of Chrysler's racing victories and amazing production car offerings. For 1971, NASCAR issued new rules requiring Chrysler's winged warriors to run de-stroked Hemi engines, which Chrysler refused to do, preferring to run 1971 stock bodied cars with the 426 Hemi engine. Thus, there was no Daytona or Superbird for 1971. The story was the same in Trans-Am; Chrysler pulled out of Trans/Am racing after 1970, so there was no Challenger T/A or AAR 'Cuda for 1971. However, Chrysler's superb Super Stock Barracudas and Darts continued to wreak havoc on the competition for years afterward.

Close-up of the 340 Six Pack induction system. The car cruised around town or on the highway on the center two-barrel, but on hard acceleration, the vacuum-operated front and rear carbs came on line. Smiles were hard to suppress.

CHAPTER SIX

The Resurgence of Chrysler Performance

As actual vehicle performance declined through the early seventies along with the market desire for musclecars themselves, Chrysler, like other manufacturers, became more committed to cleaning up emissions and improving vehicle safety. While street car performance declined, Chrysler never abandoned the amateur and semiprofessional racing enthusiasts out there. Having supported racers and street enthusiasts for many years, it felt it should continue to do so, even if Chrysler was no longer in the high-performance production car business.

In fact, Chrysler had already laid the groundwork during the musclecar heyday. Dick Maxwell, longtime Chrysler engineer and charter member of the Ramchargers, explains, "We built our race cars—production performance cars—on the assembly line. They were sold like regular production cars, and they were serviced as such. Now the mortality rate among these cars that were raced was much higher than our production cars, so there were never any parts. So we—the race group—laid out our own supply of parts. We had our own inventory of blocks, crank, pistons, heads, transmissions, and so forth. We serviced the guys we were supporting out of that. The other racers out there who were not factory sponsored came crying to us for parts because they couldn't get them out of the parts division. They were always back-ordered.

"So," Maxwell continues, "we began selling parts direct to customers. We'd ship parts C.O.D. or the guy would mail us a check and we'd send him a crankshaft or whatever, simply to keep these guys going. All the time, we were telling the parts division to stock and sell parts. This went on for a while. Finally, the parts division put together their Hustle Stuff program in 1969. The Hustle Stuff program ran well for a while, but finally it folded. Then, the race group finally got corporate approval to go into the parts business outside of the Chrysler parts division about 1971. We had our own warehouse, but distributed through the dealers. That's really how the Direct Connection program came to be. Joe Schulte, working on his own, came up with the Direct Connection name and put together the early advertising while moonlighting at home."

In an effort to expand its high-performance parts availability, corporate approval was again granted in the mid-seventies to sell Direct Connection parts through speed shops. Despite the decline of performance in the showroom, enthusiasm for keeping Mopars mighty on the street and the strips continued to grow, thanks to this program. Historically, Dodge and Plymouth never merely sold high-performance cars and parts, they offered advice as well. This advice in the form of bulletins was compiled into the Direct Connection Performance Book. Virtually all those bulletins

The Dodge Viper RT/ 10, introduced in 1992, let the world know Chrysler was back in the high-performance car business. The mighty all-aluminum V-10 engine instantly made it among the fastest and most powerful cars in the world. *Ron Strong*

The Viper RT/10 was conceived and built as a roadster with no roof or side windows. It followed the lines of the show car almost to the letter. *Ron Strong*

were painstakingly written and compiled by Larry Shepard, considered by many to be Chrysler's performance guru. In fact, Shepard has been involved in many of Chrysler's performance development programs, having joined the corporation in 1965 and moving to the race group in 1967. In 1987, the Direct Connection name was changed to Mopar Performance. This name was readily identifiable by every enthusiast and tied in with existing parts sold by Chrysler.

"Looking back over our shoulder," Shepard says, "that decision allowed us to become more visible in the performance marketplace and opened the door to very large dollars to allow capital-intensive programs."

During the late 1970s and throughout the 1980s, while GM continued building the Pontiac Firebird Trans Am and Chevrolet Camaro, and Ford its Mustang, Chrysler had no spit-into-the-wind performance car. Chrysler executives were well aware of this, but the

company, in fact, was fighting for its financial survival. The K-car series and very successful minivan programs which, established an entirely new market, put Chrysler back on its feet. Emerging technologies allowed boosting performance while reducing emissions. These events, coupled with upper management vision, would once again permit the winds of performance to blow from Highland Park.

The Viper

One day in 1988 Chrysler President Bob Lutz was out driving his Autokraft Cobra Mk IV. Lutz reveled in the car's power and handling precision and wondered why such a car, with necessary technological updating, could not be built for the 1990s. To begin with, Chrysler did not build a big enough V-8 to power the car. The largest V-8 the company built at that time was the 360 cubic-inch V-8 installed in its truck line. Nope, a real performance car had to have a big-block V-8, he reasoned. Chrysler had begun work on a new large truck line and specifically a new large displacement engine to go in it—a V-10. And then the wheels of inspiration started to turn. The V-10 was going to be engineered to deliver astounding torque and would meet all mandated truckemissions. The idea of building a V-10 sports car took hold of Lutz and would not let go.

Lutz discussed the idea with Francois Castaing, director of Jeep and Truck Engineering, and with Tom Gale, Vice President of Design. During the discussion, Gale quickly sketched up some ideas showing a car with long-enough hood to accommodate a V-10. The seed had been planted. Next, Lutz called on Carroll Shelby to bounce this idea off the sportscar great himself. Shelby was on contract to Chrysler and had built Dodge Shelbys

for the company. These cars were not V-8-powered, however, and Shelby had been thinking about how a true high-performance sports car could be built. When Lutz put the idea to Shelby, the man behind the Cobra legend smiled and told him he had been trying to drum up interest in such a car built by Chrysler Corporation for some time. Lutz could see the nucleus of a possible team forming to examine the concept.

Several weeks later, after a design review meeting, Gale showed Lutz several renderings, including a full-size rendering of the car in profile. It was considerably different from what Lutz had envisioned, but his years of experience in the business, and his respect for Gale's ability, told him to reserve judgment and mull over the design. After that meeting, Gale's studio did a full-size study in clay, accomplishing this task in only three

David Kimble's famous cutaway rendering of the Viper RT/10 reveals a wealth of engineering effort that went into the car. Team Viper succeeded in bringing the car from concept to production in less than three years. *David Kimble*

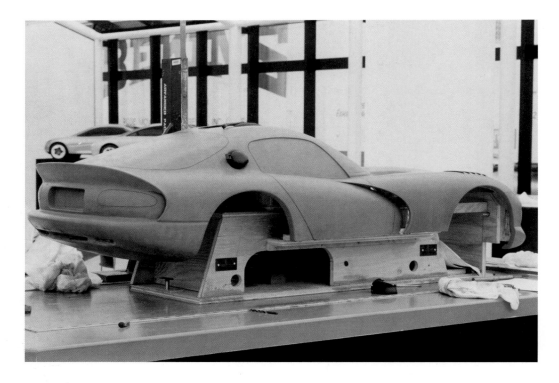

With the tremendous success of the Viper roadster, Dodge launched a program to design a coupe. The 3/8 scale clay study shows the final details of the Viper GTS, including front fender louvers and racing gas cap. *Ron Strong*

gauge public response. Metalcrafters of Newport Beach, California—which had built show cars for Chrysler before—was contracted to begin work in May of 1988.

Lutz had been toying with a name for the car but still had not come up with something to his satisfaction. On a corporate flight from California to Michigan, Lutz, Castaing and Gale kicked around some suggested monikers. They finally agreed upon Viper. Lutz kept Chrysler Chairman Lee Iacocca appraised of this car and Iacocca understood what Lutz wanted this car to accomplish should it receive a favorable response.

What Lutz wanted to accomplish was not simply to build a high-performance sports car, but actually develop the means for bringing a new vehicle to market much faster. This idea, known as the platform concept, had already been instituted at Chrysler, including a new line of cars in the LH sedan program. The Viper program was meant to bring a new car to market even faster and contribute to restoring Chrysler's image and prestige. At this point, the Viper was known to only a handful of people at Chrysler and those sworn to secrecy at Metalcrafters.

The Viper show car was to be, essentially, a running prototype, and that meant a running engine. A V-10 was decreed for the Viper, but no production or prototype V-10 existed. The largest displacement Chrysler V-8 in production was the 360 cubic-inch Wedge V-8. To achieve a V-10 configuration without prohibitive cost,

weeks. Lutz was asked to come over and take a look. As Lutz walked around the clay buck, Gale again stated this car should be unique in appearance and apart from the Cobra. The car should have its own identity, and Lutz agreed. The next step was to have a rolling, finished car to display at the key auto shows around America to

The Viper GTS, introduced in 1996, also displayed a refined front end and functional NACA hoodscoop. To pass noise drive-by standards, the side exhausts were deleted and rerouted to the rear.
Ron Strong

Castaing ordered two 360s to undergo a "siamese" operation. The back two cylinders were cut from one block and the forward four cylinders were cut from the second block. The 6+4 engine blocks were then furnace-brazed to produce a V-10 block. The resulting displacement was 450 cubic inches. The same procedure was performed on the cylinder heads. The crankshaft and camshaft were machined from billet parts. The fabricated induction system was also unique to the engine, as it had to fit below the low hoodline of the Viper. As many off-the-shelf parts were procured for the engine and the car as possible.

When the striking red Viper RT/10 was finished at Metalcrafters at the end of 1988, it was shipped to Michigan and kept under wraps at Highland Park. When the Viper display stand was ready at the North American International Auto Show in Detroit, Michigan, the Viper was transported to Cobo Hall in an enclosed trailer and moved onto the display turntable.

On January 4, 1989, the Dodge Viper RT/10 made its debut to the public, but not before the automotive press had its chance to go over the car first. The Viper proved an absolute sensation. Every automotive magazine in the world wrote about the car, and auto show visitors were bowled over. Chrysler suddenly had a snake by the tail. The story was the same in Chicago and Los Angeles.

To Build or Not to Build

To seriously examine the feasibility of manufacturing the Viper, Castaing chose Roy H. Sjoberg to assemble a small team to evaluate all aspects of building a limited-production sports car. Sjoberg was a 25-year veteran of General Motors who had come to Chrysler in 1985. Sjoberg hand-picked several engineers to attend a meeting to discuss this and other matters related to a possible Viper program. Peter M. Gladysz was one of the first men picked by Sjoberg. Gladysz had been the Shelby Program Manager in the early and

Power of the V-10 was bumped up to 450 horsepower with 490 foot-pounds of torque to coincide with the release of the Viper GTS. With power like this and world-class handling, the car is a favorite of weekend club racers—a true dual-purpose machine. *Ron Strong*

mid-1980s, oversaw the turbo 2.2 liter program, and was the 3.3 liter V-6 engine manager. Gladysz had been involved in rally and endurance racing since 1979, so he brought a great deal of racing and actual production experience to the table.

"After the auto show," Gladysz remembers, "we had our first group meeting in mid-February. We had a discussion on a broader point of view and a personnel point of view. Engineering had not been involved with the Viper prior to the show, and I was asked to bring back to Engineering an official view of 'Could we build this thing?' Bob Lutz was at the meeting and he asked, 'Do any of you want to leave your current jobs and come work on this? We are looking for volunteers.' That's how the initial team got started. It was a real mix of enthusiasts, people who knew and understood cars, right down to the grease under their fingernails. Performance-minded people. A lot of the people who eventually came on board in one way or another had prior background in racing. The working group wasn't assembled until the March/April time frame."

As part of the production evaluation program, Lutz wanted to explore new ways of production, improve ties between Chrysler and its suppliers and thus reduced time needed to get parts and subassemblies, and streamline engineering and management decision making, among other things. Herb Helbig became Viper's Vehicle Synthesis Manager. "The car was not the key to the project—it was a catalyst," Helbig explained to the editors of *Design News* magazine in the January 1992 issue.

The Viper GTS program also gave the engineers an opportunity to reengineer the chassis to make it lighter and even stronger. The same chassis is also used on the roadster. *Ron Strong*

"What we were really supposed to do was change the way our company does business."

What this entailed was establishing an autonomous platform team that would be responsible for the entire vehicle from start to finish, as opposed to the traditional approach where the engine, chassis, body, etc., were handled by separate corporate entities. The goal was to eliminate red tape, quickly produce or procure all needed parts, streamline development, bring the car to market with world-class timing and reduce the cost of doing so in the process.

"The initial goal of the team was to get the first car running in six months," Gladysz says. "The overall goal was to get to production in three years or less. We felt if we didn't make this thing happen real fast, people were going to lose interest. The program was set up as a learning experience for our people, for suppliers, and for Chrysler. We wanted to challenge the system and challenge ourselves. We had to rethink the whole production and manufacturing scenario because we didn't have the dollars to put up a plant. There was no plant we could get our hands on."

The small Viper team needed a place of their own to begin work. Fortuitously, the Jeep Truck Engineering group was vacating a portion of its offices for new offices elsewhere. Roy Sjoberg wasted no time filling the vacuum and moved his small group into those offices. The complex also had lift capability, which would allow the engineers to build the prototype cars right there in engineering. The Viper Technical Policy Committee was formed, made up of Lutz, Product Design chief Tom Gale, Engineering Vice President Francois Castaing, and Carroll Shelby as performance consultant. Shelby was brought on board to be the conscience of the Viper, to apply his wealth of knowledge to the car and ensure it would remain as light and as powerful as possible.

The Viper's appearance and drivetrain were established by the show car, so production feasibility was based on that. However, there was discussion about possible engines to go in the Viper other than a V-10. Willem L. Weertman, a Chrysler veteran with decades of engineering experience, was called out of retirement to act as consulting engineer on the Viper engine program. Weertman had spearheaded the 426 race Hemi engine program and was greatly respected regarding all his powertrain and vehicle engineering expertise over the years. He had been involved in preliminary development of the truck V-10 engine before retiring, but it was not long before his expertise was missed, and he was called back as a contract consultant. He remembers initial discussion regarding the Viper's engine.

"There was some discussion about putting the 426 Hemi engine in the Viper," Weertman remembers. "My position was this: the Hemi was supreme in its day, but that chapter is over. This Viper needs its own engine. Absolutely. It's right for the Viper to have its own engine and the V-10 is the right engine for the Viper."

Lamborghini was, at the time, owned by Chrysler, so the exotic carmaker was called on to evaluate the possibility of making an engine based on the drawings of the truck V-10. These drawings were sent to Lamborghini in February 1989, which completed the work several months later and shipped prototype parts and drawings to Chrysler later that year. Team Viper took over development of the V-10 at that point. Weertman made recommendations to the engine team on the Lamborghini design. The evolution of this engine was

The drivetrain of the Viper RT/10 and GTS is capable of withstanding grueling racing conditions. Borg-Warner engineered and builds the rugged six-speed manual transmission. *Ron Strong*

Vipers are assembled at Chrysler's Conner Avenue assembly plant In Detroit, Michigan. The Plymouth Prowler is also assembled there on its own dedicated line. *Ron Strong*

to take considerable time, however, and an engine was needed for the first mule vehicle, known as VM01.L.

Richard Winkles joined the Viper program as a development engineer. He had joined Chrysler in 1981. Winkles returned from a six-month stint at Lamborghini working on the F1 program before going over to Team Viper. The chassis and body engineering were progressing and an engine was going to be needed to power the first car. It would not be a V-10.

"My focus was to get the mule cars up and running with some sort of engine and to start developing the hardware and feed that information back to the design group," Winkles says. "Our first project was to get the first mule car—VM01—running. There was a lot of debate about the engine to go in the car. The only logical choice for the engine in the first car was a V-8. The V-8 was going to be closer to the aluminum V-10 than the iron V-10 in terms of weight and vehicle dynamics. We made a [360 cubic inch] V-8 package that ran quite well. It used the old 340 Six Pack camshaft which was something that was available and we knew it was a good design."

Dynamometer development would be essential throughout the entire Viper engine program, so Test Cell No. 13 in Highland Park was selected. It was here the induction system for the V-8 was designed and developed in order to fit underneath the hood of the Viper. Winkles was assisted in the test cell by Bob Zeimis Sr., who had many years of racing engine and production engine experience to draw on for the program.

VM01 moved forward with unprecedented speed. By the fall of 1989, the V-8 was bolted into the Viper mule's space-frame and the first body, true to the show car, was assembled to the frame. The other crucial systems to get the mule running were completed and the car began is first series of tests at the Chelsea Proving Grounds.

"From an overall handling point of view," Gladysz says, "it did a great job. Our first guess of chassis dynamics, chassis stiffness, brakes, and tire sizes, was not perfect but directionally correct. We drove that car—right out of the box—at 130 miles per hour the first day we had it out on the track at Chelsea. We were that confident in what we were doing. This first car also gave us the ability to convince management that this team which had just formed could build a car. This was extremely important because there was now a lot of confidence that a team which had never been put together this quickly could make this thing happen."

The Viper GTS ranks among the finest sports cars built in the postwar era. At speed the GTS, especially in Viper Red, is guaranteed to turn heads wherever it goes. *Ron Strong*

While VM01 was being tested, construction of VM02 began. The first prototype truck engines were procured for use in the next mule and testing in the test cell. Getting those prototype truck V-10s took some effort. Truck engineering coveted each one. Nevertheless, Team Viper prevailed, no doubt with some persuasion from Lutz and Castaing, and the prototype truck V-10 parts were delivered to Cell No. 13 for buildup. Development had progressed from the very early V-10s and displacement was now 488 ci. Instead of an iron crankshaft, several steel crankshafts were machined, using the drawings for the iron crank. The special camshaft featured the profile from the 340 Six Pack cam, with slightly more lift. This would permit the iron V-10 to be taken up to 6,000 rpm. One engine was built up for development in Test Cell 13 and the other would be assembled to go into VM02.

"We spent about three or four months developing the V-10 truck engine for VM02," Winkles says. "I don't know what the engine weighed, but it was a lot. I took that engine from the dyno after running it to verify power and calibration and we put it in the back of my Dakota pickup to take it from Jeep Truck to Hyland Park to put in VM02. That iron V-10 put my Dakota on the ground. I couldn't believe it. When it was installed in the car, it wasn't really representative of what the car was going to be because it was at least 200 pounds heavier than the eventual aluminum engine [to improve front/rear wight balance and handling]. That car had to have heavier front springs and various odds and ends. We spent a fair amount of time driving it or having someone drive it for me while I was working with the I/O [input/ouput] boxes."

In December 1989, Sjoberg felt VM01 was sufficiently refined and finished for Bob Lutz to evaluate. "We said we had a car and we wanted him to look at it," Gladysz remembers. "Lutz drove it and said he wanted to launch the program for production in January 1990."

The next big milestone in the Viper program was the long-lead press preview near Chrysler's Arizona proving grounds in June of 1990. On display and available for select test drives was VM02 finished in a brilliant Viper Red. It was fitted with the iron V-10 with a dual throttle-body induction system and functional side exhaust. This car had a pronounced hood bulge needed to clear some of the induction hardware, but this would eventually be resolved and the bulge reduced considerably. Richard Winkles, Ray Schilling, and Don Jankowski

were there to answer questions from the press and Bob Lutz was there to fan the flames. Before taking journalists for rides, Lutz took the car out to make certain the car was running to his satisfaction. At one point, Lutz was cruising next to the Sidona dry lakebed at 120 miles per hour when he was caught by police radar. Lutz obediently pulled the car over, identified himself as the president of Chrysler just evaluating the Viper, and was permitted to proceed without being ticketed. Rank has its privileges. The press preview was a great success and the new Viper received mountains of magazine copy. The Dodge Viper RT/10 would go into production in 1992.

The Pace Quickens

The Viper aluminum V-10 program was quickly moving forward. The first aluminum V-10 built from Lamborghini supplied parts was assembled in April 1990. This engine, EA03, ran for the first time on May 1. "Bob Zemis and I had just got that engine started," Winkles says, "and a car pulled up outside the test cell. Lutz, Castaing, Joe Cappy, and someone else got out of the car and came into the test cell. It was as if they had ESP. We hadn't run the engine two minutes and I hadn't called anyone—and there they were! The engine wasn't running right yet. In fact, it was running on just six cylinders because we had a few problems with the control system. Castaing walks up to it, licks his finger, and puts it on each one of the exhaust ports. And he says, 'This one's running, this one isn't . . .' and so on, without me telling him it was only running on six cylinders. He was sharp. They would show up from time to time like that during the program."

The original design for the aluminum bore liners was changed to iron and the exposed cooling length increased due to high oil temperatures. The engine also generated high crankcase pressures as a result of the original lower block bearing cap cluster that prevented breathing between cylinder bays. A change was made to separate iron main bearing caps. As a result of this, the oil pan design was also changed and incorporated an oil pan baffle and windage tray. There was also a change in the exhaust manifolds. The fabricated steel tube headers were replaced with cast-steel exhaust manifolds due to space constraints. The cast-steel manifolds were also somewhat quieter.

Other changes took place on the engine during 1990. The development team succeeded in lowering the

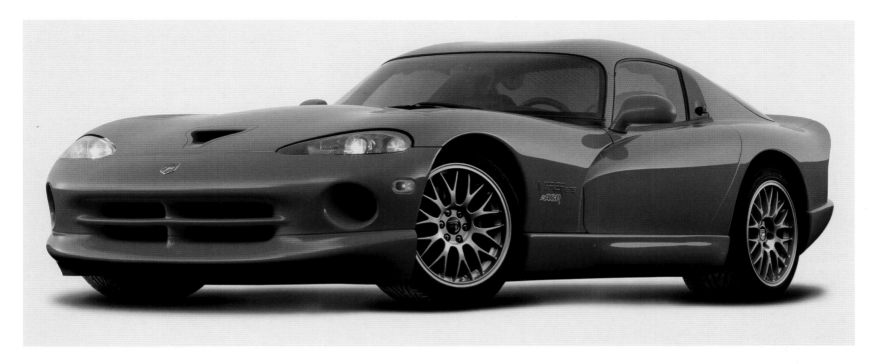

compression ratio from a relatively high 10.5:1 to 9.1:1 while actually increasing the engine's output as a result of performance development, particularly in the area of the V-10 induction system and engine control system. By December, emissions work was so successful that the electric air pump and EGR valve originally thought necessary were deleted. Releases for production parts began to be issued as various components of the V-10 were finalized.

However, a limited-production engine like this aluminum V-10 entailed procurement problems Chrysler had rarely encountered before. Charlie Brown III was brought into the engine group in July of 1989 by Jim Royer, who was in charge of the Viper engine group. Brown had joined Chrysler in 1981. He says the low volume nature of the Viper V-10 presented real challenges.

"Our biggest challenge," Brown remembers, "was trying to find vendors in our database to make our required 3,000 pieces a year, which was our original target for production. Chrysler had a lot of vendors who could make hundreds of thousands of things a year, and prototype vendors who could make 50 or 100 of something a year. So Jim Royer and I went out and surveyed vendors who could make the block, heads, et cetera. We wound up with Winters Industries as our original source for our cylinder block, cylinder heads, and intake manifold.

"All the vendors were involved from day one," Brown emphasizes. "We asked our vendors how we could make the parts better, lighter, and so on. We wanted their input while we engineered the parts. We picked their brains."

Transmission Problems and Solutions

By the first week of March in 1991, vehicle calibration and emission development started with Viper prototype vehicle VP15 running the V-10 engine EA13. A six-speed manual transmission was established as the design direction for the Viper, and only two of those existed in the world: ZF and Getrag of Germany. General Motors had ZF tied up for the Corvette program. The Getrag transmission was never designed to withstand the torque loads that would be generated by the mighty V-10.

"We got a number of those gearboxes in and we managed to break every single one," Gladysz states. "That gearbox was not designed for this torque level. We did a quick search because eighteen months before production we still had no transmission. Borg-Warner then came on board. They had a gearbox they were working on. It wasn't designed for a car, but it was a gearbox. Could it handle the torque? The answer came back yes—the gear spacing and sizes were right and the ratios weren't too far off. They signed on and within a few

In 1999, Dodge introduced the Viper ACR (for American Club Racer). It was designed for the serious club racer. The air conditioning, audio system, and fog lights are deleted to reduce weight, the suspension upgraded to full-race specifications, and power boosted as well. Production is limited to 100-200 units.
Ron Strong

months we had a transmission we could do development on and put into our development cars. It turned out to be an exceptional gearbox.

"Part of our goal with every component we touched in the car was: 'Don't just get it to production specifications. Bullet-proof the part when you are doing it because we are not going to have second-chance dollars to spend on it. So if the car evolves and we add extra horsepower and extra torque, those components can live with the program,' " Gladysz explains.

Development Testing

Vehicle development and testing is a part of every new automobile program. The Viper, however, was a very unique car and its eventual use by owners would also be unique. The car was very much the product of a racing car mentality, and it was anticipated the car would be taken club racing and no doubt highly modified for professional racing. The development testing of the Viper would evolve in such an environment.

"We spent a lot of time at the race track testing the car," Gladysz says. "We knew customers would race the car so we needed to have that experience. A lot of us knew places that were the most abusive that we could get to locally. We could run our own endurance tests and combine test schedules that take weeks or months at the Proving Grounds into literally days. This was part of the overall evolution of development within the company.

"We went back to Nelson Ledges with a mid-development car in 1991," Gladysz remembers, "and broke the car in countless places in a 24-hour race cycle. Our goal was to develop and fix everything we broke in that 24-hour race simulation that we ran by ourselves, based

The Viper GTS-R is built by Team ORECA in Signes, France, for private race teams to race in FIA GT2 class. Racing Vipers, Team ORECA won the GT2 class in FIA competition in 1997 and 1998 and the GT2 class in the 24 Hours of LeMans in 1998. *Ron Strong*

on what we did in 1983 and 1985 with Shelbys. Drawing on that progression, we knew what we had to do to a part for it to live in a 24-hour race. Roy Sjoberg told us to do 'chicken tests' on the cars. That came from the tests Lockheed used to do to test engines. They used to throw chickens into the jet engine intakes and see what broke. Nelson Ledges was our chicken test.

"There were a lot of abusive things we did to the car during the development cycle so we could make snap assessments in a short amount of time," states Gladysz. "With this car, we brought back drag cycle testing. That's something we had done in the past because people were going to use the car in that manner. We took that performance requirement, which was 300 cycles, and these were wide open throttle shift schedules. We said, 'Nope, let's make it 400 cycles. We found the car lived, so we went to 800 cycles. We wanted to see what would break. When the part was redesigned and lived through the test cycle, it went into production."

Brake testing was also crucial to the Viper. Several benchmark tests were used on the Viper. One benchmark was established by the Cobra itself. The Cobra was able to accelerate from 0 to 100 miles per hour and brake to 0 in under 15 seconds. The Viper had to do the same, or better. Similarly, Porsche had the same performance envelope, but this test was performed twenty times and the brakes could not exhibit any fade. Carroll Shelby himself was called on to do brake testing on the car and resorted to a benchmark test he had used himself in the past. At the Chrysler Arizona Proving Grounds, Shelby drove the Viper mule around the 4-1/2 mile oval track dragging the brakes, then did some acceleration runs followed by panic stops. Getting out of the car, he said, "Your brakes are going to work."

The chassis and suspension engineering was supervised by Dave Buchesky. The space-frame chassis was designed using Computer Aided Design and employed finite element analysis to locate the areas of greatest stress. Due to the very small team assigned to this major area of the car, Buchesky brought in several outside experts to assist. One of them was Larry Rathgeb, a veteran of many years' experience designing suspensions for Chrysler's NASCAR efforts with Plymouths and Dodges, including the Dodge Charger Daytona. Gladysz wanted Rathgeb to evaluate the handling of the Viper mule and come back with recommendations.

"We went out and drove the car and from my experience," Rathgeb recalls, "I told them they had a downforce problem with the back end. I suggested a rear spoiler. That nailed the car down and all the problems went away. I called Dave Buchesky and told him, but he said to take the spoiler off because Chrysler management did not want to change the basic look of the car. The only thing we could do was tune the rear suspension. Dave had called on Ralph Youngdale, one of the best chassis designers to ever walk the face of the earth. I had worked with him for years—a really good man. Ralph had retired to California but came back to set up a design shop in Detroit. He took over the task of redesigning critical areas of the front and rear suspension because Dave simply had too much to do."

Gladysz suggested Rathgeb take from two to four weeks to analyze and identify suspension performance and alignment problems, and to insure that production caster, camber, toe, and toe pattern settings would be absolutely correct. One of the most important recommendations was incorporating an inner tie-rod for the rear suspension that was adjustable up and down. Youngdale designed an inner tie-rod that permitted the fine tuning necessary to guarantee the Viper's stability at high speed.

During all this work it became clear to Rathgeb that if the front and rear suspension was not properly assembled and precisely aligned, there would be variances from car to car that would be intolerable. Rathgeb designed front and rear suspension assembly fixtures that ensured proper settings and alignment of the front and rear suspension on the Viper assembly line. It was a complex design, yet it worked perfectly on the Viper. Rathgeb and the suspension group received a patent for this revolutionary alignment fixture design.

The Viper Goes to Indy

In the midst of all this hectic development, a crisis erupted when Dodge was approved to run its Stealth as the pace car at the 1991 Indianapolis 500. This did not sit well with purists. The Dodge Stealth was based on the Mitsubishi. Any car that paced the Indy 500 had to be all-American, period! Charlie Brown remembers the initial chaos over the issue.

"Due to the uproar, everybody was running around trying to figure out what we could put in there," he recalls. "In the meantime, a few guys over on our side felt strongly enough that what we had, even as a Viper mule, was strong enough that it could go out there and at least run pace car laps for the first four laps, then pull it in. We were up to VP25 so the next car was designated VP26 and everyone was told to build the best engine, chassis, and car for Indy, and we were going to go show. Well, the guys in the back shop worked their tails off getting the car prepped to not only run right but look pretty to get it ready for pace car duty. The car went down there the first week in May. Everyone kept their fingers crossed the month of May. During that month, Carroll Shelby was down there giving joy rides to practically anyone who wanted to ride. I heard rumors he had put up to 3,000 miles on that car during the month of May. He'd pile them in the car and take them out, drive them around, and scare the hell out of them. Someone said he took one guy out and was doing 160 miles per hour on the back straight in the rain! As insurance, we actually had a second car built. We got it set up with all the lights and everything, sent it down to Indy. The original car ran so well that they never did take the Stealth out."

As it turned out, pressing the Dodge Viper into pace car duties before actually commencing production turned out to be a public relations coup. Production of the Viper was to begin during the first quarter of 1992, and putting the car on display in one of motorsports' most prestigious events was just the kick the car needed. It was a brilliant stroke.

Final Development and Introduction

The Viper development program moved forward during the last half of 1991. A major change occurred regarding the lower engine block of the V-10. In September, production approval was given to change the lower portion of the block from a one-piece casting to separate caps. The following month the engine completed its 50,000-mile emissions durability test. Also in October the first engine completed 500 continuous hours of dyno endurance testing. The dedicated Viper V-10 engine assembly line was set up at Chrysler Mound Road Engine Plant. Chrysler's Mack Avenue facility had been selected as the Viper assembly building and renamed the New Mack Avenue Viper Assembly Plant.

The first Viper V-10 production engine was assembled at Mound Road on March 2, 1992, and shipped to the Viper assembly plant. The first Viper vehicle was officially emissions certified later that month. In April, a

presentation of the Dodge Viper RT/10 was made to the Detroit Section of the Society of Automotive Engineers. Already, enthusiast magazines were testing the Viper and as a cover car ensured the issue was a sellout on the magazine stands all over the world. When the Viper went into production and deliveries to dealers began, Viper mania was launched. The Viper had a base list price of $50,000, plus a whopping $2,600 gas-guzzler tax, a $2,330 luxury tax, and a $700 delivery charge putting the as-delivered price just under $56,000. Immediately, bidding wars began among prospective buyers. Dealers took advantage of the situation; soon the price of available Vipers soared to over $100,000. Cooler and more patient heads knew the mania would eventually die down, and the price would eventually come down to earth, which it did.

Part of the problem lay in the very limited production the first year of Viper production. Dodge was determined to build each car carefully, but also to deliberately work out production problems that year. Hence, production volume was slow and low. In fact, only 285 units were built in the 1992 model year. The cars were scarce as hen's teeth. Price was a reflection of supply and demand.

And demand had everything to do with the Viper's eye-popping looks, ferocious acceleration, tenacious handling, and race-capable braking. But, above all, it was the car's ability to beat virtually anything else on the road. Brown explains:

"We met all of our original performance goals and everyone was ecstatic. The real reason the Viper is the way it is, is the V-10 is the heart of the Viper. What makes the Viper a Viper is the torque. There is no replacement for displacement. When you look at the torque curve of this beast, it makes 300 foot-pounds of torque at 700 rpm which is just off idle. By 1,200 rpm it is making 400 foot-pounds of torque. That's what makes the Viper such a kick to drive. The torque is there now. You can roll into the throttle in almost any gear and light up the tires.

Indeed, the Dodge Viper heaped untold prestige on Chrysler Corporation as a whole. The goals of effectively establishing the platform concept to bring new vehicles to market quickly had succeeded. The efforts of so many men and women at Team Viper to make the concept a reality could take great pride in their individual and collective efforts. But it would not end with the Viper RT/10.

Special Introductory Offer!

Big Savings!

Save Over <u>65%</u>

Off the $1.99 Cover Price!

▼ Detach this card and mail today! ▼

BUSINESS REPLY MAIL

FIRST-CLASS MAIL   PERMIT NO. 96   RADNOR PA

POSTAGE WILL BE PAID BY ADDRESSEE

PO BOX 5520
RADNOR PA 19088-5521

NO POSTAGE
NECESSARY
IF MAILED
IN THE
UNITED STATES

Iron 360-ci V-8-powered Vm01

Brazed-block iron V-10

Viper engine development evolved very quickly. The first engine installed in the first running Viper Mule (VM01) was an iron V-8 displacing 360 cubic inches (photo upper left). It lacked the horsepower and torque really needed, convincing the engineers that there was "no replacement for displacement" and a V-10 in the Viper was essential. However, this V-8 was crucial in establishing preliminary induction design and permitted vehicle dynamics evaluation.

When the first prototype iron V-10 blocks and heads being developed for the new Dodge line of trucks became available, Team Viper immediately began development for installation in VM02. Two iron V-10s were built for Viper development— EI00 and EI01. This engine powered the red car—still VM02—that was displayed to journalists in June 1990 several months after Lee Iacocca announced the Viper would go into production for 1992.

The iron V-10 proved much too heavy in the Viper. The engine would have to be aluminum. The development work by Lamborghini was critical at this stage, but Team Viper took over development of an aluminum V-10 in the fall of 1989 after Lamborghini supplied the first batch of blocks, heads, and other parts. The first aluminum V-10 engine assembly—EA03—was completed on April 18, 1990, and ran for the first time in test cell 13/135 on May 1.

A great deal of development work went into the aluminum V-10 between the spring of 1990 and April of 1992 when the engine received its emissions certificate from the Environmental Protection Agency. The engine was so clean, in fact, it needed neither an EGR valve nor an air pump. It displaced 488 cubic inches, developed 400 net horsepower, and churned out 450 foot-pounds of torque. The engine shown here in the test cell is a pre-production unit (photo lower right).

Viper Engine Development and Evolution

Iron V-10 E100 for VM02

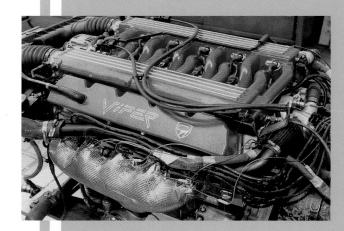

Aluminum V-10 under development testing

The Viper GTS Coupe

The original concept for the Viper had always been a roadster, in keeping with the fact the Cobra had been an open roadster. However, it was never far from the minds of the founding "four-fathers" Lutz, Castaing, Gale, and Shelby that a Viper Coupe would be very nice to have as well. After all, racing is a lot easier on the mind and body with a coupe, to say nothing of a higher top speed, better aerodynamics, and all-weather capability. These issues were raised by magazine editors as well, and letters drifted into Team Viper offices asking if such a car would ever be built. They didn't have long to wait.

At the 1993 North American International Auto Show that January, Dodge did it again. This time, a stunning Viper GTS coupe was the center of attention. Again, the car was billed as a concept car, but it was no stretch to believe the car would see production. The roofline featured a pronounced "double bubble," sweeping fastback roofline, and integral rear spoiler. A racing gas cap was located on the right-hand side. The car was finished in a blue metallic with two white racing stripes running from nose to tail. The color scheme was strongly influenced by Shelby's own Daytona Cobra Coupe. The front end featured a functional integral spoiler that enhanced the car's looks. The hood featured louvers above the front wheels and a NACA hoodscoop. The Viper GTS was a design tour de force.

"When the coupe was approved for production," Brown says, "we were told it could weigh no more than the roadster. To succeed, the entire car had to go on a weight-loss program: engine, chassis, and body."

It was estimated a coupe configuration would add roughly 200 pounds to the weight of the car, so this was the target reduction needed. All through the Viper RT/10 program, the engineers kept a laundry list of things they would like to do to improve it if the opportunity ever presented itself. The opportunity did.

"Engineers are historically tinkerers," Gladysz says. "They are not satisfied with what they've got. They want to keep pushing the envelope. What could we do to keep the enthusiasm at a heightened level? That was the basis for the next evolution. Let's do a whole new chassis, lower weight, boost power, improve emissions further. Our goal was to not allow the coupe to be heavier. Put the car on a diet and take all the weight you can out of it again. We took 40 to 50 pounds out of the frame. We went to an aluminum suspension. So, the coupe and new roadster were targeted for the 1996 time frame."

The engine was a prime example of where weight loss could be achieved. Royer tasked Brown to examine every part to see where weight savings could be achieved. For example, the cylinder heads were redesigned so there was not only considerably less aluminum in the casting, but the amount of water necessary to circulate through the block and heads was also reduced, because water is weight as well. Finite Element Analysis succeeded in reducing the weight of the main bearing cap by an entire pound and still retain the cap's necessary strength. There were many different diameter and length bolts used throughout the engine. Again, F.E.A. was used to reduce the diameter and length of these bolts, dropping another 5 1/2 pounds. The cylinder block was redesigned and a whopping 39 pounds eliminated. If a part could be eliminated or its function incorporated with another, that was done. When the engine weight loss program for the new V-10 was finished and the first engine was put on the scales, it was 80 pounds lighter than the previous engine. At the same time, output had been boosted to 450 horsepower.

The Viper GTS coupe proved a tremendous success when introduced in 1996. Many RT/10 roadster owners went back and ordered the GTS coupe. The 1996 roadster also benefited from the weight loss and performance improvement program. However, Dodge would not have the performance spotlight to itself very much longer. Plymouth had been working on its own very special car, and it was unlike anything that had ever come down an assembly line before.

The Plymouth Prowler

At the 1993 North American International Auto Show, the Dodge Viper GTS was not the only car drawing the spotlight. Over at Plymouth, show-goers were five-deep straining to see what their eyes could not believe. The Plymouth Prowler was, if anything, even more radical than the Viper. In typical auto show-speak, people were told the Prowler was a concept that would explore new ways of manufacturing, use familiar materials in new ways, and, quite simply, be an absolute blast to drive. What everyone was looking at with their mouth open was nothing less than a striking purple street rod. Was Plymouth serious? Oh yes.

Comments were heard like, "Man, if this is the new Chrysler Corporation, I want in!" That, too, was the idea. Chrysler was setting its course on building some of the most desirable cars in the world, and quite frankly,

The Plymouth Prowler began as a concept vehicle from Chrysler Pacifica in Carlsbad, California, in 1990. Among the many ideas proposed was a "retro" design reminiscent of a street rod. It progressed to model form, shown here. It was later refined and chosen to be a show car to gauge public reaction.

build cars no other company would dare build. All that auto show-speak was true, but the car was meant to reflect the radically new thinking and ways of building cars that was taking place at Chrysler.

The idea for the Prowler started at Chrysler's Pacifica Design office in Carlsbad, California, at a brainstorming session held in May 1990. Many automotive trends originate in California and the Pacifica Design office was meant to take advantage of that and draw on the rich talent in the area. Several concepts were refined over the next several months, culminating in 1/5 scale models. One of them was a modern street rod with enclosed passenger compartment but having traditional exposed tires. Pacifica's design manager, Kevin Verduyn, held discussions with Tom Gale and design director Neil Walling. Bob Lutz routinely visited Pacifica Design and encouraged the design direction the concept was taking.

Of all the designs being considered, the one that took a "retro" or street rod appearance began to be the focus of Pacifica's efforts. Its designers were encouraged to attend hot rod shows there in California to learn the current state of thinking, and also researched hot rod and street rod designs of decades past. In a lavish book

put out by Plymouth simply titled, *Plymouth Prowler*, Tom Gale explained the goal in attending these shows.

"We needed to get into the minds of the best hot rodders and make sure that we were on the right track," he said. "From the very start it was important that our design pay homage to the very essence of the hot rod culture."

The infusion of that hot rod culture was reflected in the full-size fiberglass model in the summer of 1991. It was at this time the designers knew the project and car would have to have a name. Many were considered, but finally Prowler was selected. However, the decision on production was not even an issue so the Chrysler division eventually selected to build the car was not even raised at that time. However, as the design evolved into 1992, renderings of the Prowler showed the Dodge name in the license plate area and on the wheels, and the Dodge ram logo conspicuously placed about the car's exterior.

Builders of street rods and hot rods are not burdened with federal regulations and have pretty much built what they wanted. Providing the car had headlights, taillights, brake lights, and turn-signal indicators, that was enough to satisfy the state department of motor vehicles. Car manufacturers have to meet a myriad of federal regulations regarding front and rear

bumpers, crash protection, side-impact protection, and so on. This proved a real challenge to the designers of the Prowler because the car had to be designed in anticipation of production where the car would, indeed, meet all these federal motor vehicle regulations and still remain true to the theme and aesthetic they desired of the Prowler.

The design engineering philosophy permeating Chrysler at the time was to design concept vehicles within the parameters of possible production. The reason for this was simple. Chrysler executives did not want to raise interest in a particular car as a concept to display at auto shows across the country, only to have to radically alter the car for production and lose all semblance to the concept car. The goal was to build and display concept cars with production in mind, and then build the production car as closely to the original concept as possible. The first big aesthetic and engineering hurdle to clear dealt with the bumpers.

"At this time the Prowler was still little more than a concept car theme," Verduyn stated in *Plymouth Prowler*, "so it would have been easy to do this one without any bumpers at all. But we wanted to prove this could be a production-feasible car."

With a car like the Prowler, the wheels and tires play a very large role in the car's aesthetics. While many street and hot rods are fenderless, that could not be realistically done on a production car, and it was not felt covering the tires would necessarily detract from the car looks. Pacifica's designers had noted a number of the hot rod and street rods they looked at featured minimal front wheel fenders that were fixed to the spindle, so the fender moved with the wheel and tire while still providing protection from water spray and flying stones and other debris from the road. The Prowler featured this later in the design phase. But what size to make the wheels and tires?

"Choosing the right proportion was critical because the car has a very light shape in front but a massive, heavy feel to its rear," Verduyn said in *Plymouth Prowler*. "We looked at almost two dozen wheel and tire profiles and eventually settled on 17-inch rims up front and 20-inch rims in the rear. This setup, which had to be specially supplied to us, soon became known as 'big and bigger.' "

The interior of the Prowler was every bit as important as the exterior and a great deal of design work went into it. Another rule of Chrysler design philosophy

The Plymouth Prowler show car toured the auto show and hot rod circuit in 1993. With the Viper now on the market, enthusiasts had more than a little faith the Prowler would also be built. When the production Prowler was offered in 1997, it had remained true to the showcar in form and function. *Chrysler Plymouth Jeep*

With its aluminum body and frame and other lightweight components, the weight of the Prowler was kept under 3,000 pounds. Powered by a Chrysler 3.5-liter 24-valve V-6 it offers a good power-to-weight ratio coupled with impressive handling and braking characteristics.
Chrysler Plymouth Jeep Division

regarding such concept cars was to incorporate as many off-the-the-shelf production items as possible. There were two primary reasons for this. The part would not have to be tooled in the first place, and once the car was in production, replacement parts were already in the pipeline. This approach actually was reflected throughout the car, as much as was possible. This was especially true of the engine.

Unlike the Dodge Viper that had been displayed with a new V-10 engine, the Prowler would use a V-6 from the Chrysler engine family. Due to the narrow front end, there really was not room for a V-8. Also, it was felt an advantageous power-to-weight ratio could be achieved to permit the use of a V-6. Engine controls were progressing to the point where V-6s putting out over 200 horsepower were

feasible and higher outputs were possible and planned-for. The V-6s themselves were lighter, and this would aid in the car's handling as well.

As the Prowler's conceptual design was finalized and construction of the show car itself began, the color for the car was discussed among Pacifica's designers and Tom Gale. The spectrum was wide open, but certain colors were ruled out altogether. Black, white, and various others were not selected because it was felt a powerful and dramatic color was needed for a car like the Prowler. Gale was building his own street rod and showed the designers a purple metallic he was considering for his own car. It didn't take long for the conversation to drift toward using that color on the Prowler. Gale agreed, and Prowler Purple was born.

Chrysler management made the decision that the Prowler would be displayed under the Plymouth banner. Dodge had received a great deal of prestige from the Viper program and it was felt Plymouth should get the shot in the arm this time. Thus, the car that went on display at the 1993 North American International Auto Show was the Plymouth Prowler. Reception of the car ranged from stunned disbelief to giddy euphoria. Savvy automotive editors could see a Chrysler pattern developing here, and wrote their readers, "Don't be surprised if you one day see production Prowlers cruising the streets of America."

One could argue that if a Chrysler Corporation concept car had reached this level of development and public display, eventual production was a foregone conclusion. Well, sometimes they did and sometimes they didn't. The Portofino, displayed at the 52nd Frankfurt Auto Show, was a wedge-shaped, cab-forward design that never saw production, but the cab-forward concept most certainly was employed in production cars planned for the early 1990s. The curvaceous Chrysler Atlantic strongly reflected classic lines from such 1930s cars as the Bugatti and the Talbot Lago. It took people's breath away, but this too never went into production. A bit more production-feasible was the 1992 Chrysler Thunderbolt, but this also remained nothing more than a concept. The Plymouth Prowler, however, was destined to set the automotive world on its ear.

After the rousing debut at the auto show in Detroit, the Prowler was scheduled for shows in Los Angeles, Chicago, Miami, and elsewhere. Even before the final verdicts were in from showgoers around the country, Phil Gavie, chief of engineering for the Design office, initiated a 90-day production feasibility study for the Prowler.

"Building a one-off concept car is one thing," noted Gavie in *Plymouth Prowler*, "while designing a car for actual production and public sale is quite another. The main goal of Prowler was to maintain as much as possible in the translation from concept to production."

These 90-day evaluation programs are very comprehensive, examining every aspect of the car's design engineering and manufacturing. It is often a stressful time as each designer, engineer, and other personnel involved with the program put together the information that will be combined with all other input to make a go-no go decision. Suppliers have to be selected and their ability to deliver parts determined. Full-scale frame and body engineering was be evaluated for the car's ability to withstand all crash testing, not to mention simple down-the-road and handling rigidity.

Any show-stoppers must be brought to light during this production evaluation period. "People packaging and side-impact requirements necessitated widening the body about three inches," said engineer Don Bradley in *Plymouth Prowler*, "while cooling mandates of the 3.5 liter high-output V-6 dictated a larger, wider radiator, affecting the length and shape of the hood which, by the way, became rear-hinged. The wheelbase was upped slightly from 111.5 inches to 113 inches, mainly for front visual impact. While the concept car had an aluminum flip top that disappeared electrically, the production car had to have a real folding top. There wasn't room for a spare, so we opted for run-flat tires. Even the wipers had specific zone requirements that had to be met, altering the windshield contour. We had to build a packaging buck to verify all the modifications. But by the end of the 90 days, we had an exterior surface done on the computer. We then milled the body full-size. Further changes were designed on the computer, then remilled for surface verification, or modeled directly and then digitized. Unlike the Viper, the Prowler is a completely math data car."

Much had been learned from the Dodge Viper RT/10 program and how that platform team brought the Viper to production. Many of the lessons learned from the

The interior of the Prowler also kept many of the styling cues displayed in the Prowler showcar. The dashboard structure is diecast magnesium. The interior "tub" is immensely strong and passes all federal crash and side-impact federal regulations.
Chrysler Plymouth Jeep Division

Viper program were employed on the Plymouth Prowler. During this phase, the Prowler platform team established the desire to push the technology envelope with this car.

"Part of the Prowler program was to advance as much technology as we possibly could," says Dennis Peters, Manager of Prowler Body Engineering. "That's why the body [and frame] was all-aluminum, which is something we never did before. The idea of the program was to learn as much as we could and take this knowledge and roll it into other mainstream production programs later on. For example, there is no welding on the body. Everything is rivet-bonded construction, which is something new for us. The body is made up of about 285 parts. Of those parts, maybe thirty parts are not aluminum, and the ones that are not aluminum are mainly small parts."

Thus, the materials and means of manufacture were also part of the production evaluation period. The powertrain and layout were also selected at this time. And where would the Prowler be built? After much discussion, it was decided that if the Prowler was approved for production, the New Mack Avenue plant where the Viper was being assembled could not house an additional assembly line for the Prowler. It made sense to have both cars assembled in the same building since similar assembly means and pace would be employed for the Prowler as the Viper, the manufacturing mindset, if you will. Eventually, a new building was chosen on Conner Avenue in Detroit, not far from the Mound Road Engine Plant. This decision, too, was part of the initial 90-day production evaluation phase.

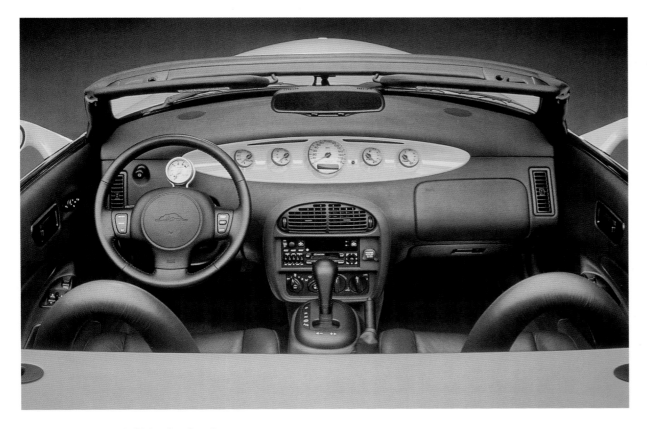

The Prowler is Plymouth's tribute to the hot rod, a purely American form of individual expression for those who don't have the time to build one of their own. Prowler is also a testbed of production ideas that Plymouth intends to introduce in the future. *Chrysler Plymouth Jeep Division*

Production Approval Given for Prowler

Without too much shock to all involved, the green light was given to build the Prowler after consideration and approval of Chrysler's upper management. Immediately, the Prowler platform team was formed. This team was deliberately kept small to ensure efficiency and speed as the design engineering and final body development and detailing moved forward.

"There were about 75 people on the Prowler platform—the core team, which is really very few people to do a car from just a concept to a final car," admits Peters. These platform teams pointed to the future for automotive design and engineering. They are a means of exploring new means and materials in a low-volume application so they can be verified and later applied to high-volume production cars and trucks.

The Prowler was precisely this kind of vehicle, and proved a rich source of materials engineering for use in future Chrysler products. From the outset it was determined to use aluminum extensively in the Prowler. The hood, decklid, door, and hood side panels are stamped from heat-treated aluminum 6022-T6. Body tub components are made of aluminum 5454-0 alloy.

Virtually the entire drivetrain is aluminum, from the 3.5-liter V-6 engine to the driveshaft and finally the rear transaxle housing. The frame is built up from thick-wall rectangular extruded 6061 and 6063-T6 aluminum sections, welded together. Upper and lower forward control arms and rear lower control arms are aluminum. The list of aluminum components in the Prowler is extensive.

Other materials are employed in unique ways on the Prowler. The instrument panel structure is diecast magnesium. The front and rear quarter panels, rear valance panel, and front fenders are made of sheet molding compound. The rear brake rotors are a metal matrix composite that significantly reduced weight. The front fascia and front and rear bumper covers are made of reaction injection-molding urethane. Injection-molded ABS was used for the front grille.

When the pre-production Prowler was put on the scales, it weighed just under 2,900 pounds. Plymouth chose the 1996 North American International Auto Show to unveil the production Prowler, three years to the day after the concept car was displayed. Sharp-eyed showgoers tried to find the changes from concept to production car but had the greatest of difficulty. In fact, the only noticeable difference appeared to be the headlights. These indeed proved most challenging to the lighting engineers, but using newly developed lighting technology, they were able to meet the federal regulations and enhance the car's looks in the process.

At the press preview at the 1996 Detroit show, Chrysler Chairman Bob Eaton and Bob Lutz, promoted from president to vice chairman, each donned a pair of cool shades, posed with the Prowler, and announced it would be offered for sale for 1997. Lutz once again was able to smile at Chrysler's next offering and explain what it was really all about: "Those who don't get it or don't like it, never will, and that's okay. We're doing this car for those who get it, want it, and can't wait to have it."

The Prowler on the Road

The month following the Detroit auto show, an extended cruise with a hand-built Prowler was begun at the new Chrysler Technology Center in Auburn Hills, Michigan, ending at the company's Phoenix, Arizona, proving grounds. It was the second shakedown cruise. In April, another road trip was taken with two Prowlers to Parkersberg, West Virginia. In May, *HOT ROD* magazine held a "Power Tour" from the Petersen Automotive Museum in Los Angeles to Norwalk, Ohio, with the likes of Boyd Coddington's 1995 Oakland Roadster Show–winner and other hot rods and street rods. In June, two Prowlers covered 5,000 miles, from Detroit to Illinois, Louisiana, Texas, Colorado, and finally Arizona.

In July, the first 18 hand-built Prowlers from the Conner Avenue assembly plant were completed. These cars were part of the assembly line shakedown and parts-approval process. In August, Plymouth released two pre-production Prowlers to a number of enthusiast magazines for initial driving impressions. That same month, Detroit's annual Dream Cruise included the Prowler, drawing crowds everywhere it was driven and parked. The final assembly line bugs and parts supply problems were worked out in the fall of 1996.

At the January 1997 North American International Automobile Show, the 1997 Plymouth Prowler was displayed, and the orders begin to pour into Plymouth dealers all across America and even in Canada. In fact, dealers have been sitting on orders for several months as they patiently waited for the first production Prowlers to arrive. Prospective buyers would have to wait several more months, while exacting effort was given at the Conner Avenue plant to ensure all Prowlers would come

off the assembly line problem-free. That spring, the Prowler began volume production at a rate of twenty cars per day in an eight-hour shift.

In its 1997 Prowler brochure, the copywriter's craft was found to be alive and well, more than up to the high-blown rhetoric that was the norm during Plymouth's musclecar heyday in the 1960s and early 1970s. Here is an excerpt:

"Who would build a tribute to hot rods in a factory? A passionate carmaker. And only Plymouth could summon the swagger to produce a two-seat suntanner with scoot that snaps off a sincere salute to hot rodding. So, here's to that inextinguishable, blue-burning flame that motivates a select few artisans to construct beautiful and awesomely competent machines from little more than a handful of junkyard parts, some raw stock, and hand tools. Building a hot rod is, of course, the most highly personalized microcosm for manufacturing an automobile—but hot rods aren't constructed to please everybody. Neither is Prowler. You either get it or you don't."

The automotive press could not help but be impressed by one of the most outrageous, innovative, and enjoyable cars to ever be built in North America. It could out-accelerate a Mercedes Benz SLK, outhandle practically everything else rolling off an American assembly line except the Viper, the Corvette, and a handful of other cars. Still, Plymouth was not entirely satisfied with the Prowler. Specifically, the division felt the car should have more power. More power was on the way, but it would not come on-line until the 1999 model year. Plymouth chose to spend 1998 doing development of the Prowler with the new 253-horsepower, overhead cam 24-valve V-6. This engine succeeded to putting the 1999 Prowler right up there with the ever-famous Road Runner of 1968.

The Future of Chrysler Performance

The platform concept proved the Chrysler could bring exciting cars to market in the shortest possible time. The Dodge Viper and the Plymouth Prowler proved Chrysler was once again in the performance car business. No company is more aware of its performance heritage than Chrysler. There can be little doubt the company that spanned the decades of performance from the Chrysler 300 to the Dodge Viper and Plymouth Prowler would offer other cars in the future that would rekindle the desire for performance enthusiasts knew years ago.

A-body: This is the designation given to, basically, the compact line of Chrysler cars during the 1960s and 1970s, i.e., Dodge Dart, Swinger, Demon, and Plymouth Valiant, Duster, Scamp.

A-engine: Small-block V-8s with wedge-shaped combustion chambers with displacements of 273, 318, 340, and 360 cubic inches.

B-body: This is the designation given to Chrysler's mid-size line of cars during the 1960s and 1970s, i.e. Dodge Coronet and Charger, and Plymouth Belvedere.

B-engine: Big-block V-8s with wedge-shaped combustion chambers with displacements 361, 383, and 400 cubic inches (see also RB-Engines).

E-body: This is the designation given to Dodge Challenger and Plymouth Barracuda.

Golden Commandos: An inter-corporate race group, which was formed in the early 1960s, patterned after the Dodge Ramchargers.

Hemi: This is the commonly used abbreviation for both the first and second generation hemispherical combustion chamber V-8s Chrysler built during the 1950s through 1971. Today, Chrysler offers complete 426 Hemi V-8s and larger displacement Hemi V-8s through its performance parts division.

Max Wedge: This phrase refers to Chrysler's maximum performance 413 and 426 cubic-inch Wedge combustion chamber V-8s the corporation built in the early 1960s for use in sanctioned drag racing. The official descriptions were the Dodge Ramcharger 413 and 426, and the Plymouth Super Stock 413 and 426.

Mopar: The origin of this word goes back to the early days of Chrysler's Motor Parts Division. This evolved into Mopar and is today a registered trademark. Over the years since it has always been used by enthusiasts to describe a Dodge, Plymouth, or Chrysler, whether or not it was a performance model.

RB-Engine: Big-Block V-8s with wedge-shaped combustionn chambers having displacements of 413, 426, and 440 cubic inches

Ramchargers: According to charter member Tom Hoover, this was a confederation of engineers who got together to swap performance knowledge, to bench race, and to drag race. Their first collective effort was the *High & Mighty*, which they raced for two years. They gave themselves the name the Ramchargers, and primarily became affiliated to the Dodge brand. They received division backing in 1962. Ramcharger was adopted by Dodge for use with its high-performance drag racing 413 and 426 Wedge V-8, its street 426 Wedge V-8, and later to its fresh-air hood induction system. The Ramchargers became the most successful corporate drag racing team in the 1960s.

Shaker: This was a fresh-air performance hoodscoop that bolted to the air cleaner assembly and was available as an option on the Dodge Challenger R/T and the Plymouth 'Cuda in 1970 and 1971. It was standard on some performance packages. The hoodscoop shook while the engine idled, hence the name.

Six Pack: Dodge introduced 3x2-barrel induction on its high-performance 440 ci V-8T in 1969 as a special package option on the Coronet Super Bee, with Six Pack X emblazoned on the sides of the fiberglass hoodscoop. In 1970, Dodge introduced the 340 Six Pack in its Challenger T/A. Plymouth used a different means to identify its six-barrel induction V-8s.

TorqueFlight: The name Chrysler gave to its very rugged and smooth-shifting automatic transmission. It was engineered in various capacities to fit all its engines. The TorqueFlight was so strong it was standard duty on the Max Wedge and Hemi V-8s used in racing.

Wedge: After the first generation Hemi V-8s, Chrysler engineered new engines having wedge-shaped combustion chambers that were more economical to manufacture.

INDEX